THE TRUMAN ADMINISTRATION

THE TRUMAN ADMINISTRATION

ITS PRINCIPLES AND PRACTICE

Harry S. Truman

Edited by Louis W. Koenig

NEW YORK UNIVERSITY PRESS
Washington Square, New York
1956

E
813
T68

PRINTED IN THE UNITED STATES OF AMERICA

To My Father and Mother

ACKNOWLEDGMENTS

The preparation of this book has been assisted by the contributions of several of my colleagues at New York University. Ray F. Harvey encouraged its undertaking, Marshall Dimock its progress, and Joseph Tannenhaus' interest in it was both taxed and abiding. I am grateful also to Carol Carter Moor and Lu Yu Kiang of the New York University library for their unfailing kindness. For the imperfections that remain I alone, of course, am responsible.

L.W.K.

CONTENTS

INTRODUCTION

i

The difficulties with which Harry S. Truman was beset and
hedged about when and just after he succeeded to the presidency
are not likely ever to be overestimated, and to overstate them would
be next to impossible. A suggestion, but only a suggestion, of their
kind and moment—though hardly of their number and complexity—
is implicit in the observation that Mr. Truman had to be both a war
President and a postwar or reconstruction President, and that he had
to accomplish the transition with hardly more forewarning than
had preceded his sudden induction into the presidency itself.

The thirty-second President was precipitated into his great office
on April 12, 1945, in the midst of a global war, the duration of which
could not then be foretold. In a matter of just over four months he
found himself confronted with the radically different problems of
demobilization. And those problems were as much civil and industrial
as military, for the United States had been for over three and a half
years totally dedicated to total war. The fortunes or misfortunes of
war had already compelled him to determine as grave an issue as
can ever have devolved on one man: whether to use or not to use
the atomic bomb and, if it were to be used, when, how, and where.
At Potsdam, he had to participate, with the minimum of preparation,
in decisions that in retrospect appear hardly less grave in their long-
run effect on a large fraction of mankind. The cessation of fighting
left Mr. Truman the chief engineer of a structure designed to ensure
enduring international peace; but its underpinnings were no more
than laid when it became clear that his country was being inexorably
drawn into war of a new kind, presently to be named "cold," against
an adversary of as yet unknown stealth, subtlety, determination, and
power. This war, whose end is still not in sight, was to remain prolific
of mounting tensions and of multiplying problems to the new President's last day in office.

Probably no one would maintain that the vice-presidency of the
United States, even if held for the full four years, is the ideal preparation for carrying such a load as Mr. Truman inherited. He held it for

1

less than three months, and that under a President little inclined
to delegate duties to his Vice-Presidents or to keep them abreast of
his cares of office—a President who, moreover, was in Washington
on fewer than thirty of the eighty-two days of his successor's vice-
presidency. Mr. Truman did, to be sure, attend Cabinet meetings;
but by reason of the President's absences they were few, and anyway
Mr. Roosevelt, according to his successor, "never discussed anything
important at his cabinet meetings." The two men saw comparatively
little of each other in private. The Roosevelt papers disclose appointments with the Vice-President only on March 8 and March 19, and
Mr. Truman computes that, as candidate, Vice-President-elect, and
Vice-President, he saw Roosevelt only eight times in the whole year
before Roosevelt's death.

He points out, too, that he took over the higher office uncoached
in the processes and the current problems of the administration, that
there was in the Cabinet no single member with a personal devotion
to him, and that he did not immediately know to whom he could
best turn for counsel. He has also testified that it was this blind and
unassisted aspect of his situation, not a sense of personal inadequacy,
that prompted his humbly prayerful declarations at the outset—
declarations that struck many persons in and out of government as
reassuring and many others as painfully self-conscious.

The enormous prestige of the dead leader would inevitably have
been a handicap to any man who followed him. For better or for
worse, Mr. Roosevelt had stamped himself into the consciousness of
the country as no other man had done since Theodore Roosevelt.
Idolaters, implacable enemies, and those who were neither were all
equally aware of him. His combination of political genius and jugglery
had held together for thirteen straight years of a working unity the
disparate, not to say motley, elements of the Democratic party—New
Dealers, Southerners, city bosses, organized labor. If the coalition
were to fall apart after his death—and so it was to do—few would
pause to ask if it had not been for some time threatening to crumble
or to wonder how much longer even a magician could have maintained it. As personage and as party leader, then, the man who had
four times swept the country was felt to be irreplaceable, and it was
a foregone conclusion that any possible successor must rise in eclipse.

Mr. Truman, moreover, had fallen somewhat short of the mission
contemplated for him when the Chicago convention of 1944 nomi-

nated him for the vice-presidency. The theory was that, as a border state politician with a mixed voting record of potential appeal to any faction, he was ideally suited to arrest the party's increasing centrifugal tendency. Catapulted into the presidency, he rather hastened than checked this tendency. He put civil rights above party unity, he alienated successively the right wing and the left wing of his party; and it seems as certain as anything that cannot be proved that in 1948 the party would summarily have jettisoned him if it could have prevailed on Dwight Eisenhower to lend an ear to the blandishments of the coalition that had detected in him the perfect candidate.

The new President's early difficulties were replaced by fresh ones faster than any man could have subdued them. Mr. Truman suffered in excelsis the obstructions that all postwar Presidents encounter in their dealings with the Congress. In war the executive branch of government is exalted and the legislative branch depressed; as soon as ostensible peace has supervened the legislative branch is intent on reasserting itself. Against the new President it reasserted itself with an obduracy hardly short of harassment; and of the elaborate Fair Deal program that he urged untiringly upon the Congress, only a microscopic fraction was enacted. The 80th Congress, with its Republican majority, he denounced as do-nothing; but his experiences with it were substantially repeated during the 81st, which had a Democratic majority. In both, the defeat of the measures that he proposed with a particular urgency became an expected and almost a routine outcome.

In foreign affairs particularly, there was a new and growing Congressional insistence on knowing the inner secrets of executive action. Not only was the Bricker amendment introduced to limit the President's power to make executive agreements, but there was also a mounting suspicion of any agreements made and of the motives behind them. General Bradley, as Chief of Staff, was put under pressure to divulge what Mr. Truman had said to him on the subject of General MacArthur's dismissal. The House of Representatives directed the Secretary of State to supply information about any secret commitments that the President might have made to Churchill in their conversations of early 1952. (There had been no commitments, and Mr. Truman said so.) One of the hottest debates of the period was produced in 1950 by Senator Taft's challenge of the

President's right to send an undisclosed number of troops to Europe without Congressional approval. Mr. Truman adduced his Constitutional authority and cited relevant bits of Our Chief Magistrate and His Powers, by the Senator's father, but General Marshall still had to disclose that the number of troops to be sent was 100,000—information that the Russians were doubtless pleased to have gratis.

Also, Mr. Truman had inherited the highest office in a period in which, thanks to the war, self-interested groups had achieved positions of advantage that they did not mean to relinquish or else had lost prerogatives that they now meant to regain. Organized labor was tenacious of its wartime winnings in income and in ancillary benefits; industrialists thought they saw new opportunities to loosen the restrictions imposed by the National Labor Relations Act. Neither labor nor agriculture had encountered much presidential resistance to its demands in the thirteen years just past, and both had come to rely on the presidency as an instrument of their own purposes. When the new President found himself obliged to resist the purposes of special groups as being at odds with the general welfare, his resistance produced a chain reaction of troublesome consequences, beginning with the mammoth strikes of 1946 and involving eventually the long-drawn battles over the Taft-Hartley Act, the injunctions and fines against John L. Lewis and his union, the Anderson and Brannan plans, and the presidential seizures of steel plants, railroads, and coal mines.

The troublous general context of the administration included a succession of personal difficulties with executive subordinates—difficulties that ranged from misunderstanding to outright collision. Mr. Truman was probably involved first and last in more clashes with his aides than any other President—even Andrew Johnson or that master of the calculated rage, Andrew Jackson. Mr. Truman, for reasons that he rehearses with candor if not completeness in Year of Decisions, broke with his first important counsellor, James F. Byrnes. He dismissed Henry Wallace, Louis Johnson, and J. Howard McGrath from their Cabinet posts; the evidence suggests that he elbowed out Henry Morgenthau. One of Mr. Roosevelt's favorite liberals, Harold Ickes, was impelled to resign in extreme dudgeon, and another, Marriner Eccles, was demoted (for reasons that he seems never to have understood) from the chairmanship of the Federal Reserve Board. Against one of the two most popular of our military half it was the mediocre or even shabby expression of a machine politician suddenly called upon for a statesmanship beyond his capacity. It will remain ˙for the future to find a hearing for the point of view to which all extremes are suspect; and even that future seems likely to be a long one when we reflect that history has not yet said its last word about Madison, Jackson, Polk, or even Buchanan.

There is every reason why there should be as yet a dearth of respectably sober and disinterested judgment. There are still those who never forgave Mr. Truman for not being Franklin Roosevelt; there are also those who will never forgive him for being insufficiently unlike Roosevelt. Practically all Americans see him as having put either sugar or poison in their tea, and they shower him with devoted thanks or with revilements accordingly. One-worlders think he bypassed the United Nations at the points where he should specially have deferred to it; America-firsters despise him for the patience of his efforts in behalf of collective security. Those who felt that General MacArthur could do no wrong abominate the Commander in Chief who dismissed him, and those who always regarded MacArthur with skepticism censure the Commander in Chief who ignored ample reasons for dismissing him earlier. Practically every transaction of the eight years produced such fiercely partisan interpretations, and we are so near to the events that partisanship can still rage unabated. There is no short-run help for such violent clashes of opinion; nearly every man in public life experiences them in some degree; the whole theory of democracy is that there is room for them, that most of them cancel one another out, and that when they have done so the sum that remains is truth and wisdom. But the process has none of the unity that totalitarians cherish, and when with characteristic promptness the ex-President publishes his candid memoirs half the old battles are fought over with almost the original ferocity.

The harsher critics of Mr. Truman can be very harsh indeed. They depict him as given to bold and defiant words followed by half-hearted actions or none. He meets with vigor the Communist challenge in Korea, and then he gets rid of the general who wants to conduct the war with corresponding vigor. He heads, if professions are the measure, the most liberal administration in our history, but his appointments show that he works the most comfortably with conservatives. He makes a fighting speech about civil rights at the nominating convention, but does not get around to mentioning the subject again until the last week of the campaign—in Harlem. He berates Wall Street with the fervor of an 1893 Populist one day and nominates a Wall Street man for an exalted post the next. In 1948, when the Marshall Plan is launched, he asks for price controls, but in 1950, when the Korean outbreak begins, he pointedly refrains from including price controls among the broad powers that he requests. Why the difference? Is it because in 1945 he knows that price controls cannot be enacted and that in the coming campaign he can make political capital out of blaming the Republicans, whereas in 1950, if he had price controls but failed to arrest living costs, he would have no politically persuasive explanation?

On this system he is discredited throughout, point by point. Some of the reservations represent, of course, honest and thoughtful disagreement. Some of them sound like the mere sniping of critics who can find a compromising inconsistency almost anywhere and who think a public figure self-condemned if he shows the slightest tendency to change his mind or to learn anything from his mistakes. Such carping, fair or not, is one of the American privileges, and doubtless several million Americans are unfailingly certain that they could run the presidency much better than it was ever run.

These add up the column by their own kind of arithmetic; but there is another kind. Sir Winston Churchill credited Mr. Truman with "great and valiant decisions which make us, I think, all feel better today than we did two or three years ago." Henry Steele Commager has declared that the historian of a half century hence will survey the Truman administration as "one of almost uninterrupted and unparalleled success." And another historian, Arnold Toynbee, holds that not the discovery of atomic energy, but the solicitude of the world's more privileged peoples for its less privileged, as vested in Mr. Truman's Point Four and the resultant program, will be remembered as the signal achievement of our age.

As for Mr. Truman's own appraisal of his stewardship, he said on his seventy-first birthday that, after two years of thought and consideration, he could not point to a thing that he would have done differently as President. He has also pronounced himself resigned to being "cussed and discussed"—his own words—for a long time to come. It is, however, permissible to put a slightly Pickwickian construction on both utterances. For his own words—including some in this volume—contain the implicit evidence that he, like any man, would have done a few things differently if he had had at the time the guidance of their later consequences; and as for his resignation, it is enough to say that important parts of his memoirs amount to a justification of his official acts and policies —a characteristically vigorous and uncompromising apologia. It seems a little unlikely that any reader of Year of Decisions will ever describe its prevailing mood and tone as resigned.

The New York Times, when it printed the last of its excerpts from Year of Decisions, spoke editorially of "the year when the sudden death of a great President left the Executive power of the United States in the hands of a man without experience, without knowledge, without prestige," and continued: "He was a man of many faults; but he was also a man of goodwill and a man of courage, and these were the qualities that stood him well during the difficult years that followed." It is the courage that stands out in his most revealing decisions and commitments—in his confrontation of Stalin at Potsdam, in his acceptance of the awful responsibility for the use of the atomic bomb, in his unhesitating answer to the challenge in Korea; above all, in the faith and fortitude that carried him through the 1948 campaign to a triumph widely regarded as impossible. To the courage he added a gift of simplification, a knack of seeing issues divested of complication and irrelevancy and of stating them in plain, blunt terms, without style but also without guile. There were those who welcomed and esteemed this subtler gift, itself a kind of courage, perhaps even rarer in political life than the more obvious kind; and it may have destined its possessor, like Grover Cleveland, to more recognition and louder acclaim as time passes.

Mr. Truman had to make many choices in situations in which there was no right way, but only an assortment of wrong ones—the situations proliferated by war and war's aftermath and increasingly typical of our age. It takes uncommon steadiness of mind to commit a nation to a choice between evils and, having made the choice, neither to misrepresent it nor to wallow in regrets and unnerving doubts. If any one thing seems more nearly certain than another about Harry Truman as President, it is that he never shrank from a necessary choice.

iii

This book is intended as documentation, not as political or personal criticism. It neither defends nor controverts any one of the many possible interpretations of the Truman administration. It will propound no retrospective views of how the manifold difficulties of the postwar years should have been met, and it will not try to anticipate the final verdicts of history—if any verdicts of history can be called final—on either the accomplishments of an administration or the characteristics of a man. The matter of these pages is simply what the difficulties were, how a man reasoned about them, what he did to meet them, and how he did it. It is, in short, a book of facts. They are such facts as may lead some readers to, or toward, conclusions of their own; indeed, they are the sort of facts without which no valid conclusions could possibly be approached. But this book steers clear of what is disputable. Its province is what a President of the United States said, did, and tried to do.

The chief purpose of this volume is to supply within reasonable compass a conspectus of the Truman administration by means of selected documents. Most of the documents are the more and less formal addresses of the President on a considerable variety of occasions—the representative addresses that, throwing light on such principles as actuated him, seem best to explain the procedures of his administration. The utterances reproduced range from campaign speeches to formal State of the Union messages, from remarks at anniversaries and dedications to the annual Economic Report to Congress. Rarely, an official letter or even a press interview is drawn upon. And when, as ex-President, Mr. Truman talks searchingly about the functions of the presidency or takes a backward look at his own conduct of the office, it seems pertinent to include remarks in which he does it; e.g. his speech at a birthday dinner in 1954. The object is, by a free treatment and arrangement, to present a comprehensive topical survey, not to assemble a chronological file.

There are, of course, drawbacks to the method of representing a presidential administration by the words and acts of the President alone. A President is naturally not the whole of his administration, and the innumerable aides and subordinates of Mr. Truman carried out many actions of moment and made many decisions that appear in these pages only by indirection and implication. But there are drawbacks to any method of surveying history so recent; and it remains true that the most comprehensive approach to a presidency is through the incumbent himself. He has the power, the responsibility; he makes the ultimate decisions; his years in office are, in sum, an expression of what he is, just as an author's shelfful of books are an expression of what the author is. A presidency has to be, with whatever else it is, a mirror of the President's personality, his philosophy, and above all his style. The style of the Truman administration is sui generis; and of this, at least, the method chosen for this book effects a high saturation.

For the sake of space-saving, some of the documents are represented only by important excerpts, and some are abridged by moderate cutting. Any President of the United States is constantly put in situations that call for expected, fully predictable sentiments, and Mr. Truman has had to voice his share of appropriate truisms. It is often possible to elide them without impairing the real substance of what he had to say, and sometimes with enhancement of its trenchancy. All elisions are made with care not to falsify the intended meaning of any context, and all are marked.

The matter interpolated by the editor by way of introducing and connecting the documents—matter kept as sparing as seemed feasible —is of two kinds, of which the first is intended to refresh the reader's memory of essential background facts and so to obviate his having constantly to fall back on reference books and newspaper files. The second kind attempts to place and to characterize various developments of the Truman administration in the history of the presidency as an institution.

The presidency is, of course, an evolving institution; and under Mr. Truman and his immediate predecessor it evolved perhaps faster than ever before. The Communist challenge made the presidency in a new sense a global affair. The postwar years put into the President's hands an immensely powerful leverage on affiliated countries to which the United States was supplying economic or military aid. Indeed, he had at times more control of some European national budgets than was vested in the ministers of finance ostensibly in charge of them. It devolved on him to initiate affiliations and alliances in several parts of the world, to stipulate the conditions of American co-operation and contribution, to propose articles of agenda and concrete programs for the General Assembly of the United Nations, even to broadcast statements of United States policies and attitudes through the Voice of America. The exigencies first of war and then of the cold war thrust upon him enormous powers, including powers of expenditure, that not only could be, but also had to be, exercised in almost absolute secrecy. And by virtue of his duty as Commander in Chief he could, and in Korea did, commit his country to hostile action on the scale of war without any Congressional declaration of war—more than a hint that the Constitutional assumption of an absolute alternative between war and peace has become in modern conditions an unreal technicality and something of an anachronism.

In short, the presidency has insensibly accumulated enhanced powers that reinforce and extend the obvious latterday tendency of administrative functions to absorb prerogatives once thought inherent in the legislative function. Under Mr. Roosevelt, in both peace and war, this extension proceeded fast and far; under Mr. Truman, in war, in peace, and in the misty mid-region between the two, it continued, though not without criticism, challenge, and resistance.

The topical arrangement of this book begins with this very subject of the presidency itself—how Mr. Truman conceived the office, what he said about it, and what he made of it. From that point it proceeds through the major departments and categories of the multifarious presidential task. The President has to administer the vast, protean executive branch of the government. He has to lead not only his party, but also his whole people, and, as a part of that leadership, to initiate legislation. He has to preside over the foreign policy and the international relations of his country. And he has to exercise at least a broad strategic command of his country's armed forces.

How history will one day judge the thirty-second President's way of shouldering these great burdens is a question beyond the scope and province of the present treatment. But the pages that follow contain the central nuclei of the record on which such future judgments will necessarily be based; and on the detailed personal account that Mr. Truman gives of his stewardship in the volumes of his memoirs they provide an important gloss.

I
THE PRESIDENCY

1. THE GENERAL CHARACTERISTICS OF THE OFFICE

Mr. Truman's conception of his role as President underwent some change under the pressure of changing tactical considerations. At the outset he thought of himself as primarily the heir and executor of Franklin Roosevelt's policies—a stage that lasted approximately until the Congressional elections of 1946. When the outcome of these upset the Democrats' sixteen-year control of the legislature it was evident to him that his administration could no longer meet new exigencies by remaining a mere extension of his predecessor's, and he is supposed to have told political aides that the Democrats could win in 1948 only if in the interim the presidency were placed above politics and made the vehicle of fresh initiatives. On this theory he acted with vigor for two years; and when, in 1948, he won what could reasonably be construed as a national mandate to make the office express his own political philosophy he made the most of his new freedom from inherited trammels.

He had throughout, however, a solid continuum of conviction about the essence and meaning of the presidential function. There is perhaps no subject about which Mr. Truman has thought longer

15

or more searchingly than about the presidency itself. From his long preoccupation with American history he learned much about the office; from his own exercise of its responsibilities and powers in conditions that crucially tested both, he inevitably learned more. He incorporated findings from both kinds of education in remarks prepared over a year after his own incumbency had become a thing of the past—the remarks delivered at the dinner given in New York City on May 8, 1954 in honor of his seventieth birthday.

There's never been an office—an executive office—in all the history of the world with the responsibility and the power of the presidency of the United States. That is the reason in this day and age that it must be run and respected as at no other time in the history of the world, because it can mean the welfare of the world or its destruction.

When the founding fathers outlined the presidency in Article II of the Constitution, they left a great many details out. . . . I think they relied on the experience of the nation to fill in the outlines. The office of chief executive has grown with the progress of this great republic. It has responded to the many demands that our complex society has made upon the government. It has given our nation a means of meeting our greatest emergencies. Today, it is one of the most important factors in our leadership of the free world.

Many diverse elements entered into the creation of the office, springing, as it did, from the parent idea of the separation of powers.

There was the firm conviction of such powerful and shrewd minds as that of John Adams that the greatest protection against unlimited power lay in an executive secured against the encroachment of the national assembly. Then there were the fears of those who suspected a plot to establish a monarchy on these shores. Others believed that the experience under the Confederation showed above all the need of stability through a strong central administration. Finally, there was the need for compromise among these and many other views.

The result was a compromise—a compromise which that shrewd observer, Alexis de Tocqueville, over a hundred and twenty years ago, believed would not work. He thought that the presidential office was too weak. The President, he thought, was at the mercy of Congress. The President could recommend, to be sure, he thought, but the President had no power and the Congress had the power.

The Congress could disregard his recommendations, overrule his vetoes, reject his nominations. De Tocqueville thought that no man of parts, worthy of leadership, would accept such a feeble role.

This was not a foolish view, and there was much in our early history which tended to bear it out. But there is a power in the course of events which plays its own part. In this case again, Justice Holmes's epigram proved true. He said a page of history is worth a whole volume of logic. And as the pages of history were written they unfolded powers in the presidency not explicitly found in Article II of the Constitution.

In the first place, the President became the leader of a political party. The party under his leadership had to be dominant enough to put him in office. This political party leadership was the last thing the Constitution contemplated. The President's election was not intended to be mixed up in the hurly-burly of partisan politics.

I wish some of those old gentlemen could come back and see how it worked. The people were to choose wise and respected men who would meet in calm seclusion and choose a President, and the runner-up would be Vice-President.

All of this went by the board—though most of the original language remains in the Constitution. Out of the struggle and tumult of the political arena a new and different President emerged—the man who led a political party to victory and retained in his hands the power of party leadership. That is, he retained it, like the sword Excalibur, if he could wrest it from the scabbard and wield it.

Another development was connected with the first. As the President came to be elected by the whole people, he became responsible to the whole people. I used to say the only lobbyist the whole people had in Washington was the President of the United States. Our whole people looked to him for leadership, and not confined within the limits of a written document. Every hope and every fear of his fellow citizens, almost every aspect of their welfare and activity, falls within the scope of his concern—indeed, it falls within the scope of his duty. Only one who has held that office can really appreciate that. It is the President's responsibility to look at all questions from the point of view of the whole people. His written and spoken word commands national and often international attention.

These powers which are not explicitly written into the Constitution are the powers which no President can pass on to his successor. They go only to him who can take and use them. However, it is these powers, quite as much as those enumerated in Article II of the Constitution, which make the presidential system unique and which give the papers of Presidents their peculiarly revealing importance.

For it is through the use of these great powers that leadership arises, events are molded, and administrations take on their character. Their use can make a Jefferson or a Lincoln administration; their nonuse can make a Buchanan or a Grant administration.

Moreover, a study of these aspects of our governmental and political history will save us from self-righteousness—from taking a holier-than-thou attitude toward other nations. For, brilliant and enduring as were the minds of the architects of our Constitution, they did not devise a foolproof system to protect us against the disaster of a weak government—that is, a government unable to face and resolve, one way or another, pressing national problems. Indeed, in some respects the separation of powers requires stronger executive leadership than does the parliamentary and cabinet system.

As Justice Brandeis used to say, the separation of powers was not devised to promote efficiency in government. In fact, it was devised to prevent one form of deficiency—absolutism or dictatorship. By making the Congress separate and independent in the exercise of its powers, a certain amount of political conflict was built into the Constitution. For the price of independence is eternal vigilance and a good deal of struggle. And this is not a bad thing. On the contrary, it is a good thing for the preservation of the liberty of the people—if it does not become conflict just for its own sake.

I've always said that the President who didn't have a fight with the Congress wasn't any good anyhow. And that's no reflection on the Congress. They are always looking after their rights. You needn't doubt that.

Having been in these two branches of government, legislative and executive, I think I am expressing a considered and impartial opinion in saying that the powers of the President are much more difficult to exercise and to preserve from encroachment than those of the Congress. In part, this comes from the difficulty of the problems of our time, and from the fact that upon the President falls the responsibility of obtaining action, timely and adequate to meet the nation's needs. Whatever the Constitution says, he is held responsible for any disaster which may come.

And so a successful administration is one of strong presidential leadership. Weak leadership—or no leadership—produces failure and often disaster.

This does not come from the inherent incapacity of the people of the nation. It is inherent in the legislative government, where there is no executive strong and stable enough to rally the people to a sustained effort of will and prepared to use its power of party control to the fullest extent.

Today, also, one of the great responsibilities and opportunities of the President is to lead and inspire public opinion. The words of a President carry great weight. His acts carry even more weight.

All of us remember the words of Franklin D. Roosevelt in his first inaugural address which did so much to rally the spirit of the nation struggling through the depths of a depression. He said: "The only thing we have to fear is fear itself." Those words, however, would have had little effect if President Roosevelt had not backed them up by action. Following that speech, President Roosevelt plunged into a vigorous course, striking at the depression on all fronts. He backed his words by his action, and words and action restored the faith of the nation in its government and in its form of government, too.

Today, there is the same need for a combination of words and action concerning the hysteria about communism. Our country has acted firmly and resolutely to hold the communist imperialism in check. Nevertheless, that concern has created fear, and fear has been played upon by persons who see in it an easy way to influence votes. There is no dispute any more that this unreasonable fear exists. The leaders of both political parties have acknowledged it. I do not wish to go into this subject at length tonight. I have talked a good deal about it of late and most recently at Westminster College in Missouri, where Winston Churchill made his famous Iron Curtain speech. We all know the corrosive effect of this hysteria and the dangers it holds.

But, as I have said, the office of the presidency is the one office to which all the people turn when they are beset by fears like these. It is to the President that they look to say a firm "No" to those who wish to destroy others through fear and innuendo. It is his duty to defend the unjustly accused and demonstrate in the executive branch of the government that the ancient principles of fair play and decency prevail all the time. By such deeds and acts the President can reassure the nation and stem the growth of hysteria.

Again, we see today history repeating itself as the legislative branch of the government, under the overshadowing fear of communism, expands its functions and activities into the very center of the power of the executive branch.

The President is responsible for the administration of his office. And that means for the administration of the entire executive branch. It is not the business of Congress to run the agencies of government for the President.

Unless this principle is observed, it is impossible to have orderly government. The legislative power will ooze into the executive offices. It will influence and corrupt the decisions of the executive branch. It will affect promotions and transfers. It will warp and twist policies.

Not only does the President cease to be a master in his own house, but the whole house of government becomes one which has no master. The power of decision then rests only in the legislative branch, and the legislative branch by its very nature is not equipped to perform these executive functions.

To this kind of encroachment it is the duty of the President to say firmly and flatly: "No, you can't do it." The investigative power of Congress is not limitless. It extends only so far as to permit the Congress to acquire the information that it honestly needs to exercise its legislative functions. Exercised beyond these limits, it becomes a manifestation of unconstitutional power. It raises the threat of a legislative dictatorship, and that's the worst dictatorship in the world.

Our nation was once almost torn apart by such an expansion of Congressional power. That was in the age of President Andrew Johnson, when the Radical Republicans of that time tried to take over the functions of the President. But we cannot afford such an attack on the presidency by today's version of the Radical Republicans.

Today the perils and problems which threaten us and our allies make all the difficulties of the Reconstruction period—that tragic era—seem rather pale. Today the tasks of leadership falling upon the President spring not only from our national problems but from those of the whole world. Today that leadership will determine whether our government will function effectively, and upon its functioning depends the survival of each of us and also on that depends the survival of the free world, if I may be so bold as to say that.

And today our government cannot function properly unless it follows the provisions of the Constitution. Our government cannot function properly unless the President is master in his own house and unless the executive departments and agencies of the government, including the armed forces, are responsible only to the President.

I hope and believe that we will pass through this present crisis successfully. I do not believe that the Congress will succeed in taking over the functions of the executive if the President presents the problem in its constitutional light. I have always maintained that the internal security of the executive branch was a matter for the President himself to handle. President Eisenhower in his first State of the Union message announced the same principle. If this administration under his leadership will act upon this principle, we can look forward to the continuation of constitutional government as our founding fathers intended it to be.

§ No one who reads the foregoing address can miss its conviction that the United States needs a strong executive leadership, that the Constitution provides for this, and that it is incumbent on a President to be alert in resisting encroachment on his prerogatives. It is, however, Congressional encroachment alone that Mr. Truman chiefly deals with here. He says, in this context, nothing about the co-operation that the President may and should require of his appointive subordinates—his Cabinet members and heads of administrative bureaus. This is an issue that was constantly coming up, especially at the outset of his administration, and it was one about which he developed as strong views as any President has ever held or acted on. An integral and important part of his conception of the President's mastery of his own house was his subordinates' absolute loyalty in the application of any policy on which he had decided.

At Cabinet meetings and other conferences Mr. Truman has pointed out, he encouraged the utmost frankness of discussion and freedom of disagreement as long as a policy was in the making.

To himself he reserved, as being both a right and a duty, the ultimate decision among conflicting possibilities. Once a policy was framed and understood, he expected his appointees to stand by it. If they could not in good conscience overtly support it or, at the least, refrain from betraying their private reservations about it, he expected —and, if compelled, demanded—their resignations. A public advocacy of some alternative policy he regarded as sabotage, and he could not regard presidential tolerance of such sabotage as a virtue. This requirement of a working unity in the executive branch is the other half of his resistance to whatever tended to erode the strength of the office. The same requirement is a recurring motif in Year of Decisions. It will be found at the bottom of his contentions with a succession of subordinates over whom he had the power of dismissal, and it is of course the rationale of his dismissal of General MacArthur, from whom he asserted as Commander in Chief a right to faithful application of politico-military policies to which as President he had committed himself.

2. THE LEADERSHIP OF PAST PRESIDENTS

At Raleigh, North Carolina, on October 19, 1948, in the midst of his campaign for re-election, Mr. Truman spoke at the dedication of a monument to the three Presidents born in North Carolina, Jackson, Polk, and Johnson, and in doing so he drew further upon his reflections as a student of constitutional and political history.

We are in the midst of a political campaign upon which depends much of the country's future. It is good at such a time to pause to take strength and guidance from our country's past.

This year, as in all the years, the State of North Carolina has much to teach the country. Its great sons have important things to say to us still. And we have important things to learn from them. We deal here today not merely with the dedication of a monument. Our task is the rededication of ourselves.

Each of the three men whose fame this monument celebrates held the office of President in time of trouble.

Andrew Jackson had to face the nullification crisis, which was the first threat of secession.

James K. Polk was confronted by the Mexican War.

Andrew Johnson was caught in the mass hysteria following a

war in which more American blood was spilled than in both the World Wars of our time.

Because they lived through days when reason was overcome by emotion, their acts were misunderstood and misinterpreted. And because they were misunderstood they were libeled beyond the lot of most Presidents. Intense feeling obscures the truth. And so it is not surprising that the estimates of these men made by their contemporaries have been almost completely discarded by later generations.

In these new estimates, not one of the three has diminished in stature. On the contrary, each is now regarded as a stronger and wiser man.

What each of them meant to his time, you have been told by many learned men. So I shall not repeat what you already know —what Jackson meant in 1832, or Polk in 1845, or Johnson in 1865.

I prefer to offer some suggestions as to what they all mean in 1948—and what they should mean in the years that lie ahead.

Jackson, Polk, and Johnson are gone. Yet they are forever a part of North Carolina. They represent the glory of the past. But that is not all. If that were all, I venture to say that this monument would serve only half its purpose. To the young men and women, to the boys and girls of the State who pass this way, it would say, "We have produced great men." That is true and should be said, but it has no bearing on the future.

It should say more. And to anyone who has studied the careers of these three Presidents it will say more. It has a message that is not only true as to the past, but is also encouraging as to the future.

That message is this: "Do your duty, and history will do you justice."

Each of these men did his duty as President of the whole nation against the forces of pressure and persuasion which sought to make him act as a representative of a part of the nation only.

Each of them provoked the wrath of some sincere and honest men—which is a serious thing. A President may dismiss the abuse of scoundrels. But to be denounced by honest men honestly outraged is a test of greatness that none but the strongest men survive.

Consider, for example, the career of Andrew Jackson. He has always been held up as a symbol of courage, but too often for reasons that are not the best. It takes courage to face a duelist with a pistol, and it takes courage to face a British general with an army. But it takes still greater and far higher courage to face friends with a grievance. The bravest thing Andrew Jackson ever did was to stand up and tell his own people to their faces that they were wrong.

It was all the braver because he knew in his heart that they had some cause for discontent. The tariff of 1828, which provoked the Nullification movement, was well named the Tariff of Abominations. It did inflict injustice upon South Carolina and the other Southern states. Andrew Jackson knew that as well as John C. Calhoun.

But Jackson also knew that the way to correct injustices in a democracy is by reason and debate, never by walking out in a huff. To attempt to correct injustice by disunion is to apply a remedy that is worse than the disease.

It would not have been pleasant for Andrew Jackson to say this to any State. It was doubly unpleasant to say it to South Carolina, a state composed of people of his own blood, his own faith, of his own qualities of mind and heart, a state to which he was bound by ties of memory, pride, and affection. The closing paragraph of the great Nullification Proclamation is eloquent of the pain it cost him to stand against people so closely allied to him.

But it was his duty, and he did it.

We know now what they could not know then. We know what a pliant, supple man in the White House in that crisis might have cost us. A man more careful to preserve his own peace than to "preserve, protect and defend the Constitution of the United States" might have drifted into ways that would have ended in the destruction of the Union. It is because Andrew Jackson did his duty in agony of mind as well as agony of body that this monument is raised in his honor.

Let me say, too, how fine a thing it is that this monument was raised in the South by Southerners. Democracy is safe among a people who are too just to withhold respect from a man because his duty once forced him to oppose them.

Consider, then, the case of James K. Polk. Thomas Jefferson has been endlessly praised for adding 827,000 square miles to the United States by the Louisiana Purchase. But the average American is astonished when reminded that Polk added 814,000 square miles.

This is not the place either to defend or attack Polk's policy in regard to the Mexican War. But there is one aspect of it that is worth serious attention by this generation. Even when the war was won, Polk's efforts to negotiate a generous peace were interfered with by the House of Representatives in such a way as to draw the lines for great internal conflict in later years.

That interference took the form of the Wilmot Proviso, which the House attached to the appropriation bill that supplied the first installment of our payment to Mexico. It was a condition that no area purchased with the money appropriated should be slave territory.

I am not questioning now the merits of the Wilmot Proviso. But it was, nevertheless, an attempt to use foreign policy as a lever in the settlement of a domestic question. Such an attempt is always fraught with peril. We should have learned that fact from the experience of Polk's day and its tragic consequences in the Civil War. Unfortunately, we did not. It took another great foreign war and another disastrous injection of domestic politics into foreign affairs—in the fight on the League of Nations—to drive the lesson home.

But now, I trust, we have learned it. In the midst of the Second World War President Roosevelt and his great Secretary of State, Cordell Hull, proposed, and certain of the wiser Congressional leaders of the opposition agreed, that, as far as they could bring it about, politics should stop at the water's edge. It has been my duty to carry out that agreement and to urge all Americans to abide by it faithfully.

The wisdom of that bipartisan policy should be very clear indeed to North Carolinians. They have before them not only the case of Woodrow Wilson, but also that of Polk. You know that Polk's greatest achievement was clouded for many years because, in his time, we had not learned to keep our domestic quarrels at home and present a united front to the rest of the world.

Andrew Johnson came to the presidency by reason of a death that was tragic not merely for America, but for all mankind. Suddenly, without a moment's preparation, he was called upon to take up and complete the work of one of the greatest men that ever occupied the White House.

Andrew Johnson needs no defense. But it is a simple statement of fact to point out that in 1865 no man alive could have succeeded Abraham Lincoln without being subject to unfavorable comparisons. And it was Johnson's misfortune to encounter more than that. It is one of the major tragedies of war that the passions it unleashes do not automatically subside with the fighting. They must be subdued gradually. And it usually takes long, patient, courageous effort.

In 1865 passions were as furious as the war had been long and bloody. There were men in and out of Congress who had lost their heads completely. In their madness they were determined that the blood-letting should not stop. They would have sent scores of brave and honorable men to the gallows and stripped thousands more of all they possessed. They wanted to keep a whole region in chains.

That no such disgrace has occurred in the United States is due largely to the bulldog courage of Andrew Johnson. I have no wish to prettify him. He doesn't need it. He was stubborn. He was tactless. Often he was ungracious to the point of being surly. The fact remains that he faced such a storm of hatred as never before had swept this country. And in facing it, he defended not so much certain individuals as the principle that the Constitution of the United States and not the desire of angry men is the supreme law of the land.

His courageous stand has made it easier for every President who has had to cope with postwar hysteria since his day. That task is still no child's play. We have among us today men who, blinded by their fury and their fears, are ready to condemn on suspicion and punish without trial. To them no President dare yield an inch. If he yielded, he would be unworthy to stand before the monument of Andrew Johnson.

It is a happy circumstance that this is a monument not to one man but to three. Americanism is not embodied in any one man. It is a distillation of the spirits of all the heroes who have labored and fought and died for the common good.

The Constitution declares that there shall be no *titles* of nobility in this republic. It does not say that there shall be no nobility. We do have what may be described with exact justice as a nobility. But it is not attained by birth. One may come to it from the camp, as Jackson did, or from a university, as Polk did, or from a tailor's bench, as Johnson did.

The test is long and brave and honest labor for our country's good.

And this is the thing that these three men, different as they were in origin and in temperament, held in common. But it is no exclusive possession. Most certainly, it is not confined to Presidents or other officers of state. Our country would not last long if that were true. The strength of the republic lies in the fact that so many millions of men, and women, who hold no office and aspire to none, recognize as clearly as Jackson and Polk and Johnson did that they must serve their country before they serve themselves.

3. THE LATTERDAY CHALLENGE

How the scope of the presidential office became enlarged with America's postwar leadership of the Western nations is a subject on which Mr. Truman touched briefly in his final State of the Union message on January 7, 1953.

The President is Chief of State, elected representative of all the people, national spokesman for them and to them. He is Commander in Chief of our armed forces. He is charged with the conduct of our foreign relations. He is Chief Executive of the nation's largest civilian organization. He must select and nominate all top officials of the executive branch and all federal judges. And on the legislative side, he has the obligation and the opportunity to recommend, and to approve or veto, legislation. Besides all this, it is to him that a great political party turns naturally for leadership, and that, too, he must provide as President.

This bundle of burdens is unique; there is nothing else like it on the face of the earth. Each task could be a fulltime job. Together, they would be a tremendous undertaking in the easiest of times.

But our times are not easy; they are hard—as hard and complex, perhaps, as any in our history. Now, the President not only has to carry on these tasks in such a way that our democracy may grow and flourish and our people prosper, but he also has to lead the whole free world in overcoming the communist menace—and all this under the shadow of the atomic bomb.

This is a huge challenge to the human being who occupies the presidential office. But it is not a challenge to him alone, for in reality he cannot meet it alone. The challenge runs not just to him but to his whole administration, to the Congress, to the country.

Ultimately, no President can master his responsibilities save as his fellow citizens—indeed, the whole people—comprehend the challenge of our times and move, with him, to meet it.

It has been my privilege to hold the presidential office for nearly eight years now, and much has been done in which I take great pride. But this is not personal pride. It is pride in the people, in the nation. It is pride in our political system and our form of government —balky sometimes, mechanically deficient perhaps, in many ways— but enormously alive and vigorous; able through these years to keep the republic on the right course, rising to the great occasions, accomplishing the essentials, meeting the basic challenge of our times.

4.   DELEGATION OF AUTHORITY

A formidable aspect of the presidency is the impossibility of delegating the smallest fraction of its responsibility, combined with the necessity of delegating large fractions of its authority. For whatever is done wrong the Chief Executive has ultimately to accept the onus; yet there is a vast amount that he cannot himself undertake to do. As Mr. Truman saw it, a President's one hope of keeping abreast of his duties—to say nothing of surviving a notoriously man-killing job—is to delegate his authority freely to the right persons. On this subject he made some observations to Anthony Leviero of the New York Times in an interview of December 26, 1952.

The President said it was . . . difficult to lighten the burden of the presidency, which he regards as the most powerful office in all history. He said neither Genghis Khan, nor Alexander the Great, nor Napoleon, nor Louis XIV of France had as much power as the President of the United States, whose acts or utterances might affect as many as one and one half billion people.

Under the Constitution, he did not see how the role of the President could be changed, . . . adding that the job was one for five men. The only way that the job could be done . . . was to select responsible and experienced people for key jobs in the administration, give them authority, and then to back them up in carrying out presidential decisions. . . .

Mr. Truman cautioned that some Presidents had not delegated authority and had got into trouble by trying to do too much themselves.

"I provided myself with the best information that could be accumulated and surrounded myself with the best minds I could get, and reached the best conclusions that I could reach.

"Then when I issued a directive I knew that it would be carried out properly, and I could sleep nights. I know that when I am carried out feet first it can be said of me, 'He did his damnedest.'"

5. THE PRESIDENT AS PERSUADER

Greatly as President Truman was concerned at times with the powers and prerogatives of his office, he was acutely aware of the areas into which his peremptory powers did not reach—the areas in which even a President has no powers except those of persuasion. In May 1948 Mr. Truman was trying to effect, between the Association of American Railroads and the Brotherhood of Locomotive Engineers and others, an agreement that would spare the United States the stress of a nation-wide railway strike. In a speech in Washington on May 7 he said:

I am only a servant of the people of the United States. I can only do what the law authorizes me to do as President of the United States. I am the enforcement part of the government of the United States for the laws that are passed by the Congress. That is my duty. That is what I am sworn to do.

And people talk about the powers of a President, all the powers that a Chief Executive has and what he can do. Let me tell you something from experience.

The President may have a great many powers given to him in the Constitution and may have powers under certain laws which are given to him by the Congress of the United States, but the principal power that the President has is to bring them in and try to persuade them to do what they ought to do without persuasion. That's what I spend most of my time doing. That's what the powers of the President amount to. . . .

The President can't solve problems by himself. The Congress can't solve problems, but the President and the Congress and the country can solve any problem that comes before us.

6. SOME INCIDENTAL OBSERVATIONS

Mr. Truman has made at one time and another a variety of scattered remarks on the presidency, some of them about the office in general and some about his specific conduct of it. Reviewing the stresses of April 1945 to a gathering of party workers in 1949, he characterized the legacy that had descended on him as an "almost unbearable burden." He said: "No one, I think, in the history of the country ever assumed a greater responsibility than I did"; and the same sentiment is repeatedly affirmed and amplified in Year of Decisions. In a lighter vein he expressed it, after six weeks in office, at a luncheon of the Jesters, a Kansas City Masonic group: "This thing of being President just means responsibility on a grand scale. Every time I sign a document, it affects the welfare of groups of citizens or of States."

It is clear from the record—the record of both declaration and performance—that Mr. Truman conceived the presidency in primarily human terms and that he was determined to resist so far as possible the tendency of an exalted executive office to set its holder apart at an altitude of inhuman grandiosity. In unveiling a statue of Andrew Jackson at the Jackson County courthouse in his native state on December 26, 1949, he said: "There isn't any difference between the work that you do and the work which I have to do as President of the United States, only [my work] is on a larger scale. In fact, I imagine you see as many people in one day as I see, because there is a limit to which a man can go in transacting the business of the government." And one of Mr. Truman's favorite ideas, expressed on a number of occasions, is that the President is essentially a lobbyist for the people in a scheme of government in which every special interest has its lobby and the plain people have none. ". . . government is for all the people and not for any one group or for any special groups. The people have no lobby in Washington looking out for their interests except the President of the United States, and it's too bad if the President does not work for their good." One of the President's unheralded visits to the Senate in 1949 brought forth the declaration that he had been trying his level best to work for the general welfare, and that he hoped historians would not say that he had failed.

Aware of the inherent dignity of his office and quite capable of asserting it against trespassers, he was nevertheless resolved that he was not going to be made self-important or inaccessible by the servile flatteries that seem inseparable from life in the White House. He sometimes admonished himself, in words of the Gospel according to Luke: "Woe unto you when all men shall speak well of you, for so did their fathers to the false prophets." Within a month after taking office, he had a letter sent to the governors of all the states telling them that his latchstring would always be out to them. "If as we go along to complete the unfinished work, you are confronted with a problem which the President can help you with, do not hesitate to ask me for an opportunity for you to discuss it with him." And he had no unwelcome list. Two prominent members of his predecessor's unwelcome list, ex-President Hoover and Senator Taft, were conspicuous among Mr. Truman's early visitors; and General de Gaulle, hitherto persona non grata at the White House, received an early invitation to visit it. Nor can all of his hospitality be explained by the manifest importance of giving his foreign policy a bipartisan underpinning—the consideration that at least partly explains his early consultations with the former Republican presidential candidates, Governor Landon and Governor Dewey.

Mr. Truman soon came to perceive that to be President is an inveterate process of self-subordination, and in a letter to a Postmaster General of the Roosevelt administration, Frank Walker, he wrote: "I have learned in a very short time that the President of the United States all too often has to act in ways which are very different from the personal wishes and feelings of the President himself."

He was, of course, well aware, and sometimes wrily aware, that a President has to be at least five persons in one: "He is the executive officer of the government. He is the leader of his party. He has certain legislative duties, consisting of signing bills or vetoing them. He is the social head of the state. And he is Commander in Chief of the armed forces." On the other hand, he was cheered and impressed by the unique exhaustiveness of the factual information available to a President. In a press interview on his seventy-first birthday, May 8, 1955, he said revealingly, with the current administration inevitably in mind: "The President has the information available to him to know more than any other person what is going on around the world, and he shouldn't let others tell him what to do."

7. EMERGENCY POWERS

Mr. Truman clearly belongs in the succession of Presidents who have been jealous guardians of their powers and have tended to make rather a broad than a narrow construction of them—such Presidents as Jefferson, Madison, Jackson, Lincoln, both Roosevelts, and Wilson, all of whom did something to apply and perhaps extend the Hamiltonian concept of the presidency. It was Hamilton's theory that the President is endued by the Constitution with a good deal of autonomous discretion inherent in his possession of the executive power of the United States—that he has a vast, not precisely definable authority in addition to his specifically named constitutional powers. On this theory Mr. Truman acted; and some important applications that he made of it in the field of labor-management contentions led eventually to a crucial testing of theory and application.

In May of 1946, in not the first of the successive emergencies brought to a head by John L. Lewis as chief of the United Mine Workers, Mr. Truman declared a federal seizure of the soft coal mines. Though under pressure from political critics to act under the authority of the Smith-Connally Act, the President by-passed this piece of legislation and acted under a declaration of authority as follows:

Because the coal produced by the bituminous coal mines "is required for the war effort and is indispensable for the continued operation of the national economy during the transition from war to peace," the President said he had decided "that the exercise . . . . of the powers vested in me is necessary to insure the operation" of the mines.

"Now, therefore, by virtue of the power and authority vested in me by the Constitution and laws of the United States, . . . as President of the United States and Commander in Chief of the Army and Navy of the United States," the President said he is ordering the Secretary of the Interior to take possession of the struck mines and to arrange for their protection and operation.

§ The resultant situation led in the following November to what was theoretically and actually a strike of the United Mine Workers against the government of the United States, to a federal injunction,

and to the massive fines levied upon Mr. Lewis and his union for civil
and criminal contempt of court. But a partly analogous assertion of
the same emergency powers late in the Truman administration produced a strikingly different outcome.

On April 8, 1952, the President's answer to an impending strike
in the steel industry was government seizure of the steel mills. What
evoked this action was a controversy involving complex issues that
affected some 600,000 United Steel Workers of America and the
ninety-two steel companies that accounted for ninety-five per cent
of the national production. On the evening of the day of the executive
order for the seizure Mr. Truman made to the nation the following
statement of the history, considerations of policy, and legal justifica-
tions behind the situation.

Tonight our country faces a grave danger. We are faced by the
possibility that at midnight tonight the steel industry will be shut
down. This must not happen.

Steel is our key industry. It is vital to our defense effort. It is vital
to peace.

We do not have a stock pile of the kinds of steel we need for
defense. Steel is flowing directly to the plants that make it into
defense production.

If steel production stops, we will have to stop making the shells
and bombs that are going directly to our soldiers at the front in
Korea. If steel production stops, we will have to cut down and delay
the atomic energy program. If steel production stops, it won't be long
before we have to stop making engines for the Air Force planes.

These would be the immediate effects if the steel mills close down.
A prolonged shutdown would bring defense production to a halt and
throw our domestic economy into chaos.

These are not normal times. These are times of crisis. We've been
working and fighting to prevent the outbreak of world war. So far
we have succeeded. The most important element in this successful
struggle has been our defense program. If that is stopped, the situation
can change overnight.

All around the world, we face the threat of military action by the
forces of aggression. Our growing strength is holding these forces in
check. If our strength fails, these forces may break out in renewed
violence and bloodshed.

Our national security and our chances for peace depend on our defense production. Our defense production depends on steel.

As your President, I have to think about the effects that a steel shutdown here would have all over the world.

I have to think about our soldiers in Korea, facing the Chinese Communists, and about our soldiers and our allies in Europe, confronted by the military power massed behind the Iron Curtain. I have to think of the danger to our security if we are forced, for lack of steel, to cut down on our atomic energy program.

I have no doubt that if our defense program fails, the danger of war, the possibility of hostile attack, grows much greater.

I would not be faithful to my responsibilities as President if I did not use every effort to keep this from happening.

With American troops facing the enemy on the field of battle, I would not be living up to my oath of office if I failed to do whatever is required to provide them with the weapons and the ammunition they need for their survival.

Therefore, I am taking two actions tonight.

First, I am directing the Secretary of Commerce to take possession of the steel mills, and to keep them operating.

Second, I am directing the Acting Director of Defense Mobilization to get the representatives of the steel companies and the steel workers down here to Washington at the earliest possible date in a renewed effort to get them to settle their dispute.

I am taking these measures because it is the only way to prevent a shutdown and to keep steel production rolling. It is also my hope that they will help bring about a quick settlement of the dispute.

I want you to understand clearly why these measures are necessary, and how this situation in the steel industry came about.

In normal times—if we were not in a national emergency—this dispute might not have arisen. In normal times, unions are entitled to whatever wages they can get by bargaining, and companies are entitled to whatever prices they can get in a competitive market.

But today, this is different. There are limitations on what wages employees can get, and there are limitations on what prices employers can charge.

We must have these limitations to prevent a wage-price spiral that would send prices through the roof and wreck our economy and our defense program.

For more than a year, we have prevented any such runaway inflation. We have done it by having rules that are fair to everyone—that require everyone to sacrifice some of his own interests in the national interest. These rules have been laid down under laws enacted by Congress, and they are applied by fair, impartial government boards and agencies.

Those rules have been applied in this steel case. They have been applied to the union, and they have been applied to the companies. The union has accepted these rules. The companies have not accepted them.

The companies insist that they must have price increases that are out of line with the stabilization rules. The companies have said that unless they can get these increases they will not settle with the union. The companies have said, in short, that unless they can have what they want, the steel industry will shut down. This is the plain, unvarnished fact of the matter.

Let me tell you how this situation came about.

The steel companies and the steelworkers' union had a contract that ran until December 31, 1951.

On November 1, 1951, the union gave notice that in view of the higher cost of living and the wage increases already received by workers in other industries, the steel workers wanted higher wages and better working conditions in their new contract for 1952.

The steel companies met with the union, but the companies never really bargained. The companies all took the same position. They said there should be no changes in wages and working conditions—in spite of the fact that there had been substantial changes in many other industries, and in spite of the fact that the steel industry was making very high profits.

No progress was made, and a strike was threatened last December 31.

Before that happened I sent the case to the Wage Stabilization Board. I asked them to investigate the facts and to recommend a settlement that would be fair to both parties, and would also be in accordance with the rules for preventing inflation. Meanwhile, I asked both sides to keep the steel industry operating, and they did.

The wage board went into the facts very thoroughly. And about three weeks ago, on March 20, the wage board recommended certain wage increases and certain changes in working conditions.

The wage board's recommendations were less than the union thought they ought to have. Nevertheless, the union accepted them as a basis for settlement.

There has been a lot of propaganda to the effect that the recommendations of the wage board were too high, that they would touch off a new round of wage increases, and that a new wage-price spiral would set in.

The facts are to the contrary. When you look into the matter, you find that the wage board's recommendations were fair and reasonable. They were entirely consistent with what has been allowed in other industries over the past eighteen months. They are in accord with sound stabilization policies.

Under these recommendations, the steel workers would simply be catching up with what workers in other major industries are already receiving.

The steel workers have had no adjustment in their wages since December 1, 1950. Since that time the cost of living has risen, and workers in such industries as automobiles, rubber, electrical equipment, and meat packing have received increases ranging from 13 to 17 cents an hour.

In the steel case, the wage board recommended a general wage increase averaging 13¾ cents an hour in 1952. Obviously, this sets no new pattern and breaks no ceiling. It simply permits the steel workers to catch up to what workers in other industries have already received.

The board also recommended a 2½-cent wage increase to go into effect next January if the union would agree to an eighteen-month contract. In addition, the board recommended certain other provisions concerning such matters as paid holidays and extra pay for Sunday work. The steel industry has been lagging behind other industries in these matters, and the improvements suggested by the board are moderate.

When you look at the facts, instead of the propaganda, it is perfectly plain that the wage board's recommendations in the steel case do provide a fair and reasonable basis for reaching a settlement on a new management-labor contract—a settlement that is consistent with our present stabilization program.

Of course, neither party can ever get everything it thinks it deserves; and, certainly, the parties should bargain out the details.

But in the present circumstances, both the companies and the union owe it to the American people to use these recommendations as a basis for reaching a settlement.

The fact of the matter is that the settlement proposed by the board is fair to both parties and to the public interest. And what's more, I think the steel companies know it. They can read figures just as well as anybody else—just as well as I can or anybody in the business.

I think they realize that the board's recommendations on wages are reasonable, and that they are raising all this hullabaloo in an attempt to force the government to give them a big boost in prices.

Now, what about the price side? Is it true that the steel companies need a big increase in prices in order to be able to raise wages?

Here are the facts.

Steel industry profits are now running at the rate of about $2,500,000,000 a year. The steel companies are now making a profit of about $19.50 on every ton of steel they produce. On top of that, they can get a price increase of close to $3 a ton under the Capehart Amendment to the price-control law. They don't need this, but we are going to have to give it to them, because the Capehart Amendment requires it.

Now add to this the $19.50 a ton they are already making and you have profits of better than $22 a ton.

Now, what would the wage board's recommendations do to the steel profits? The way the steel companies talk, you would think the wage increase recommended by the board would wipe out their profits altogether. Well, the fact of the matter is that if all the recommendations of the wage board were put into effect, they would cost the industry about $4 or $5 a ton.

In other words, if the steel companies absorbed every penny of the wage increase, they would still be making profits of $17 or $18 a ton on every ton of steel they make.

Now, a profit of $17 or $18 a ton for steel is extremely high. During 1947, 1948, and 1949, the three years before the Korean outbreak, steel profits averaged a little better than $11 a ton. The companies could absorb this wage increase entirely out of profits and still be making much higher profits than they made in the three prosperous years before Korea.

The plain fact is—though most people don't realize it—the steel industry has never been so profitable as it is today; at least not since the "profiteering" days of World War I.

And yet, in the face of these facts, the steel companies are now saying they ought to have a price increase of $12 a ton, giving them a profit of $26 or $27 a ton. That's about the most outrageous thing I ever heard of. They not only want to raise their prices to cover any wage increase; they want to double their money on the deal.

Suppose we were to yield to these demands. Suppose we broke our price-control rules, and gave the steel companies a big price increase. That would be a terrible blow to the stability of the economy of the United States of America.

A big boost in steel prices would raise the prices of other things all up and down the line. Sooner or later, prices of all the products that use steel would go up—tanks and trucks and buildings, automobiles and vacuum cleaners and refrigerators, right on down to canned goods and egg beaters.

But even worse than this, if we broke our price control rules for steel I don't see how we could keep them for any other industry.

There are plenty of other industries that would like to have big price increases. Our price control officials meet every day with industries that want to raise their prices. For months they have been turning down most of these requests, because most of the companies have had profits big enough to absorb cost increases and still leave a fair return.

The paper industry has been turned down. So have the brass industry, and the truck industry, and the auto parts industry, and many others.

All these industries have taken "no" for an answer, and they have gone home and kept right on producing. That's what any law-abiding person does when he is told that what he'd like to do is against the rules.

But not the steel companies. Not the steel companies. The steel industry doesn't want to come down and make its case, and abide by the decision like everybody else. The steel industry wants something special, something nobody else can get.

If we gave in to the steel companies on this issue, you could say good-by to stabilization. If we knuckled under to the steel industry, the lid would be off. Prices would start jumping up all around us—not just prices of things using steel, but prices of many other things we buy, including milk and groceries and meat.

You may think this steel dispute doesn't affect you—you may think it's just a matter between the government and a few greedy companies. But it isn't. If we granted the outrageous prices the steel industry wants, we would scuttle our whole price control program. And that comes pretty close to home to everybody in the country.

It is perfectly clear, from the facts I have cited, that the present danger to our stabilization program comes from the steel companies' insistence on a big jump in steel prices.

The plain fact of the matter is that the steel companies are recklessly forcing a shutdown of the steel mills. They are trying to get special, preferred treatment, not available to any other industry. And they are apparently willing to stop steel production to get it.

As President of the United States it is my plain duty to keep this from happening. And that is the reason for the measures I have taken tonight.

At midnight the government will take over the steel plants. Both management and labor will then be working for the government. And they will have a clear duty to heat up their furnaces again and go on making steel.

When management and labor meet down here in Washington, they will have a chance to go back to bargaining and settle their dispute. As soon as they do that, we can turn the steel plants back to their private owners with the assurance that production will continue.

It is my earnest hope that the parties will settle without delay—tomorrow if possible. I don't want to see the government running the steel plants a minute longer than is absolutely necessary to prevent a shutdown.

A lot of people have been saying I ought to rely on the procedures of the Taft-Hartley Act to deal with this emergency.

This has not been done because the so-called emergency provisions of the Taft-Hartley Act would be of no help in meeting the situation that confronts us tonight.

That act provides that before anything else is done, the President must first set up a board of inquiry to find the facts on the dispute and report to him as to what they are. We would have to sit around for a week or two for this board to report before we could take the next step. And meanwhile, the steel plants would be shut down.

Now there is another problem with the Taft-Hartley procedure. The law says that once a board of inquiry has reported, the government can go to the courts for an injunction requiring the union to postpone a strike for eighty days. This is the only provision in the law to help us stop a strike.

But the fact is that in the present case the steelworkers' union has already postponed its strike since last December 31—ninety-nine days. In other words, the union has already done more, voluntarily, than it could be required to do under the Taft-Hartley Act. We do not need further delay and a prolonging of the crisis. We need a settlement, and we need it fast.

Consequently, it is perfectly clear that the emergency provisions of the Taft-Hartley Act do not fit the needs of the present situation. We've already had the benefit of an investigation by one board. We've already had more delay than the Taft-Hartley Act provides.

But the overriding fact is that the Taft-Hartley procedure could not prevent a steel shutdown of at least a week or two.

We must have steel. We have taken the measures that are required to keep the steel mills in operation. But these are temporary measures, and they ought to be ended as soon as possible.

The way we want to get steel production—the only way to get it in the long run—is for management and labor to sit down and settle their dispute. Sooner or later that's what will have to be done. So it might just as well be done now as any time.

There is no excuse for the present deadlock in negotiations. Everyone concerned knows what ought to be done. A settlement should be reached between the steel companies and the union. And the companies should then apply to the Office of Price Stabilization for whatever price increase they are entitled to under the law.

That is what is called for in the national interest.

On behalf of the whole country, I ask the steel companies and the steelworkers' union to compose their differences in the American spirit of fair play and in obedience to the law of the land.

§ On April 9, the day after the seizure, the President informed the Congress of his action and offered to co-operate if Congress deemed it necessary to enact "legislation establishing specific terms and conditions with reference to the operation of the steel mills by the government." Meanwhile, litigation in the Federal District Court of the District of Columbia challenged the legality of the President's action. Mr. Truman himself explored the matter at his press conference on April 24. Not only did the President have inherent powers under conditions of emergency to seize the steel industry, he declared: the same powers were equally available to seize the press and radio, though he could not imagine that any government would take them over. The President mentioned the Louisiana Purchase, the territorial annexations of Polk and Seward, Lincoln's response to the outbreak of the rebellion, and Roosevelt's initiative in World War II as like instances of inherent presidential powers exercised to meet emergencies. He had seized the steel industry because the country was confronted with one of the greatest emergencies in its history.

Three days later Mr. Truman described his powers more circumspectly in a letter to C. S. (Casey) Jones of Washington Crossing, Pennsylvania, who had written to the President questioning his powers of seizure. Mr. Truman replied: "The powers of the President are derived from the Constitution, and they are limited, of course, by the provisions of the Constitution, particularly those that protect the rights of individuals.

"The legal problems that arise from these facts are now being examined in the courts, as is proper, but I feel sure that the Constitution does not require me to endanger our national safety by letting all the steel mills shut down in this critical time."

The Supreme Court of the United States thought differently. On June 2, 1952, by a majority of 6 to 3, it voided the seizure in the case of Youngstown Sheet and Tube Company vs. Sawyer, 343 U.S. 579. The Court ruled in effect that when the President seized the steel mills he seized the lawmaking power, and that only Congress could authorize the taking of private property for public use. In the Court's opinion no statute, express or implied, authorized the President to seize the steel mills. Indeed, Congress in considering the Taft-Hartley Act had refused to authorize government seizure of property as a method of preventing work stoppages or settling labor disputes. Nor was such authority deducible from the aggregate of executive powers in Article II or from the President's powers as Commander in Chief.

Immediately after the decision President Truman ordered the

return of the steel mills to the companies and appeared before a joint session of Congress to request specific statutory authority to deal with labor disputes in major industries in time of emergency. The Senate, dominated by a coalition of Republicans and Southern Democrats, quickly rejected the request. The Congress then requested the President, in its amendments of 1952 to the Defense Production Act, to apply to the steel problem the relevant provisions of the Taft-Hartley Act. He had previously rejected these provisions as "unfair, harmful and futile" in bringing about a settlement and restoring production. From this view he never retreated. Through the summer of 1952 the steel talks continued, though without success. On August 9 they were suspended indefinitely after both sides had agreed to turn out essential military material.

8. PRESIDENTIAL SUCCESSION

During his first weeks in office President Truman was greatly concerned about what he deemed the inadequacies of existing law covering selection of a successor in the event of his own death or incapacity. His proposal of new legislation on presidential succession was incorporated in a special message to Congress on June 19, 1945.

I think that this is an appropriate time for the Congress to reexamine the question of the presidential succession.

The question is of great importance now because there will be no elected Vice-President for almost 4 years.

The existing statute governing the succession to the office of President was enacted in 1886. Under it, in the event of the death of the elected President and Vice-President, members of the Cabinet successively fill the office.

Each of these Cabinet members is appointed by the President with the advice and consent of the Senate. In effect, therefore, by reason of the tragic death of the late President, it now lies within my power to nominate the person who would be my immediate successor in the event of my own death or inability to act.

I do not believe that in a democracy this power should rest with the Chief Executive.

Insofar as possible, the office of the President should be filled by an elective officer. There is no officer in our system of government, besides the President and Vice-President, who has been elected by all the voters of the country.

The Speaker of the House of Representatives, who is elected in his own district, is also elected to be the presiding officer of the House by a vote of all the representatives of all the people of the country. As a result, I believe that the Speaker is the official in the federal government whose selection, next to that of the President and Vice-President, can be most accurately said to stem from the people themselves.

Under the law of 1792, the President pro tempore of the Senate followed the Vice-President in the order of succession.

The President pro tempore is elected as a Senator by his state and then as presiding officer by the Senate. But the members of the Senate are not as closely tied in by the elective process to the people as are the members of the House of Representatives. A completely new House is elected every two years, and always at the same time as the President and Vice-President. Usually it is in agreement politically with the Chief Executive. Only one third of the Senate, however, is elected with the President and Vice-President. The Senate might, therefore, have a majority hostile to the policies of the President, and might conceivably fill the presidential office with one not in sympathy with the will of the majority of the people.

Some of the events in the impeachment proceedings of President Johnson suggested the possibility of a hostile Congress in the future seeking to oust a Vice-President who had become President, in order to have the President pro tempore of the Senate become the President. This was one of the considerations, among several others, which led to the change in 1886.

No matter who succeeds to the Presidency after the death of the elected President and Vice-President, it is my opinion he should not serve any longer than until the next congressional election or until a special election called for the purpose of electing a new President and Vice-President. This period the Congress should fix. The individuals elected at such general or special election should then serve only to fill the unexpired term of the deceased President and Vice-President. In this way there would be no interference with the normal four-year interval of general national elections.

I recommend, therefore, that the Congress enact legislation placing the Speaker of the House of Representatives first in order of succession in case of the removal, death, resignation, or inability to act of the President and Vice-President. Of course, the Speaker should resign as a Representative in the Congress as well as Speaker of the House before he assumes the office of President.

If there is no qualified Speaker, or if the Speaker fails to qualify, then I recommend that the succession pass to the President pro tempore of the Senate, who should hold office until a duly qualified Speaker is elected.

If there be neither Speaker nor President pro tempore qualified to succeed on the creation of the vacancy, then the succession might pass to the members of the Cabinet as now provided, until a duly qualified Speaker is elected.

If the Congress decides that a special election should be held, then I recommend that it provide for such election to be held as soon after the death or disqualification of the President or Vice-President as practicable. The method and procedure for holding such special election should be provided now by law, so that the election can be held as expeditiously as possible should the contingency arise.

In the interest of orderly, democratic government, I urge the Congress to give its early consideration to this most important subject.

§ *The House quickly approved, but through 1945 and 1946 the Senate failed to act on the proposal. In February 1947 the President renewed his request, and on July 18, 1947, the Congress repealed the Act of 1886 and enacted a new law embodying Mr. Truman's original plan except for its special-election feature. Congress in the meantime had passed under Republican control; but the President saw no reason to change his mind, and he signed the bill the day after its enactment.*

II
ADMINISTRATIVE CHIEF

One of the things that a President of the United States presides over is a mammoth administrative organization—the hugest and most complex in the free world. It is, moreover, a perpetually growing organization; it grows by accretion of functions and responsibilities, and the burden carried by the President grows pari passu. A part of what the President has to do as administrator is, of course, routine and does not greatly alter from one incumbency to another. But any presidency is also characterized by the emergence of special administrative problems, some of them formulated on the President's own initiative and expressive of his own sense of what the country needs, others crystallized by current events as outgrowths of inevitable change. Mr. Truman's insistence on reorganizing the executive branch of the government toward efficiency and economy is an example of the first kind; the dismaying new problem of divided loyalty, of assuring the ideological and practical fidelity of the civil service to American and democratic principles, is an example of the second kind.

It is wholly natural that a President shall give his attention and his enthusiasm, so far as the march of events will let him, to the proposals that grow out of his own thinking and represent his own initiative. It is by these that he hopes to prove his capacity and to *make himself remembered. Mr. Truman, in the main, was intent on preserving and increasing the effectiveness of the civil service. And he did not mind involving himself in repelling attacks on its integrity from Congressional and other quarters whenever he deemed the attacks unwarranted. He was also intent on reducing the complexity and the costs of administration and on the reorganization of departments to that end. It is, then, not surprising that he should have spoken and acted with the utmost vigor in these areas, whereas by comparison he tended to brush off all suggestions that there was a grave question of loyal patriotism in high places or that his administration had provided a startling foothold for petty grafters, corruptionists, and receivers of baksheesh in the form of mink coats, deepfreeze apparatus, and percentages on contracts influenced.*

The utterances that follow, grouped around the subjects just mentioned and some ancillary topics, make clear this difference of enthusiasm.

1. TRAINING FOR PUBLIC SERVICE

Mr. Truman's general concern for the civil service and for its progressive improvement is implicit in his address at the Bicentennial Convention at Princeton University on June 17, 1947.

On an earlier occasion of equal significance in the history of this university the President of the United States, Grover Cleveland, spoke in 1896 at the Princeton sesquicentennial ceremonies. President Cleveland seized that opportunity to charge our colleges and universities with the task of supplying a "constant stream of thoughtful, educated men" to the body politic—men who were eager to perform public service for the benefit of the nation. He chided our institutions of higher learning for their lack of interest in public affairs and held them responsible for the disdain with which many of the best-educated men of the day viewed politics and public affairs.

Happily for us, that attitude on the part of our universities vanished long ago. I am certain that no observer of the American scene in recent years has detected any reluctance on the part of our educators to enter the political arena when their services have been needed. And our schools have made much progress in supplying the "constant stream of thoughtful, educated men" for public service called for by President Cleveland half a century ago.

That task is more important today than at any previous time in our national history.

In our free society, knowledge and learning are endowed with a public purpose—a noble purpose, close to the heart of democracy. That purpose is to help men and women develop their talents for the benefit of their fellow citizens. Our advance in the natural sciences has led to almost miraculous achievements, but we have less reason to be proud of our progress in developing the capacity among men for co-operative living. In the present critical stage of world history we need, more than ever before, to enlist all our native integrity and industry in the conduct of our common affairs.

The role of the United States is changing more rapidly than in any previous period of our history. We have had to assume world-wide responsibilities and commitments. Our people have placed their trust in the government as the guardian of our democratic ideals and the instrument through which we work for enduring peace.

The success of the government's efforts in achieving these ends will depend upon the quality of citizenship of our people. It will also depend upon the extent to which our leaders in business, labor, the professions, agriculture, and every other field appreciate the role of their government and the greatness of its tasks.

Our schools must train future leaders in all fields to understand and concern themselves with the expanded role of government and— equally important—to see the need for effective administration of the government's business in the public interest.

I call your attention particularly to the problem of effective administration within the government, where matters of unprecedented magnitude and complexity confront the public servant. If our national policies are to succeed they must be administered by officials with broad experience, mature outlook, and sound judgment. There is, however, a critical shortage of such men—men who possess the capacity to deal with great affairs of state.

The government has recruited from our academic institutions many members of its professional staffs—geologists, physicists, lawyers, economists, and others with specialized training. These men are essential to the conduct of the government and the welfare of the nation. But we have been much less effective in obtaining persons with broad understanding and an aptitude for management. We need men who can turn a group of specialists into a working team and who can combine imagination and practicability into a sound public program.

All large organizations, public or private, depend on the teamwork of specialists. Co-ordination is achieved by administrators trained to assemble the fruits of specialized knowledge and to build on that foundation a sound final decision. Men trained for this kind of administrative and political leadership are rare indeed.

In the task of finding and training men and women who will add strength to the public service, universities have a particular responsibility. They should develop in their students the capacity for seeing and meeting social problems as a whole and for relating special knowledge to broad issues. They should study the needs of government and encourage men and women with exceptional interests and aptitudes along the necessary lines to enter the government service.

The Woodrow Wilson School of Public and International Affairs of this university was established with this purpose in mind. It seeks to prepare students for public careers. It is significant that the school bears the name of a statesman whose concept of civic duty contributed so much to the nation and to the world.

Of course, the government cannot and does not expect to rely entirely upon our educational institutions for its administrators. It must bring into service from business and labor, and the professions, the best qualified persons to fill posts at all levels.

The government must take several steps to make its career service more attractive to the kind of men and women it needs.

Salary limitations prevent the government, in many instances, from securing the kind of executives required to manage its vital activities. Capable administrators are too frequently drawn away from government to private positions with salaries many times what they could earn in government service. This situation can be remedied only by laws to bring salaries more nearly into line with the heavy responsibilities that executives carry at the higher levels in the public service.

The complexities of the tasks now facing our top officials force them to spend most of their time in studying matters of policy. These officials should be supported by a career group of administrators skilled in the various aspects of management. If capable men and women can look forward to holding such posts as a reward for able service, they will be more eager to accept government employment.

Because of the difficult tasks of government today, we should plan a program for the systematic training of civilian employees once they have entered the public service. It is not generally possible at the present time for the Federal government to send its employees to universities for special short-term training programs. Nor is it permissible under existing law to spend federal funds for government schools to develop the knowledge and techniques required by officials in their work.

This is a problem that can be solved only by the joint efforts of the government and the universities. Training programs can be formulated, both on the job and on the campus. The government must make provision for its employees to participate. The universities will need to provide courses well adapted to increasing the effectiveness of the employee in his job. Such a plan is certain to pay substantial dividends.

2. IMPROVEMENT OF THE CIVIL SERVICE

President Truman, like some other modern Presidents, wanted to extend the competitive basis of appointment and correspondingly to reduce the incidence of patronage. He also wanted to enhance the prestige of government employment, a perennial problem seriously aggravated in his administration by the complicating issue of loyalty. His views were set forth in an address to the National Civil Service League in Washington on May 2, 1952.

I have a deep appreciation and admiration for the loyal, hardworking, and able men and women who make up our civil service. I have worked in all kinds of government. In fact, I know government from precinct to President, I know it in the country, I know it in federal, state, legislative and executive . . . of the United States.

I have been interested in public service for over thirty years; in fact, on the third day of next January I will have been in elected public office exactly thirty years. Ever since I was first elected judge of the county court for Jackson County, Missouri, I've been interested in Government. Now don't get the idea that a judge of the county court of Missouri knows anything about law—he doesn't. It's an administrative office.

Let me tell you something I have learned in my thirty years of public office: Good government is good politics; and the best politics is what is best for all the people.

Of course, there are very important differences between being an elective official and serving in the civil service. Our elective officials are politically responsible; they must answer to the people. And they must make the major policy decisions. The role of our civil servant is to (and sometimes we have a terrible time in getting them to do it) carry out these policy decisions. But there is the great bond of public service, holding both groups together. Both are working together for the good of all the people of this great country.

The people are entitled to the most efficient public service we can devise. The way to provide such service is to make sure that all government employees, except those in top policy jobs, are under the merit system. It has consistently been my goal to bring this about. I am happy to report that the goal is now in sight.

We have made great progress since 1881, when the National Civil Service League was organized. Then there was virtually no civil service. By the turn of the century 50 per cent of federal employees were under civil service.

And now over 93 per cent of all federal employees in the United States are under the competitive civil service. This is a remarkable achievement, but it is by no means the whole story. In addition to our regular civil service, special merit systems have been set up for various agencies, such as the Atomic Energy Commission, the Tennessee Valley Authority, and the Federal Bureau of Investigation. When these are taken into account, the number of employees covered by the merit system comes to 99 per cent of the total.

I am proud that during my term of office we have extended the merit system to cover virtually all Federal positions.

Our career civil service is still a long way from perfect; but it is in better shape than it's ever been before. We are going forward with our plans to eliminate the last remnants of the patronage system. But these efforts meet with the same kind of resistance, the same kind of hypocritical opposition, that has greeted every effort to make the civil service better. The patronage seekers are still on the prowl.

Just a few weeks ago, for example, I sent to Congress my plan to reorganize the Bureau of Internal Revenue. The purpose of this plan is to place under the civil service all the positions in the bureau, with the sole exception of the Commissioner of Internal Revenue. In short, this plan takes all our tax collectors out of politics. Of course it also takes that much patronage away from the members of the Senate.

And what a howl of anguish went up from the patronage boys. Just as you might expect, those who cried the loudest were the very ones who had been making the most noise about the misdeeds of political employees. If you want to know who these gentlemen are, get out the Congressional Record and read the list of those who voted against the plan. Well, we fought them and we beat them, and we won a major victory for the merit system.

On April 10 I sent three more reorganization plans to the Congress. Reorganization Plan No. 2 would take postmasters out of partisan politics by abolishing the requirement that they be appointed by the President and confirmed by the Senate. Under Reorganization Plan No. 3, all political offices in the Bureau of Customs would be eliminated and the work would be carried on by qualified civil service appointees. Reorganization Plan No. 4 would place the positions of United States marshals under Civil Service. You'll hear a bigger roar about that than you did about the Collectors of Internal Revenue.

When these three reorganization plans are approved, only a handful of positions will remain outside the merit system. But that doesn't mean the job of the National Civil Service League is finished—far from it. We have created a career public service throughout the federal government—now we must fight to protect and to keep it. There is a new attack on the Civil Service—an attack which holds more dangers than the spoilsman. This new attack is an attempt to gain political ends by the shameful method of defaming and degrading the people who work for the government of the United States.

To understand exactly what we are up against calls for another lesson in politics.

In the normal operation of our democratic system, every administration is held to account every four years for its policies, its programs, and its conduct of the government. That is as it should be. In recent years the programs and the policies of the administration in office have been upheld, time after time, by the popular verdict. Today, the time for another accounting is approaching, and the opposition is becoming rather frantic.

They know that they cannot persuade the people to give up the gains of the last twenty years. But they think they can undermine those gains by attacking the men and women who have the job of carrying out the programs of the government. And so they have launched a campaign to make people think that the government service as a whole is lazy, inefficient, corrupt, and even disloyal.

Now these confusers do not for a moment believe their own charges. The government servant is not the real target of their attack. They are engaged in a ruthless, cynical attempt to put over a gigantic hoax and fraud on the American people.

They say: "Let's make the public think that the government service is full of crooks and thieves. Let's create the impression that all public servants are bad. Let's tell the people that the government servants are Reds. Let's confuse innuendo with fact, rumor with evidence, charge with guilt.

"If the real people get mad enough and confused enough we won't have to take a position on any of the great public policy issues: we can sneak into office by the back door."

Now that's what they think they can do, but I'll tell you right now they're not going to be able to do it. They tried it in 1948, much to their sorrow.

There is only one effective way to deal with this attack, and that is to wage a campaign of truth. Chairman Ramspeck has courageously started such a campaign, but he needs the help of all of us. He needs the help of every government employee in order to let the people know that the government employees are honest men and good workers. It is time to blast the rumors, the false inferences and innuendoes, and the downright lies about public service.

Take the charge that most federal employees are unnecessary. This is completely untrue. It's just as false as it can be.

Fifty per cent of our civilian employees are in the Defense Department—engaged directly in military activities of the Army, Navy, and Air Force. They man our arsenals, shipyards, supply depots, and weapons laboratories. Most of them are mechanics, steel workers, riveters, electricians, and other artisans.

In addition to that, another 28 per cent of the total are in the Post Office Department and the Veterans' Administration.

That adds up to 78 per cent in just three agencies.

The remaining 22 per cent perform all the other functions of the government—staffing such vital agencies as the F.B.I. and the Atomic Energy Commission, the Soil Conservation Service and Reclamation, the Employment Service and Public Health. This 22 per cent covers a great many peacetime activities of the government, as well as all the national security activities outside the Department of Defense. Except for these national security emergency activities, employment in the normal peacetime operations of the government has been cut back since Korea. Now you never hear that. You won't see that in the paper, and unless you're listening to me over the radio you'll never find out if that's true.

The people who carry on these operations are not useless bureaucrats. If they are, so am I. They are performing necessary services for the good of the American people, for their protection and welfare. They are performing services which the American people have demanded and the Congress has authorized by law. And they are performing them well and efficiently.

But the detractors are not satisfied with attacking the federal services as a whole. They have launched a personal campaign against the government worker himself. He is pictured as mediocre, shiftless, lazy, and nonproductive, a feeder at the public trough who couldn't get a job anywhere else. At one moment he is berated as a low-salaried nonentity with no standing in his field, and in the next breath he is called a high-salaried drain on the public purse.

What are the facts? Government workers are like any other American citizens throughout the country. Only 10 per cent are employed in Washington, D.C.; the remainder are in every state in the Union. California has more federal employees than the nation's capital. Get that now. California has more federal employees than the nation's capital.

More than 850,000 of all federal employees, one third of the total, are artisans and skilled craftsmen. The others include scientists, doctors, nurses—people in almost every trade and profession.

Are these people mediocre, shiftless, lazy, nonproductive?

Not at all, of course they're not. Government workers come out at the top in nearly every contest for efficiency and ingenuity. In 1950 a business efficiency organization sponsored a contest "for the best productive ideas." Government employees took the top honors. Their proven ingenuity and initiative had saved the taxpayers 22 million dollars in one year alone.

There are hundreds of examples of outstanding public service in the records of our federal employees.

Last year, for example, Dr. Thomas L. McMeekin, a chemist in the Agriculture Department, won top honors from the American Chemical Society for his outstanding work on the chemistry of milk proteins.

An employee of the Maritime Administration, Clarence Mercer, has invented a water blast method of removing scale from ships, which will save the Government over one million dollars. An employee of the Air Force, Irving Gordy, has carried on research in the electronics field that makes it possible to use a simple mechanism costing $30 in place of a machine costing $6,000.

And all these inventions and works belong to the government of the United States, and these men do not profit a penny by having brought them to light.

In engineering, in medicine, in the field of ordnance, the scientific and technical advances made by federal employees are saving the government millions and millions of dollars. Literally thousands of government employees have achieved high recognition in their special fields and are using their skills and abilities for the good of us all.

They're patriotic citizens. And if you don't think they could do better in private industry you're just as mistaken as you can be. But they like government service. They want to do something for the welfare of the people and they stay there and do it.

The demagogues say that government employees are responsible for high taxes. That's a good one; that's one that goes into every campaign. You'll hear it time and again around this time. The fact is that only 13 per cent of our budget is for wages and salaries. Our budget is large and our taxes are high because of the threat of Soviet imperialism. We have to build strong defenses. This is an expensive business, and lots of people grumble about it.

But it is a costly and destructive luxury to take our feelings out on our public servants. Berating our public servants doesn't help our defense, it weakens us. In this time of crisis we should try to improve our public service—not tear it down.

Now let me take up one other kind of charge against our public servants—and this is the most vicious and insidious of all. I say, with all the emphasis at my command, that there is no more cancerous, no more corrosive, no more subversive attack upon the great task of our government today than that which seeks to undermine confidence in government by irresponsible charges against the loyalty and integrity of government employees.

There is no room in government service for anyone who is not true to his public trust. We have had a few bad people turn up in government, just as they do in business and industry. They are not in the government now, and we are prosecuting all those who have violated the criminal statutes. If we turn up any more, they can expect the same treatment—and if there are any more we will turn them up, kick them out, and prosecute them if they need to be prosecuted.

But I will not tolerate the smearing and slandering of government employees as a group. We have every right to protest and to raise the roof against the deliberate creation for private political purposes of these unjust charges, of an atmosphere of suspicion and distrust against public employees. I'm not just starting now, and I'm giving warning to the people who've been slandering the government employees that they're going to have trouble with me from now until November.

And the best part of it is I'm not running for anything.

We have a right to protest against the creation of an atmosphere in which a charge is a conviction in the public mind despite the lack of evidence. We're not defending evildoers when we demand that the whole truth be stated—that the other side of the ledger be examined.

The truth is that the government service, in the light of its tremendous size and scope, has a remarkable record of honesty and integrity. I firmly believe that its ethical standards are as high as those of any government in the history of the world. I firmly believe that its ethical standards are higher than those prevailing in the American business community, and the Senate's own Committee on Ethics in Government agrees with me wholeheartedly. You read the report they made on the subject.

It is a curious fact that those in the business world who shout the loudest about corruption in government are those who most often approach the government with their hands out. It is a tragic fact that those in the political world who shout the loudest about corruption in government are motivated by such a lust for power that they are willing to wreck the lives and the careers of innocent public servants.

Of course, the worst kind of attack upon government employees has been the attack on their loyalty. Here, the technique of the attackers is the same; innuendo and smear and just plain lies. And the motivation is the same; they want to get more votes.

The truth is that we can be more confident of the unswerving loyalty of employees in the executive branch of our government than of any other group of people in the nation. They are the only large group of employees in the nation, public or private, subjected to such systematic and thoroughgoing investigation. And the record is one of which they can well be proud. Every employee in the executive branch is checked by the F.B.I. Only 384 employees, or nine one thousandths of one per cent of all those checked, had to be discharged on loyalty grounds. Think of that.

This is the real picture, based on hard fact. It is a shameful and degrading thing to try to mislead the American people into thinking it is otherwise.

We must always be vigilant in guarding the public service against the infiltration of disloyal elements.

But we must be just as vigilant in protecting employees against unjust accusations.

The loyalty program was designed to protect innocent employees as well as the government. When I set it up I intended it to expose the guilty and at the same time to safeguard the rights and reputations of those who were innocent. But I have become increasingly concerned in recent months by attempts to use the loyalty program as a club with which to beat government employees over the head.

Political gangsters are attempting to pervert the program into an instrument of intimidation and blackmail, to coerce or destroy any who dare to oppose them. These men and those who abet them have besmirched the reputations of decent, loyal public servants. They have not hesitated to lie, under cover of Congressional immunity, of course, and repeat the lies again and again.

This is a matter of great concern to me. These tactics contain the seeds of tyranny. Can we be sure that people who employ such tactics are really loyal to our form of government, with its Bill of Rights, its tradition of individual liberty? The fact is that they are breaking these things down. They are undermining the foundation stones of our Constitution. I believe such men betray our country and all it stands for. I believe they are as grave a menace as the communists; in fact, I think they're worse than communists, and I think they're partners with them.

It is not your job to take sides in partisan political controversy.

But it is your duty and the duty of all citizens to demand the truth about the government service and to reject the smear campaign as base, and call it immoral and the evil that it is.

In particular, it is your job to fight the attempt to reduce the civil servant to the status of a second-class citizen. This can be done, without taking sides in politics, by placing the facts about the civil service before the people. It can be done, without partisanship, in the name of ordinary decency and fair play.

The history of the National Civil Service League shows that it is well equipped to deal with the problem before us.

You can count on me, in office or out, to keep on fighting to uphold the government service, and I am confident that I can count on you as well.

3. SCREENING FOR LOYALTY

In the circumstances that produced the following address President Truman found himself under prolonged fire as a result of his plan for guaranteeing the loyalty of federal employees in the fight against domestic communism.

The plan had been made operative March 22, 1947, by Executive Order 9835, which was at least partly designed to head off more drastic Congressional action. The order provided for (1) the investigation of applicants for posts in the executive branch and (2) removal of disloyal employees. Investigation was mainly the responsibility of the Civil Service Commission. Removal was made the responsibility of the head of each department, assisted by loyalty boards of not fewer than three representatives of the department. The Truman order also required the Civil Service Commission to set up out of its membership "a Loyalty Review Board of not less than three impartial persons with authority to review cases of persons recommended for dismissal on grounds of disloyalty by any loyalty board." The order set forth various standards for refusal of employment and for dismissal.

Inextricable from the process was the President's frank policy of exercising executive discretion about requests by Congressional committees for access to confidential files and records of the executive branch. Mr. Truman had denied several requests from Congressional committees for the personnel files and for Federal Bureau of Investigation reports on employees whose loyalty was under question, and he issued the following directive to all federal officials:

Any subpoena or demand or request for information, reports, or files (relative to the loyalty of employees or prospective employees) received from sources other than those persons in the executive branch of the government who are entitled thereto by reason of their official duties, shall be respectfully declined, on the basis of this directive, and the subpoena or demand or other request shall be referred to the Office of the President for such response as the President may determine to be in the public interest in the particular case. There shall be no relaxation of the provisions of this directive except with my express authority.

§ This manifesto was strictly applied. In a report of August 28, 1948, the Un-American Activities Committee of the House said that it had been "hampered at every turn by the refusal of the executive branch of the government to co-operate in any way . . . due to the President's loyalty freeze order."

To the screening process as a whole two main schools of opposition developed. One, represented by a letter of April 13, 1947, to the New York Times by four Harvard Law School professors, protested that the plan did not sufficiently protect the individual. The other insisted that the plan did not deal drastically enough with the problem of subversion. (See the comment by James Rorty and Moshe Decter in McCarthy and the Communists, a study sponsored by the American Committee for Cultural Freedom, pp. 8-11, Boston, 1954.)

The President surveyed some of the attacks in the following address to the Federal Bar Association on April 24, 1950.

We've been fully aware of the threat of communist subversion within our own borders. Through the Federal Bureau of Investigation and other security forces, through prosecutions in the courts by the Department of Justice, through our federal employee loyalty program, and in many other ways, we have vigorously attacked communists wherever their activities become a threat to our liberty.

There's been so much confusion recently about who's doing what to defeat communism in this country that I think the record should be set straight.

This administration has fought communism with action and not just with words. We've carried on this fight with every law on the statute books, and we've recommended new laws when we found they were necessary and could be framed without impairing the very freedoms we are seeking to protect.

No known instance of communist subversion—or any other kind of subversion—has gone uninvestigated.

No case where the facts warranted has gone unprosecuted.

We have prosecuted and obtained convictions of eleven top-ranking members of the Communist party in this country. We have successfully prosecuted many other persons for crimes related to communism. We have also prosecuted and obtained conviction of a large number of alleged communists on charge of contempt for refusing to testify before federal grand juries or Congressional committees.

And these prosecutions have been carried on by the Attorney General's office in the executive part of the government.

We now have under investigation the cases of over 1,000 citizens to determine whether steps should be taken to revoke their citizenship on grounds involving subversive activities. One hundred and thirty-eight persons are under orders of deportation on grounds involving communism.

There is no area of American life in which the Communist party is making headway, except, maybe, in the deluded minds of some people. The communists have done their best to penetrate labor unions and the government, but they are being successfully fought on both fronts. Labor has been doing a splendid job of cleaning its house. In the federal government the employee loyalty program has been an outstanding success, and your government lawyers have contributed greatly to its results.

I set up the employee loyalty program three years ago with two objectives in mind.

I was determined, as far as it was humanly possible, to see that no disloyal person should be employed by our government, whether he was a communist or a native American fascist of the Silver Shirt or Ku Klux Klan variety. I was equally determined that loyal government employees should be protected against accusations which were false, malicious, and ill founded. And that's just as important as the other part of the program.

The loyalty program was drafted by able and experienced persons to protect the security of the government and to safeguard the rights of its employees. It is the first time in the history of this country that we have had such a program. The communists and their friends, as well as some sincere idealists, say that it is too drastic. The false patriots and even some honest reactionaries say that it is entirely too mild. They want us to dismiss employees on the basis of unsupported charges. They actually resent the democratic safeguards of the loyalty program. All this confirms me in the conviction that it is a sound and effective program conceived and carried out in the American tradition. And that's just what it is.

The F.B.I., the agency loyalty boards, the Loyalty Review Board have quietly and effectively carried out their job of protecting the integrity and security of the government of the United States. The Loyalty Review Board is the central organization which directs the whole program. It is divided about half and half between Democrats and Republicans and is headed by a distinguished Republican lawyer, Mr. Seth Richardson, who served as Assistant Attorney General of the United States under President Hoover.

Under the supervision of this board the loyalty program has rid the government of all employees who were found to be disloyal —and they were only a tiny fraction of one per cent.

Not a single person who has been adjudged to be a communist or otherwise disloyal remains on the government payroll today.

The able men charged with carrying out the loyalty program know that keeping disloyal persons out of the government is a business which must be done carefully and objectively. They know that the job cannot be done by publicly denouncing men as communists without having evidence to support such a charge, or by blackening the character of persons because their views are different from those of the accuser, or by hurling sensational accusations based on gossip, hearsay, or maybe just a hunch. They know that no one whose principal concern was the security of this country would try to do it that way. They know that anyone who had information about communist activity or who placed the security of this country above selfish or partisan considerations would turn that information over to the F.B.I., so that it could be properly investigated and the necessary action taken.

I've been surprised to see how much ignorance and misunderstanding there is about this loyalty program—even on the part of persons who should know better. It has occurred to me that, perhaps, they do know better—or perhaps there is some element of politics in their accusations. Of course that couldn't be the case.

A large part of the hue and cry about the loyalty program has centered on my refusal to turn over to a Congressional committee confidential loyalty files concerning individual employees. I've already stated several times the reasons why these files must not be disclosed. I want to restate them briefly, now.

The preservation of the strictest confidence with respect to loyalty files is the single most important element in operating a loyalty program which provides effective security for the government and justice for the individual employee.

The disclosures of these files would not only destroy the whole loyalty program, but it would seriously damage the future usefulness of the F.B.I. Information is given to the F.B.I. in confidence, which the F.B.I. has sworn to protect. Breaking the confidence would not only greatly embarrass and even endanger the informants involved, but would gravely impair the F.B.I.'s ability to get future information from other confidential sources.

Opening these files would reveal F.B.I. procedures and methods. It might reveal highly secret information vital to our national security and of great value to foreign nations.

Disclosure of the files would result in serious injustice to the reputation of many innocent persons. This is true because the F.B.I. investigative files do not contain proved information only. They include unverified charges and statements, as well as mere suspicions which, upon investigation, are found to be untrue.

If I should now open these files, I would create a precedent for future cases in which access to these files is demanded—and there would be many of those requirements. This would completely destroy the loyalty program, since, as experience shows, it would mean an attempt to try all loyalty cases over again in newspaper headlines, although they had already been carefully considered and fairly decided by a bipartisan board of loyal and distinguished Americans.

This question of maintaining the confidential character of information which the President determines it would not be in the public interest to disclose is not new. It goes back to the beginnings of our government.

It started with Washington, was upheld by Monroe and Jackson and Grover Cleveland and Theodore Roosevelt and Franklin Roosevelt and half a dozen other Presidents I could name to you who have taken the same position which I am taking.

Nothing new at all. All you need to do is read your history and study the situation and you will find out that I'm right on it.

Despite the historic precedents, with which I was thoroughly familiar, I gave the most careful consideration to the recent request of the Senate committee for access to the loyalty files. I obtained the views of Attorney General McGrath, the Loyalty Review Board chairman, Seth Richardson, and the F.B.I. director, Edgar Hoover, before I reached my decision to deny this request. All three were unanimous in recommending to me in the strongest possible terms that I refuse to make the files available. The decision was mine to make, and I made it. I am confident that no President, whatever his party, would have acted otherwise. I'd do it again if necessary.

Now, the federal employee loyalty program has demonstrated that the United States has the most loyal civil service in the world. It's a splendid organization, and I'm proud to head it.

Of course, in an organization as large as the United States government it is always possible, despite the greatest precautions, that there may be a few bad individuals. We shall not for one minute relax our vigilant efforts to protect the security of the government of the United States. That's what I have sworn to do, and that's what I intend to proceed to do to the best of my ability.

The present Attorney General and his predecessor have repeatedly asked that if any person has any information about the presence of any communist in the government it be furnished to them.

I now repeat that request.

That if there was anybody in the country who has any information that he feels would contribute to the safety and the welfare of the government, all he has to do is to put it through the regular channels, and if results are to be obtained they will be obtained. That's the only way you can do it, too.

If any citizen knows of the presence of a single communist or other subversive person in any federal job, let him furnish that information, and the evidence which supports his belief, to the Attorney General or to the F.B.I. Any information that may be furnished in response to this request will be promptly investigated and will be acted upon if the allegations are found to be true.

The fact of the matter is—because of measures we are taking— the internal security of the United States is not seriously threatened by the communists in this country. There are proportionately fewer communists in this country than in any other large country on earth. They are noisy and they're troublesome, but they are not a major threat.

Moreover, they have been steadily losing ground since their peak in 1932, at the depth of our greatest depression, when they polled the largest number of votes in their history in this country.

There is a right way and a wrong way to fight communism. This administration is doing it the right way and the sensible way.

Our attack on communism is embodied in a positive threefold program:

One, we are strengthening our own defenses and aiding free nations in other parts of the world so that we and they can effectively resist communist aggression.

Two, we are working to improve our democracy so as to give further proof, both to our own citizens and to people in other parts of the world, that democracy is the best system of government that men have yet devised.

Three, we are working quietly but effectively, without headlines or hysteria, against communist subversion in this country wherever it appears, and we are doing this within the framework of the democratic liberties we cherish.

That's the way this administration is fighting communism. That's the way it's going to continue to fight communism.

Now I'm going to tell you how we are not going to fight communism. We are not going to transform our fine F.B.I. into a Gestapo secret police. That's what some people would like to do. We are not going to try to control what our people read and say and think. We are not going to turn the United States into a Right-Wing totalitarian country in order to deal with a Left-Wing totalitarian threat.

In short, we're not going to end democracy. We're going to keep the Bill of Rights on the books. We're going to keep those ancient, hard-earned liberties which you lawyers have done so much to preserve and protect.

If we all work together to maintain and strengthen our democratic ideals, communism will never be a serious threat to our American way of life. The example we set for free men everywhere will help to roll back the tide of communist imperialism in other parts of the world.

Now, I have outlined for you my program against communism. This is the way I've worked against it.

This is the way I shall continue to work against it.

And now, I call on all fair-minded men and women to join me in this good fight.

4. EXAGGERATION OF SECURITY RISKS

The President's consistently asserted position, both during his incumbency and since, is that the allegation of numerous security risks in the federal service is grossly exaggerated. It is a position that made the phrase "red herring" a household word of the late 1940's.

It was at a press conference on August 5, 1948, when the hearings on Alger Hiss were under way in the Committee on Un-American Activities, that Mr. Truman denounced Congressional investigations into spy rings and Communist infiltration as diversions and red herrings. He first caught up the phrase from a reporter's question. At another press conference, that of September 2, he made the same application of the term on his own initiative, in seeming reference to the Committee on Un-American Activities. And in a press conference of December 16, 1948, he said that the indictment the day before of Alger Hiss for perjury had not altered his view that the agitation was a red herring.

On several occasions he amplified his views. Once he affirmed that, in the course of a concerted effort ever since the outbreak of the Second World War to see that disloyal persons were not employed in the government, very few disloyal persons had been found, and that these had been promptly discharged. In an exclusive interview with Arthur Krock of the New York Times in February 1949 Mr. Truman said that in using the terms "hysteria" and "red herrings" he had been denouncing the methods rather than the objectives of legislative committees and individual legislators.

Mr. Krock reported this phase of the discussion as follows:

When the President was chairman of the special Senate committee during the war, he followed a method which he sought to endorse by contrast when he made . . . comments about hysteria and red herrings. Whenever he found something wrong or some indication of potential wrong in the war program, he privately communicated the facts to the departments concerned, and usually it was corrected or averted without the kind of publicity that unfairly shakes public confidence and spreads through the more than two millions in government employ a feeling of insecurity in their jobs which hampers and damages their work.

The result was that no major scandal occurred in the war. This is the responsible method which, because it was not followed in these other matters, impelled him to say what he did. The Government service is 99-per-cent-plus loyal and secure.

If the facts about a government employee show contrary, out the man will go at no expense to public stability—though, it is true, without a headline for a politician who has that chiefly in his mind.

§ *In addition to attacks by Senator McCarthy, Mr. Truman's management of the loyalty problem had to cope with attacks from Republicans generally in the 1952 campaign and after. Early in the Eisenhower administration Republican spokesmen were asserting the presence of security risks in the Truman administration in numbers that even the Senator from Wisconsin had never dreamed of. It soon transpired that the Republicans' data included alcoholics, excessive talkers, and other such misfits. Mr. Truman took up the Republican charges in a speech to the Americans for Democratic Action on February 5, 1954.*

First, let me say that I am sure we are all against communism. I understand that one of the prime objectives of A.D.A.—and one of the main reasons it was brought into being in the first place— is to fight against the communist movement. For that, I salute you. Keep up the fight. Communism is an evil, wicked thing and we should oppose it utterly.

However, we can be against communism without being dishonest about it—without slinging mud and smearing everyone with whom we disagree. At least Democrats can. The Republican party, on the other hand, has set out deliberately to mislead and deceive the American people on this question in order to smear the Democratic party. And their effort to deceive runs through the Republican party all the way to the top.

In the campaign of 1952 the Republican orators did their best to make the people believe that the government was honeycombed with communists. They knew this was not true, of course. At least most of them did. Some of them knew so little about the facts of life in the United States government that they might have believed anything.

But by now even the political newcomers in the Republican ranks are bound to know better. They know, and know full well, that any communists they may have found in the government were few and far between. The Republicans know, and know full well, that they found an employee loyalty program that had cleaned communists out of the government effectively and efficiently before the subject was ever made a political issue.

I established this loyalty program by executive order in 1947. To put it above partisan politics I deliberately put Republicans in charge of its operation. They did an honest and thorough job of cleaning out the communists and everyone else whose loyalty was doubtful. They may have missed a few. We all know how the communists practice tactics of secret infiltration, and some may have slipped by without being caught. But you can be absolutely sure of this: When the Republicans took over the government on January 20, 1953, if there were any communists in the government service they were very, very few, indeed.

Now, what did these self-styled Republican "crusaders" do when they took over the government and found that the facts were not what they had represented them to be? . . . They set out to create the impression that they actually were finding hundreds of communists in the government. This is the Republican administration I am talking about—not irresponsible members of Congress. They didn't say flatly that they had found hundreds of communists. Oh no, they knew the absolute falsity of that could be proved beyond a doubt. But they announced from the White House, with much fanfare, that they were doing a wonderful job—simply magnificent—of cleaning the communists out of the government, and that, as a matter of fact, already they had gotten rid of 1,456 "security risks."

The number had grown to 2,200 by the time of the State of the Union message. But they were still talking about a vague category they called "security risks" in an effort to make the American people believe they had found hundreds of communists. It seems to me that the presidential press conference and the State of the Union message ought not to be used for such deceptive practices as this.

Who is included in the 2,200? The administration refuses to say. How was that number arrived at? The administration refuses to say. But some of the facts are beginning to come out just the same.

Few of them do any credit to the "great crusade."

Many of the 2,200 are said to be employees who resigned from the government voluntarily without ever having any charges brought to their attention. The number is even said to include many employees who were cleared on further investigation and are still in government service. Responsible Washington correspondents report that "there was not a single case of actual subversion in all the State Department's security findings—and it is doubtful if there was one such case throughout the government." These same correspondents go on to point out that, despite the actual facts, "to ninety-nine out of one hundred people the news that there have been a large number of security firings means that this number of communists and subversives have actually been uncovered in the government."

"Under the circumstances," they say, "it is surprising that any self-respecting person will work for the government at all. In fact the morale of the government worker has been thrown completely out the window."

Another thoughtful commentator on Washington events points out the deplorable conditions in the Department of State, as follows:

". . . I am told that there is the minimum of forthright, even of honest speaking, out of fear of talebearing. Eavesdropping is rampant. A hiatus exists, in consequence, between the policy-making and the working levels, and efficiency and morale are nonexistent. The State Department, often and rightly called our first line of defense, is just 'getting by.'

"So," he continues, "we are witnessing a loss to the government service of some very skilled technicians and some very accomplished officials. The amazing thing is that few at the top appear to care."

I believe the President owes a duty to the American people— and especially to all the government employees whose good names are involved—to tell us just how many communists and other actual subversives he has found. If he does not do this, he will leave our government service and many loyal American citizens under a cloud of grave suspicion. . . .

In standing firm in your liberal faith you get called a lot of names by people who would rather call you names than answer your arguments. You can expect that. Read your American history and see the names they called Presidents Washington and Jefferson and Lincoln and, to come down to date, Woodrow Wilson and Franklin Roosevelt.

5. REFUSAL TO BE SUBPOENAED

On November 9, 1953, the House Committee on Un-American Activities subpoenaed former President Truman to testify before it, presumably about Harry Dexter White, an Assistant Secretary of the Treasury alleged to have played a central part in communist conspiratorial activities of the 1940's. In the following letter to the committee chairman Mr. Truman refused the subpoena and gave his reasons. The Committee did not challenge his refusal.

Dear Sir:

I have your subpoena dated November 9, 1953, directing my appearance before your committee on Friday, November 13, in Washington. The subpoena does not state the matters upon which you seek my testimony, but I assume from the press stories that you seek to examine me with respect to matters which occurred during my tenure of the presidency of the United States.

In spite of my personal willingness to co-operate with your committee, I feel constrained by my duty to the people of the United States to decline to comply with the subpoena.

In doing so I am carrying out the provisions of the Constitution of the United States; and am following a long line of precedents, commencing with George Washington himself in 1796. Since his day, Presidents Jefferson, Monroe, Jackson, Tyler, Polk, Fillmore, Buchanan, Lincoln, Grant, Hayes, Cleveland, Theodore Roosevelt, Coolidge, Hoover, and Franklin D. Roosevelt have declined to respond to subpoenas or demands for information of various kinds by Congress.

The underlying reason for this clearly established and universally recognized constitutional doctrine has been succinctly set forth by Charles Warren, one of our leading constitutional authorities, as follows:

"In this long series of contests by the Executive to maintain his constitutional integrity, one sees a legitimate conclusion from our theory of government. . . . Defense by the Executive of his constitutional powers becomes in very truth, therefore, defense of popular rights—defense of power which the people granted to him.

"It was in that sense that President Cleveland spoke of his duty to the people not to relinquish any of the powers of his great office. It was in that sense that President Buchanan stated the people have rights and prerogatives in the execution of his office by the President which every President is under a duty to see 'shall never be violated in his person' but 'passed to his successors unimpaired by the adoption of a dangerous precedent.'

"In maintaining his rights against a trespassing Congress, the President defends not himself, but popular government; he represents not himself but the people."

President Jackson repelled an attempt by the Congress to break down the separation of powers in these words:

"For myself I shall repel all such attempts as an invasion of the principles of justice as well as of the Constitution, and I shall esteem it my sacred duty to the people of the United States to resist them as I would the establishment of a Spanish Inquisition."

I might commend to your reading the opinion of one of the committees of the House of Representatives in 1879, House Report 141, March 3, 1879, Forty-fifth Congress, Third Session, in which the House Judiciary Committee said the following:

"The Executive is as independent of either house of Congress as either house of Congress is independent of him, and they cannot call for the records of his actions, or the action of his officers against his consent, any more than he can call for any of the journals or records of the House or Senate."

It must be obvious to you that if the doctrine of separation of powers and the independence of the presidency is to have any validity at all, it must be equally applicable to a President after his term of office has expired when he is sought to be examined with respect to any acts occurring while he is President.

The doctrine would be shattered, and the President, contrary to our fundamental theory of constitutional government, would become a mere arm of the legislative branch of the government if he would feel during his term of office that his every act might be subject to official inquiry and possible distortion for political purposes.

If your intention, however, is to inquire into any acts as a private individual either before or after my Presidency and unrelated to any acts as President, I shall be happy to appear.

Yours very truly,

HARRY S. TRUMAN

6.   HONESTY IN GOVERNMENT

Like the administrations that followed the Civil War and the First World War, Mr. Truman's postwar administration was marred by practices of more than questionable ethics by executive officials. A focal point of the startling revelations of Congressional Committees in 1949 and 1950 was the President's military aide, Harry Vaughan. A typical disclosure was that Vaughan had interceded to obtain a lumber permit for repairs at a San Francisco race track during acute shortages of building materials and heavy demands for housing. The worst trouble spots were the Reconstruction Finance Corporation and the Internal Revenue Bureau. An R.F.C. director testified to a Senate subcommittee that he had so far departed from accepted procedure as to do a favor for a friend who was seeking a $300,000 loan, the favor being the personal assignment of the R.F.C. examiner in the affair of the loan, and the friend being a person who subsequently became an R.F.C. director himself and was serving as vice chairman at the time of the investigation.

In the face of these disclosures Mr. Truman staunchly supported his aides. Despite the accumulating scandal he renominated each of the five R.F.C. directors, including those specifically criticized in a unanimous report by a Senate committee headed by James Fulbright, Democrat of Arkansas. In commenting on the report Mr. Truman declared, through his press secretary, that he knew of no evidence of illegal influence on the R.F.C. Senator Fulbright retorted: "I think it is setting a low level if our only goal for official conduct is that it be legal instead of illegal." Another move of the President was to acquire from the R.F.C. a ten-year accumulation

of letters addressed to it by members of Congress in behalf of prospective borrowers. *Senator Paul Douglas, Democrat of Illinois, said
that there would be no yielding before the President's counterattack.*

With public resentment rising, the administration altered its
policy in late 1951. In November, in a letter to party leaders, the
President attacked grafters in government and asked that the Democratic party be made morally strong for the coming campaign.
Numerous dismissals from the Bureau of Internal Revenue followed,
and Mr. Truman himself removed the Assistant Attorney General
in charge of the Tax Division. Newbold Morris, a liberal Republican
of New York City, was brought to Washington to investigate corruption. He promptly devised an exhaustive questionnaire calling
for precise information about personal income. But his superior,
Attorney General McGrath, apparently with Mr. Truman's approval,
refused to distribute the questionnaire and notified Morris that he
was dismissed. In an unexpected move the President then asked
McGrath for his resignation. The new Attorney General announced
that he would drop the project of a special inquiry and rely on the
Federal Bureau of Investigation.

Mr. Truman's most nearly definitive speech on the issue of corruption was delivered in Washington on March 29, 1952.

Now, I want to say something very important to you about this
issue of morality in government.

I stand for honest government. I have worked for it. I have
probably done more for it than any other President; I have done
more than any other President to reorganize the government on an
efficient basis and to extend the civil service merit system.

I hate corruption not only because it is bad in itself, but also
because it is the deadly enemy of all the things the Democatic party
has been doing all these years. I hate corruption everywhere, but
I hate it most of all in a Democratic officeholder; because it is a
betrayal of all that the Democratic party stands for.

Here is the reason. To me, morality in government means more
than a mere absence of wrongdoing. It means a government that
is fair to all. I think it is just as immoral for the Congress to enact
special tax favors into law as it is for a tax official to connive in
a crooked tax return. It is just as immoral to use the lawmaking
power of the government to enrich the few at the expense of the

many as it is to steal money from the public treasury. That is stealing money from the public treasury.

All of us know, of course, about the scandals and corruption of the Republican officeholders in the 1920's. But to my mind the Veterans Administration scandals, in those days, and the Teapot Dome steal, were no worse—no more immoral—than the tax laws of Andrew Mellon, or the attempt to sell Muscle Shoals to private owners. Legislation that favored the greed of monopoly and the trickery of Wall Street was a form of corruption that did the county four times as much harm as Teapot Dome ever did.

Private selfish interests are always trying to corrupt the government in this way. Powerful financial groups are always trying to get favors for themselves.

Now, the Democratic administration has been fighting against these efforts to corrupt the powers of government. We haven't always won, but we have never surrendered, and we never will.

For all these years, we have been fighting to use our natural resources for the benefit of the public, to develop our forests and our public oil reserves and our water power for the benefit of all, to raise the incomes of all our citizens, to protect the farmer and the worker against the power of monopoly.

And where have the Republicans been in this fight for morality in government? Do they come out and vote with us to keep the special interests from robbing the public? Not at all. Most of them are on the other side.

It's the same thing when you come to the question of the conduct of government officials. The Republicans make a great whoop and holler about the honesty of federal employees, but they are usually the first to show up in a government office asking for special favors for private interests, and raising Cain if they don't get them.

These Republican gentlemen can't have it both ways—they can't be for morality on Tuesday and Thursday, and then be for special privileges for their clients on Monday, Wednesday, and Friday. The press recently, for a wonder, has been giving some facts on this subject that have been very hard to get at.

I'm disgusted with these efforts to discredit and blacken the character and reputation of the whole federal service. We have a higher percentage of federal employees under civil service than ever before, and, on the whole, they are a finer, better type of men and women than ever. It is just as much our duty to protect the innocent as it is to punish the guilty. If a man is accused, he ought to have his day in court, and I don't mean a kangaroo court either.

I hate injustice just as much as I hate corruption.

Of course, we must always work to keep our government clean. Our Democratic Senators and Congressmen have been working to clean up bad conditions where they exist and to devise procedures and systems to prevent them in the future. And I would like to have help in this fight from everybody, Democrats and Republicans alike.

I have just got one reorganization plan through the Congress, and I am going to send up some more plans to Congress soon—to put more of our federal officials under civil service and out of politics.

7. FISCAL MANAGEMENT

The Truman administration undertook some not insignificant revisions and reforms in fiscal management. These and other developments in the same field were discussed by Mr. Truman when he laid the cornerstone of the new General Accounting Office building in Washington on September 11, 1951.

Many people in the government have wrongly considered the General Accounting Office a sort of bugaboo that keeps them from doing what they want to do. Many people outside the government, when they think of the General Accounting Office at all, consider it a dry and boring subject.

But the General Accounting Office is neither a bugaboo nor a bore. It is a vital part of our government. Its work is of great benefit to all of us.

Under Lindsay Warren the General Accounting Office has handled the biggest auditing job in the history of mankind and has done it well. It has continuously improved its operations so it could serve the people of this country better and more efficiently.

The General Accounting Office is an agency responsible to the Congress. But this does not mean that it works at cross-purposes with the executive agencies of the government. On the contrary, the General Accounting Office co-operates with the executive agencies, for they are working for the same great purpose, to give good government to the American people at the lowest possible cost.

One of the outstanding achievements has been the joint accounting program which the Controller General worked out in 1947 with the Secretary of the Treasury and the director of the Bureau of the Budget.

As a result of this joint program, accounting improvements have been made in agency after agency of the federal government. These improvements have given us new machinery for tighter and more efficient control of the public funds.

The success of this accounting program can be attributed largely to teamwork—co-operation of the highest degree among those responsible for fiscal affairs. On this team, the Controller General has played a leading role.

It is especially important in this day and time for the financial affairs of the government to be prudently managed. Taxes are high, and the people who pay the taxes are entitled to see that they get a dollar's worth of value for every dollar they pay.

Nobody likes to pay taxes. That's just human nature. A man will go into a night club and throw away forty or fifty dollars and think nothing of it. But let him get a tax bill for $30 and hear him scream! But we have to pay them, and for very good reasons. Since this is true, we are all entitled to know what those reasons are and what is done with our money.

I wish everybody in the country could read the budget message of the federal government. I don't mean the whole big book. That's full of tables and as thick as a Sears Roebuck catalogue. But in the front of the book is a message to Congress, about sixty or seventy pages long, that explains what the budget is all about—where the money goes and what the citizen gets for his tax dollar.

I am proud of the budgets that have been prepared since I've been President. I want to say to you I know every figure in every one of them. I want the people to understand them. I would not want anyone to give up his time-honored right to complain about paying taxes. If people couldn't blow off steam that way sometimes, they might explode. Half of the fun of being a citizen in this country comes from complaining about the way we run our governments—federal, state, and local.

But I don't think anyone ought to take his complaints about

government spending too seriously until he has gone to the trouble of finding out what it is all about. Most people talk about the budget and don't know a figure in it.

I suppose it is impossible for everybody to get a copy of the regular budget message and read that. But it is possible for you to get a copy of a little book called the "Budget in Brief." This little book gives the highlights of the budget story. Every citizen who pays taxes ought to read it. You can get a copy by sending twenty cents to the Government Printing Office in Washington and asking them to send you a copy of the "Federal Budget in Brief." [Holding up book.] There it is. It's got about thirty-eight pages in it.

I don't get any commission for selling these little books. I will be amply repaid just by having people read them. I am proud of the way the financial affairs of the government are handled, and I want just as many people as possible to know the whole story—the facts as they actually are. I can't tell you the whole story here today. We don't have time. But I would like to mention part of it.

The most obvious fact about the federal budget is that it is big. Everybody knows that, but there are many people who do not know why it has to be big and what the money is used for.

I would like to tell you something about that.

In the first place, most of the money is used to provide for the national security. In the current fiscal year, national security programs will require nearly $50,000,000,000, or 70 per cent of all federal expenditures.

That is a very large sum of money. The question is: "Is it worth it?" I think the answer will come back from most of us that it is. I think most of us will say that our national independence and our freedom are important enough for us to spend whatever is required to preserve them. That is my answer. And I am humbly thankful that this nation is strong and powerful enough to bear this mighty program for security.

Now what else is included in the budget?

It includes $6,000,000,000 to pay interest on the public debt. I suppose that is noncontroversial. Surely there is no one who objects to paying this. We can't repudiate the signed obligations of the United States and don't intend to.

Then there is nearly $5,000,000,000 in the budget for services and benefits to veterans. I hope that is noncontroversial, too. I don't believe in economizing at the expense of the men who have bared their breasts to save their country.

The budget includes more than a billion dollars for grants-in-aid to the states for assistance to the aged and the blind and other needy persons. Some people don't approve of this. I will say frankly that I welcome their criticism. I never saw any money spent for a better purpose. I think we can afford it.

Then the budget has close to $500,000,000 for grants to the states to help them build highways. I'm in favor of that, too. Highways cost money. But let me tell you something else: They also help to make money. I have no doubt that the money we spend on highways more than repays itself in greater prosperity for the country. Indeed, the same thing is true of many of the expenditures of the government.

The things I have mentioned add up to more than $60,000,-000,000, out of the total estimated expenditures of $68,000,000,000. And yet some people are saying you can cut $6,000,000,000 from the budget. If you did that, there wouldn't be anything left to maintain the ordinary operations of the government, like the Coast Guard, and the Federal Bureau of Investigation, and the Public Health Service.

I could go on down through every item in the budget and show you that there is a vital reason for its being there.

I don't mean to claim that there is not a single dollar wasted. In an operation as big as the federal government there are bound to be some cases of waste or extravagance. One of the reasons we have the General Accounting Office is to help us find those cases and put a stop to them.

But the main point I want to make is that, although federal expenditures are very large, they are all made for purposes that are necessary to our national welfare; and our budget is as tight and solid as we can make it. There is a great deal of misinformation circulated on this subject. Some of it is done in ignorance and some with malice aforethought. But it won't stand up under honest analysis.

Let me give you an example.

In a recent issue of a magazine which is circulated widely in this country and abroad, there appeared an article purporting to show that "waste" and "extravagance" were running wild in the federal government. It was just a pack of lies. Accompanying the article was a table of figures supposedly showing that nondefense expenditures of the government had increased anywhere from 100 per cent to 1,000 per cent between 1940 and 1950.

This table was a typical example of what I once heard described as "butterfly statistics"—statistics so meaningless that they seem to have been plucked right out of the air with a butterfly net. And that's where these came from.

The fact is that the expenditures of the government, other than those arising out of past wars or out of our efforts to prevent another world war, increased 68 per cent in dollar terms from 1940 to 1950. Adjusting for changes in the price level, they actually declined. During the same time the country was growing, of course, and the government had a bigger job to do. The total national output of goods and services rose about 50 per cent in real terms.

In 1940 the cost of these civilian government services not connected with our national security took about six per cent of our total national output; in 1950 this had been reduced to about four per cent. And this year it is going to be an even smaller percentage than it was in 1950. If people want to be fair about this, it seems to me that is the way to look at it.

I would like to say a word of comfort and console those who fear that we are spending our way into national bankruptcy. This alarming thought has some currency in certain circles, and it is used to frighten voters—particularly as visions of elections dance through the heads of gentlemen who are politically inclined.

I want to say to these gentlemen who are spreading this story, "Don't be afraid." This is something that has been worrying you for a number of years now. It's something you've been saying over and over again. It wasn't true when you began to say it, it has not been true as you have repeated it over and over since then, and now it's further from the truth than ever.

The country is stronger economically than it has ever been before. Its people are more prosperous. After paying their taxes, the people have an average per capita income that will buy forty per cent more than it did in 1939, in spite of increases in prices. Corporations are making more money than they ever did, and, even after paying taxes at the new high rates, their profits are running at a higher rate than in any year except the record-breaking 1950.

I know taxes are high and I know they are burdensome, but we ought to keep this thing in the proper perspective.

The world has some great problems before it today. The United

States has great responsibilities in helping to meet those problems. We must face up to these problems and do whatever is required to meet them—and it is going to cost a lot of money.

If we want to keep the country on a sound financial basis and hold down inflation, we must pay this money as we go.

One of the benefits of using the pay-as-we-go approach is that it results in a tighter check on expenditures. It is so unpleasant to increase taxes that before doing it we try to hold down on expenditures wherever we can. That is the way it ought to be. All I ask is that we do not cut our expenditures to the point where we lose more than we gain. We must not be penny wise and pound foolish. I don't want to lose a horse through being too stingy to buy a strong enough rope to tie him with—or have him starve by being too stingy to buy the oats and corn to feed him.

I believe in operating the government's finances on a sound basis. I think the record shows that. Over the last five years we have operated the government with a surplus—a surplus of nearly $8,000,-000,000 altogether. That may be a surprise to most people, but it's true. That's something for us to be proud of.

It is difficult to overstate how much the whole future of the world depends upon the financial condition of the United States government. We've got to keep it solvent. We've got to keep it sound. We've got to be sure that the government's financial affairs are well managed. They are, thanks to the Secretary of the Treasury.

8.   IMPROVING THE POST OFFICE DEPARTMENT

The Post Office Department was subjected to an intensive study by the Hoover Commission, many of whose recommendations were carried out. These Mr. Truman cites by chapter and verse in one context of his speech of September 17, 1951, to the National Association of Postmasters.

It seems to be open season, these days, on government employees. There are a lot of people who are trying to make political capital by slurring the loyalty and efficiency of government employees and trying to bring the public service into disrepute.

I think that is a contemptible way to try to get votes.

We have the greatest government in the world, and the most

loyal and efficient government servants. I am proud to be a part of it. I think you are proud to be part of it, too.

It is time we made it perfectly plain that we feel it is an honor to work for our fellow citizens through the public service.

The postal service is one of the key activities of the federal government. It employs over half a million people, one fourth of all civilian employees of the whole government. It is one of the biggest businesses in the country. And without it the rest of the country would not be able to do business at all. Without the postal service all our activities would come to a standstill—business, the national defense, family life, everything.

Last year the postal service carried over 27,000,000,000 letters and 1,000,000,000 parcels. It carried over 6,000,000,000 copies of newspapers and magazines and nearly 40,000,000 packages of books.

The postal service is not only big business, it is public business. We all ought to be concerned about the way the postal service is run. We ought to be sure that it is run on a businesslike basis— that it pays for itself.

Today, it does not pay for itself. Postal rates are not set by the Post Office Department, but by the Congress. And these rates are not high enough to cover the cost of carrying the mail.

Right now the postal service is being run at a deficit of more than $500,000,000 a year. The biggest part of the deficit is caused by the low rates on second- and third-class mail—that is, newspapers, magazines and circulars, and advertising matter. Now, first-class mail pays its own way. There are lobbyists who are trying to raise the rate on it. But the publishers and advertisers who use second and third class to reach the public are not paying fully for the services they get.

To put it bluntly, the taxpayers of the country are subsidizing these business interests to the tune of several hundred million dollars a year. That is not right, and I have asked the Congress to raise these rates. The Congress has been considering this matter very diligently, and I hope that they will soon pass legislation to raise these second- and third-class rates substantially.

However, there is a lot of opposition to raising these rates, and I am sorry to say that most of it comes from the slick magazine publishers who are getting the benefit of millions of dollars of the taxpayers' money each year. I mean that word in two ways. About

$200,000,000 is going to carry second-class mail; that is, newspapers and magazines. I am glad to say that a large number of newspapers know this is not right and are entirely willing to pay their own way.

It's the slick magazine boys who don't want to pay their way. We are subsidizing them for all that bunch of advertising that we have to read in order to find something to look at in those slick magazines.

Some of these concerns have come down here and lobbied members of Congress from breakfast to bedtime, trying to prevent them from raising second-class postal rates. Some of the biggest magazine publishers in the country are fighting tooth and toenail to keep their juicy subsidies, and then they write editorials about somebody else getting a subsidy.

They are strongly against subsidies—for everybody but themselves. Here they are, costing the taxpayers millions of dollars every year, and they have the nerve to complain about the high cost of government. The next time any of you see an article or editorial in one of those magazines attacking government subsidies, I just wish you would write them a polite little letter asking when they will be ready to pay the full cost of sending their own publications through the mail.

In addition to fair rates for postal service, I believe in fair salaries for postal workers and other government employees. A while back I sent recommendations to the Congress on this subject too, asking them to raise the salaries of government employees, including postal workers.

In addition, I asked the Congress to remove the inequities they allowed to creep into postal pay scales. This is something that affects postmasters as well as postal employees. I hope the Congress will straighten out this situation the way it ought to be done. And there are some postmasters who are not getting as much money as the people who are working for them. And that is not fair.

Fair rates and fair salaries are the responsibility of the Congress. But there is something equally important which is the responsibility of you who work in the postal service. That is the responsibility of constantly using new ideas and new techniques to increase the efficiency of postal operations. And I want to tell you that in this field I am proud of you.

Since 1945 the output of postal employees per man-hour worked has increased by more than ten per cent. That is a record to be proud of.

A lot of new equipment has been put into service, and more new equipment is being tested. The postal service has new mail sorting machines, for example. It is using helicopters for short air hauls. Postal engineers have developed a new kind of light motor vehicle for mailmen who work in suburban districts where houses are far apart. And if I ever get retired from the presidency I am going to get me one of these machines to ride around in.

All these and many more mechanical improvements are being tried out in the effort to find more efficient ways to handle and transport the mails.

Another way in which we are improving the postal service is through administrative reorganization. Ever since I have been President I have been working for greater efficiency through the reorganization of government departments. The Commission on Government Organization, headed by former President Hoover, studied this field thoroughly—and Mr. Acheson was vice chairman of that organization —and made some very valuable recommendations for improving the efficiency of the government.

The other day a member of Congress said that we had not carried out any of the recommendations of the Hoover Commission regarding the Post Office. That man was just as wrong as he could be. He should talk to some of the other members of Congress, who have been putting some of these reorganization measures through and who know what the situation really is.

The fact is that we either have put into effect or have submitted to the Congress virtually every recommendation the Hoover Commission made concerning the Post Office—and some of them have been in effect for more than two years.

One of the first recommendations of the Hoover-Acheson Commission was that the Postmaster General should continue to be a Cabinet member, but should not be an official of a political party. I had already accomplished that, before the Commission's report was made. And I have kept in office, as Postmaster General, a career man who came up from the ranks in the postal service, a fine public servant, Jesse Donaldson.

Then the Hoover Commission recommended that the top level of the Post Office Department be reorganized. And we've done that too. I sent up to the Congress a reorganization plan to give the Postmaster General more authority over the department, along with a Deputy Postmaster General and four Assistant Postmasters General to help him, and a national advisory board to consider methods and policies for improving the postal service. The Congress approved that plan, and it has been in effect for two years, and it is working fine.

The Hoover Commission also recommended that the fiscal affairs of the Post Office be reorganized. And that has been done, largely as a result of the financial control act of 1950, which gave the Post Office Department, for the first time, the authority to establish and maintain its own accounting set-up.

We have been making a lot of reorganizations like this in other departments of the government too.

There has been a great deal of misinformation put out around the country lately to the effect that nothing much has been done about the Hoover Commission's recommendations for any part of the federal government. Well, that is just poppycock. I've been surprised to see that a lot of people have been taken in by it—including some newspapers that should have known better.

Anyone who looks at the record will see that our achievements in government reorganization and management improvement have been outstanding. Out of the thirty-six reorganization plans I have submitted to the Congress, twenty-seven have been approved. The other nine were voted down—and some of the members of Congress who talk the loudest about efficiency and economy voted against them.

As a result of these reorganization plans and other actions, I can report that we already have in effect a majority of the recommendations of the Hoover Commission for the whole government. The Department of Defense has been brought under more unified direction. The Department of State has been substantially strengthened. Reorganization plans have gone into effect for the Department of Commerce, the Department of the Interior, the Department of Justice, and many other departments, agencies, and regulatory commissions. The supply and property management activities of the government have been consolidated in the General Services Administration.

Those and many other changes have stepped up the efficiency of the federal government. They have saved the taxpayers money.

And they are standing us in good stead as we face the large new problems brought on by the defense emergency. Now, don't let anybody tell you that the President of the United States is not for efficiency and economy. Whenever there is any economy and efficiency in the government, the President of the United States has been responsible for it, and don't let anybody tell you different.

But that job is not finished, of course. In fact, the job of making the federal government more efficient will never be finished. There are other recommendations of the Hoover Commission to consider.

I also have an advisory commission of experts on administrative management who are constantly finding new ways to improve the operations of the government. One of the members of that commission is the Deputy Postmaster General, Vincent Burke.

There will always be new ideas to be tried, better ways of doing things found. There will always be new challenges to be met as the government is called on to serve the people of our country under new conditions. Now, they are always talking about going back to something.

You can't turn the clock back. You have got to go forward. And these people who talk about going back are thinking about a government for seventy or eighty millions. We have got 156,000,000 of people now, and you have to have a government in proportion to the size of its population, and it has to expand, if we are going to run.

All of us who work for Uncle Sam should continue to strive for good government at the lowest possible cost. That is the spirit, I am sure, in which you postmasters are doing your work.

Let us continue, in everything we do, to encourage every postal employee, and every other federal worker, to give his energy, imagination, and talents to continually improving the service he renders to the people of our great country.

§ *In 1952, it should be added, the President tried to place all postmasters under the merit system. The Congress did not accede.*

9. A DEPARTMENT OF HEALTH, EDUCATION, AND SOCIAL SECURITY

In 1949 the Hoover Commission emphatically recommended a new federal department in the welfare-education field. The President

*reshaped this proposal to include public health measures and trans-
mitted it to Congress on June 20, 1949. In doing so he said:*

We must make possible greater equality of opportunity to all our
citizens for an education. Only by so doing can we insure that our
citizens will be capable of understanding and sharing the responsibilities of democracy.

The government's programs for health, education, and security
are of such great importance to our democracy that we should now
establish an executive department for their administration.

§ *The Congress declined to approve, and it was not until the
administration of President Eisenhower that a Department of Health,
Education, and Welfare was finally established.*

10.   PRESIDENTIAL PAPERS

*Mr. Truman, as an indefatigable student of history, has exhibited
both in and out of office a firm conviction that the official papers
of our Presidents, past, present, and future, should be preserved in
a way both to keep them the property of the people and to make
them accessible to scholars. In office, he affirmed this conviction in
connection with the publication by the Princeton University Press
of the papers of Jefferson. Out of office, he had something to say
about the progress of the Harry S. Truman Library, a project launched
by friends just after his retirement from the presidency.*

His remarks on the Jefferson papers were made on May 17, 1950.

This is a big undertaking. It will take a long time. It should be
done as far as possible by private groups and not by the federal
government, although the federal government can and will be of
assistance whenever possible.

The editions should be in every instance completely objective
and should maintain the same high editorial standards that are
evident in this first volume of *The Papers of Thomas Jefferson*. They
should aim to place the facts beyond debate and distortion.

At a time when democracy is meeting the greatest challenge in
its history, we need to turn to the sources of our own democratic
faith for new inspiration and new strength. These volumes of Thomas
Jefferson will be a great reservoir of hope and faith during the critical
years ahead. I sincerely hope that similar editions of the writings of

other great men and women who have made our nation what it is today can be placed with them.

Since the United States today scarcely resembles the United States when Jefferson knew it, why should the publication of his letters be so important to us?

The answer should be obvious, as we turn the pages of this first volume. Throughout his life Jefferson waged an uncompromising fight against tyranny. The search for human liberty was a goal which he pursued with burning zeal. The spirit of democracy shines through everything he ever wrote.

Today, when democracy is facing the greatest challenge in its history, the spirit which Jefferson expressed in his battle against tyranny, and in his search for human liberty, stands out as a beacon of inspiration for free peoples throughout the world.

Jefferson lived in a time of great struggle, when this Nation was trying to establish itself as a democracy of free men. We today, in a different time and under different conditions, are in a great struggle to preserve and expand human freedom.

Our stage is larger—our struggle must be waged over the whole world, not merely in our own country. But the essential nature of the struggle is the same: to prove, by hard work and practical demonstration, that free men can create for themselves a good society, in which they live together at peace and advance their common welfare.

When freedom is at stake we need to draw upon every source of strength we can. Jefferson thought deeply about how to make liberty a living part of our society, and he proved the rightness of his thinking by practical demonstration. That is why I think it is particularly important that we are reasserting Jefferson's ideals by publishing these volumes.

History can be fairly written only when all the facts are on record. Jefferson has suffered at the hands of unscrupulous biographers and biased partisans ever since his death. The publication of his papers should correct the mistakes that have been made about him and should help prevent misinterpretations in the future.

There are others like Jefferson whose lives have enriched our history, but about whom we know too little. Many of them have been victims of unfair treatment at the hands of historians; others have been neglected because the record of their work is scattered about in remote places.

I hope that this edition of the writings of Thomas Jefferson will inspire educational institutions, learned societies, and civic-minded groups to plan the publication of the works of other great national figures.

In far too many cases, there are incomplete and inaccurate editions of the writings of the great men and women of our country. In some distressing instances, we have only fragmentary records of men whose ideas and actions have helped shape our history.

I am convinced that we need to collect and publish the writings of the men and women who have made major contributions to the development of our democracy.

I am, therefore, requesting the National Historical Publications Commission, under the chairmanship of the Archivist of the United States, to look into this matter and to report to me. I am sure this commission will wish to consult with scholars in all fields of American history, and to report what can be done—and should be done— to make available to our people the public and private writings of men whose contributions to our history are now inadequately represented by published works.

I am interested not just in political figures, but in the writings of industrialists and labor leaders, chemists and engineers, painters and lawyers, of great figures of all the arts and sciences who have made major contributions to our democracy.

Obviously, we cannot hope to collect, edit, and publish all the writings of all such leaders, but we can and should select the works of those who have been too long neglected and who need to be better known if we are to understand our heritage.

§ About the project of a Harry S. Truman Library, Mr. Truman had this to say in New York on his seventieth birthday:

This library of mine will not be mine. It will be yours. It will belong to the people of the United States. That great pile of papers of mine, as were those of former President Roosevelt, are and will be the property of the people of the United States and be accessible to all the people of the United States.

And that is as it should be, because the actions of a President are shown in the records of his office. The papers of the Presidents are among the most valuable sources of material for history. They ought to be preserved and they ought to be used.

I think that the method we are following in our plans for this library—that is, having these papers placed under the care of the National Archives facilities, which permit study and research—is a method which ought to be applied to the papers of all future Presidents. It is a method which keeps the papers as the property of the people and makes them available to scholars as soon and as completely as possible. In this way we can be sure that the historical facts are not lost or misrepresented.

The papers of Presidents of the United States are important because of the unique character and importance of the presidential office.

III
POPULAR LEADER AND LEGISLATOR

As a leader of the American people and of a political party, as an initiator of legislation, and as a maker of decisions to sign or to veto legislation, Mr. Truman was mainly and centrally preoccupied with the advancement of the principles that came to be summarized in the phrase "Fair Deal." The phrase itself, which did not gain currency until 1949, was (like "New Deal") of quasi-accidental origin; it first occurred, not with capital letters, in a State of the Union message—that of January 5, 1949. ("Every segment of our population and every individual has a right to expect from his government a fair deal.") Nevertheless the Fair Deal in its essence existed from the moment when Harry Truman took the oath of office. As a collection of specific measures it was an extension of the New Deal and also a modification of it.

Mr. Truman stated the nuclear principle of what he meant by the Fair Deal when, dedicating Hyde Park as a national shrine, he said: "This government exists not for the benefit of a privileged few, but for the welfare of all the people"—not excluding, as he once said, those who attacked it the most bitterly. Such a statement is, of course, one of those large and unexceptionable generalizations that mean nothing until translated into concrete proposals and pro-

93

grams. Nevertheless, there is every evidence that Mr. Truman meant it with deep sincerity, that he judged concrete proposals in the light of it, and that his Fair Deal as a sum total represented his idea of the large generalization turned into realizable actualities. What he actually meant when he referred to "the progressive and humane principles of the New Deal" was a set of adjustments designed to use the combined resources of the nation in the interest of all its people, and especially to improve the purchasing power of the mass of people and thereby incidentally to help the great industries and businesses flourish.

The actualities that Mr. Truman had on his mind he urged on the Congress in season and on the nation in and out of season. He stated it in twenty-one points; he stated it in ten points; he stated it on occasion in isolated points that he considered to be the burning issues of the hour. After all his untiring persistence, only a trifling fraction of what he meant by the Fair Deal was enacted into law by the Congresses of his administration. From the point of view of practical politics narrowly construed, he was a failure as a legislative leader. Was his leadership, in larger definitions, actually a failure?

It is possible to see it as a delayed success. One must always remember that the words of Presidents are themselves acts, especially when spoken with conviction and persistence. They affect the shape of things even when they do not sway Congressional majorities. They change the climate of opinion, the balance of opposition and sympathy. Who can affirm with certainty, for example, that what Mr. Truman said about civil rights in the 1940's was devoid of effect on some decisions that the Supreme Court handed down in the 1950's, or of effect on the reception of the Court's decisions in innumerable places from coast to coast? A sympathizer with the Fair Deal will interpret it, temporary failure or no, as a political force that kept the atmosphere of political and social reform from being dissipated and heartened masses of people with solid expectations of better things at hand, whatever recalcitrant members of the Congress might say or vote for. A despiser and contemner of the Fair Deal will see it as a deplorable collectivistic program. Either way, the Fair Deal has to be admitted to have been a force that made itself felt entirely out of proportion to its embodiment in law.

The pronouncements put together in this section all bear more or less directly on the several components of the Fair Deal; and taken in sum, they convey a fairly comprehensive idea what it was made up of and what it meant.

1. CIVIL RIGHTS

At the Archives Building in Washington there was dedicated on December 15, 1952, a new shrine for the Constitution of the United States, the Declaration of Independence, and the Bill of Rights. At this dedication Mr. Truman spoke; and what he said is surcharged with his interpretation of the American heritage of freedom.

We are assembled here on this Bill of Rights Day to do honor to the three great documents which, together, constitute the charter of our form of government.

The Declaration of Independence, the Constitution, and the Bill of Rights are now assembled in one place for display and safekeeping. Here, so far as is humanly possible, they will be protected from disaster and from the ravages of time.

I am glad that the Bill of Rights is at last to be exhibited side by side with the Constitution. These two original documents have been separated far too long. In my opinion, the Bill of Rights is the most important part of the Constitution.

We venerate these documents not because they are old, not because they are valuable historical relics, but because they still have meaning for us. It is 161 years today since the Bill of Rights was ratified. But it is still pointing the way to greater freedom and greater opportunities for human happiness.

So long as we govern our nation by the letter and the spirit of the Bill of Rights, we can be sure that our nation will grow in strength and wisdom and freedom.

Everyone who holds office in the federal government or in the government of one of our states takes an oath to support the Constitution of the United States. I have taken such an oath many times, including two times when I took the special oath required of the President of the United States.

This oath we take has a deep significance. Its simple words compress a lot of our history and a lot of our philosophy of government into one small space. In many countries, men swear to be loyal to their king, or to their nation. Here we promise to uphold and defend a document.

This is because the document sets forth our idea of government. And beyond this, with the Declaration of Independence, it expresses our idea of man. We believe that man should be free. And these documents establish a system under which man can be free and set up a framework to protect and expand this freedom.

The longer I live, the more I am impressed by the significance of our simple official oath to uphold and defend the Constitution. Perhaps it takes a lifetime of experience to understand how much the Constitution means in our national life.

You can read about the Constitution and you can study it in books, but the Constitution is not merely a matter of words. The Constitution is a living force—it is a growing thing.

The Constitution belongs to no one group of people and to no single branch of the government. We acknowledge our judges as the interpreters of the Constitution, but our executive branch and our legislative branch alike operate within its framework and must apply it and its principles in all that they do.

The Constitution expresses an idea that belongs to the people—the idea of the free man. What this idea means may vary from time to time. There was a time when people believed the Constitution meant that men could not be prevented from exploiting child labor or paying sweatshop wages.

We no longer believe these things. We have discovered that the Constitution does not prevent us from correcting social injustice or advancing the general welfare. The idea of freedom which is embodied in these great documents has overcome all attempts to turn them into a rigid set of rules to suppress freedom.

As we look toward the future, we must be sure that what we honor and venerate in these documents is not their words alone, but the ideas of liberty which they express.

We are engaged here today in a symbolic act. We are enshrining these documents for future ages. But unless we keep alive in our hearts the true meaning of these documents, what we are doing here could prove to be of little value.

We have treated the documents themselves with the utmost respect. We have used every device that modern science has invented to protect and preserve them. From their glass cases we have excluded everything that might harm them, even the air itself.

This magnificent hall has been constructed to exhibit them, and the vault beneath, that we have built to protect them, is as safe from destruction as anything that the wit of modern man can devise. All this is an honorable effort, based upon reverence for the great past, and our generation can take just pride in it.

But we must face the fact that all this pomp and circumstance could be the exact opposite of what we intend. The ceremony could be no more than a magnificent burial. If the Constitution and Declaration of Independence were enshrined in the Archives Building, but nowhere else, they would be dead, and this place would be only a stately tomb.

The Constitution and the Declaration can live only as long as they are enshrined in our hearts and minds. If they are not so enshrined, they would be no better than mummies in their glass cases, and they could in time become idols whose worship would be a grim mockery of the true faith. Only as these documents are reflected in the thoughts and acts of Americans can they remain symbols of a power that can move the world.

That power is our faith in human liberty. That faith is immortal, but it is not invincible. It has sometimes been abandoned, it has been betrayed, it has been beaten to earth again and again, and although it has never been killed, it has been reduced to impotence for centuries at a time. It is far older than our Republic.

The motto on our Liberty Bell, "Proclaim liberty throughout all the land unto all the inhabitants thereof," is from the book of Leviticus, which is supposed to have been written nearly 1,500 years before Christ. In the thirty-five centuries since that date, the love of liberty has never died, but liberty itself has been lost again and again.

We find it hard to believe that liberty could ever be lost in this country. But it can be lost, and it will be, if the time ever comes when these documents are regarded not as the supreme expression of our profound belief, but merely as curiosities in glass cases.

Today, the ideals which these three documents express are having to struggle for survival throughout the world. When we sealed the Declaration and the Constitution in the Library of Congress, almost a year and a half ago, I had something to say about the threat of totalitarianism and communism. That threat still menaces freedom. The struggle against communism is just as crucial, just as demanding, as it was then.

We are uniting the strength of free men against this threat. We are resisting communist aggression, and we will continue to resist the communist threat with all our will and all our strength.

But the idea of freedom is in danger from others as well as the communists. There are some who hate communism but who, at the same time, are unwilling to acknowledge the ideals of the Constitution as the supreme law of the land.

They are people who believe it is too dangerous to proclaim liberty throughout all the land to all the inhabitants. What these people really believe is that the Preamble ought to be changed from "we, the people" to read "some of us—some of the people of the United States, but not including those we disapprove of or disagree with—do ordain and establish this Constitution."

Whether they know it or not, those people are enclosing the spirit as well as the letter of the original Constitution in a glass case, sealed off from the living nation. They are turning it into a mummy, as dead as some old Pharaoh of Egypt, and in so doing they are giving aid and comfort to the enemies of democracy.

The first article of the Bill of Rights provides that Congress shall make no law respecting freedom of worship or abridging freedom of opinion. There are some among us who seem to feel that this provision goes too far, even for the purpose of preventing tyranny over the mind of man. Of course, there are dangers in religious freedom and freedom of opinion.

But to deny these rights is worse than dangerous, it is absolutely fatal to liberty. The external threat to liberty should not drive us into suppressing liberty at home. Those who want the government to regulate matters of the mind and spirit are like men who are so afraid of being murdered that they commit suicide to avoid assassination.

All freedom-loving nations, not the United States alone, are facing a stern challenge from the communist tyranny. In the circumstances, alarm is justified. The man who isn't alarmed simply doesn't understand the situation—or he is crazy. But alarm is one thing, and hysteria is another. Hysteria impels people to destroy the very thing they are struggling to preserve.

Invasion and conquest by Communist armies would be a horror

beyond our capacity to imagine. But invasion and conquest by communist ideas of right and wrong would be just as bad.

For us to embrace the methods and morals of communism in order to defeat communist aggression would be a moral disaster worse than any physical catastrophe. If that should come to pass, then the Constitution and the Declaration would be utterly dead, and what we are doing today would be the gloomiest burial in the history of the world.

But I do not believe it is going to come to pass. On the contrary, I believe that this ceremony here today marks a new dedication to the ideals of liberty.

Since 1789 we have learned much about controlling the physical world around us. In 1789 they had nothing to compare with our modern methods of preserving priceless documents. They did not know how to place these sheets under conditions that, left undisturbed, may keep them intact and legible for a thousand years.

Perhaps our progress in learning the art of government has been less spectacular, but I for one, believe it has been no less certain. I believe the great experiment that we call the United States of America has taught much to mankind.

We know more than our forefathers did about the maintenance of popular liberty. Hence it should be easier, not harder, for us to preserve the spirit of the Republic, not in a marble shrine, but in human hearts. We have the knowledge; the question is, have we the will to apply it?

Whether we will preserve and extend popular liberty is a very serious question, but, after all, it is a very old question. The men who signed the Declaration faced it. So did those who wrote the Constitution. Each succeeding generation has faced it, and so far each succeeding generation has answered yes. I am sure that our generation will give the same answer.

So I confidently predict that what we are doing today is placing before the eyes of many generations to come the symbols of a living faith. And, like the sight of the flag "in the dawn's early light," the sight of these symbols will lift up their hearts, so they will go out of this building helped and strengthened and inspired.

§ *From 1948 on, Senator McCarthy and others had raised serious questions about what Americanism is and what conduct does and does not qualify as American. These issues Mr. Truman faced in a speech of August 14, 1951, in dedicating the Washington headquarters of the American Legion.*

In the preamble to the Legion's constitution, its members pledged themselves—among other things—to "uphold and defend the Constitution of the United States . . . to foster and perpetuate a 100 per cent Americanism . . . to safeguard and transmit to posterity the principles of justice, freedom and democracy."

At the present time, it is especially important for us to understand what these words mean and to live up to them.

The keystone of our form of government is the liberty of the individual. The Bill of Rights, which protects our individual liberties, is a fundamental part of our Constitution.

When the Legion pledged itself to uphold the Constitution, and to foster one-hundred-per-cent Americanism, it pledged itself to protect the rights and liberties of all our citizens.

Real Americanism means that we will protect freedom of speech— we will defend the right of people to say what they think, regardless of how much we may disagree with them.

Real Americanism means freedom of religion. It means that we will not discriminate against a man because of his religious faith.

Real Americanism means fair opportunities for all our citizens. It means that none of our citizens should be held back by unfair discrimination and prejudice.

Real Americanism means fair play. It means that a man who is accused of a crime shall be considered innocent until he has been proved guilty. It means that people are not to be penalized and persecuted for exercising their Constitutional liberties.

Real Americanism means also that liberty is not license. There is no freedom to injure others. The Constitution does not protect free speech to the extent of permitting conspiracies to overthrow the government. Neither does the right of free speech authorize slander or character assassination. These limitations are essential to keep us working together in one great community.

Real Americanism includes all these things. And it takes all of them together to make one-hundred-per-cent Americanism—the kind the Legion is pledged to support.

I'm glad the Legion has made that pledge. For true Americanism is under terrible attack today. Americanism needs defending—here and now. It needs defending by every decent human being in this country.

Americanism is under attack by communism, at home and abroad. And we are defending it against that attack. We are protecting our country from spies and saboteurs. We are breaking up the communist conspiracy in the United States. We are building our defenses, and making our country strong, and helping our allies to help themselves.

If we keep on doing these things—if we put our best into the job—we can protect ourselves from the attack of communism.

But Americanism is also under another kind of attack. It is being undermined by some people in this country who are loudly proclaiming that they are its chief defenders. These people claim to be against communism. But they are chipping away our basic freedoms just as insidiously and far more effectively than the communists have ever been able to do.

These people have attacked our basic principle of fair play that underlies our Constitution. They are trying to create fear and suspicion among us by the use of slander, unproved accusations, and just plain lies.

They are filling the air with the most irresponsible kinds of accusations against other people. They are trying to get us to believe that our government is riddled with communism and corruption—when the fact is that we have the finest and the most loyal body of civil servants in the whole world. These slandermongers are trying to get us so hysterical that no one will stand up to them for fear of being called a communist.

Now, this is an old communist trick in reverse. Everybody in Russia lives in terror of being called an anticommunist. For once that charge is made against anybody in Russia—no matter what the facts are—he is on the way out. And what I mean, he's on the way out!

In a dictatorship, everybody lives in fear and terror of being denounced and slandered. Nobody dares stand up for his rights.

We must never let such a condition come to pass in this great country of ours.

Yet this is exactly what the scaremongers and hatemongers are trying to bring about. Character assassination is their stock in trade. Guilt by association is their motto. They have created such a wave of fear and uncertainty that their attacks upon our liberties go almost unchallenged. Many people are growing frightened—and frightened people don't protest.

Stop and think. Stop and think where this is leading us.

The growing practice of character assassination is already curbing free speech and it is threatening all our other freedoms. I daresay there are people here today who have reached the point where they are afraid to explore a new idea. How many of you are afraid to come right out in public and say what you think about a controversial issue? How many of you feel that you must "play it safe" in all things —and on all occasions?

I hope there are not many, but from all that I have seen and heard, I am afraid of what your answers might be.

For I know you have no way of telling when some unfounded accusation may be hurled at you, perhaps straight from the halls of Congress.

Some of you have friends or neighbors who have been singled out for the pitiless publicity that follows accusations of this kind— accusations that are made without any regard for the actual guilt or innocence of the victim.

That is not fair play. That is not Americanism. It is not the American way to slur the loyalty and besmirch the character of the innocent and the guilty alike. We have always considered it just as important to protect the innocent as it is to punish the guilty.

We want to protect the country against disloyalty—of course we do. We have been punishing people for disloyal acts, and we are going to keep on punishing the guilty whenever we have a case against them. But we don't want to destroy our whole system of justice in the process. We don't want to injure innocent people. And yet the scurrilous work of the scandalmongers gravely threatens the whole idea of protection of the innocent in our country today.

Perhaps the Americans who live outside of Washington are less aware of this than you and I. If that is so, I want to warn them all. Slander, lies, character assassination—these things are a threat to every single citizen everywhere in this country. And when even one American—who has done nothing wrong—is forced by fear to shut his mind and close his mouth, then all Americans are in peril.

It is the job of all of us—of every American who loves his country and his freedom—to rise up and put a stop to this terrible business.

This is one of the greatest challenges we face today. We have got to make a fight for our real one-hundred-per-cent Americanism.

You Legionnaires, living up to your constitution as I know you want to do, can help lead the way. You can set an example of fair play. You can raise your voices against hysteria. You can expose the rotten motives of those people who are trying to divide us and confuse us and tear up the Bill of Rights.

No organization ever had the opportunity to do a greater service for America. No organization was ever better suited or better equipped to do the job.

I know the Legion. I know what a tremendous force for good it can be and what a tremendous force for good it has been.

Now go to it. The job's up to you.

God bless you.

§ *Mr. Truman's thoughts on one of the principal dilemmas of his administration—how to reconcile civil rights with the requirements of national security—are set forth in the following letter to Arthur J. Freund, Chairman of the Section of Criminal Law of the American Bar Association.*

September 1, 1951

Dear Mr. Freund:

I regret that I cannot accept your generous invitation to address the general session of the Section of Criminal Law of the American Bar Association on "The Protection of Individual Rights and Government Security in Times of Stress." I am glad, however, that this subject is being given consideration by the American Bar Association, since it is one of the most serious problems facing the American people and our government today.

The great peril of Soviet aggression which confronts the United States and, indeed, all free nations today makes it necessary that we continuously scrutinize our national security measures directed against treason, espionage, and subversion, to make sure that they are entirely adequate for the critical times in which we live. The federal government is doing that and will continue to do so. As I have pointed out in the past, however, the greatest contribution that the United States has to make to its own citizens and to the world is the heritage of freedom—freedom of speech, freedom of religion, and freedom of political belief. That heritage is not only the object of all our protective security measures, it is also the basic source of our true over-all national security.

Although the nation has always united against any external peril, blind obedience to authority has never been characteristic of Americans. Rather, they have been questioners, doubters, experimenters, and very often articulate and vociferous dissenters. This attitude is perhaps our unique and most valuable national asset. It has promoted our moral and spiritual welfare. It has made possible great material advances. It has forced discussion, examination, and re-examination of policies on every level. The free interchange of opinion and criticism thus made possible is in a very real sense the most important element of national security we possess, for it provides a greater likelihood that we will take the right course than does any system in which policies are determined by a few leaders whom none dares criticize.

The fact is—and what an object lesson there is for us in that fact—that the repressive security measures of the police states do not promote their over-all national security. On the contrary, they hurt it. They hurt it because the dictators of those countries have thereby made certain that they will not receive any opinions which do not conform with their own preconceived opinions—that even the intelligence reports which they receive about the strength and vulnerability of other countries will be slanted to conform with the party line view about those countries, however distant that may be from the real facts, lest the men who prepare those reports be suspected of being too friendly to foreign powers. Thus, in their mistaken zeal to promote their security by excessive police measures the totalitarian countries have actually undermined their security by making certain that their national policy decisions will be the product of the intuition or hunches or biases of the dictators rather than of actual facts and full discussion.

Full discussion can take place only in an atmosphere of freedom —an atmosphere in which a different or even an unpopular idea does not render the motives and patriotism of its proponent suspect, as would be the case in a totalitarian country. This national asset must be preserved. Unfortunately, the very crisis which requires that we take action to protect our security generates fear and suspicion. Because of this, there appears to be a growing confusion as to what are wise and appropriate security measures and what are measures that have little or no merit in terms of security, but which may and often do inflict irreparable harm upon innocent individuals and at the same time gravely injure real national security by enforcing conformity of political expression and thought. Too many Americans have not made a sufficient distinction between the two, and a few others—often posing as superpatriots—are, I believe, taking advantage of confusion and fear for partisan purposes. Let us beware of "the impostures of pretended patriotism" which George Washington warned us against in his Farewell Address.

The Bar is in a peculiarly strategic position to provide leadership in solving the problem of reconciling our security measures with the essentials of our heritage of freedom. Its tradition of leadership in public affairs and devotion to civil liberties, together with its understanding of the importance of fair procedure in the maintenance of liberties, place special responsibilities upon it. There are two specific suggestions that I have as to the manner in which the Bar might discharge its responsibilities in this regard.

First, action has been taken by many different bodies in the field of security. The federal government has intensified its efforts against sabotage, espionage, and related offenses. It has successfully completed prosecution of a number of important criminal cases in these fields, and it has recently initiated other such cases. It is carrying on security and loyalty programs with respect to its own employees. At the same time measures affecting the question are being introduced in the Congress continuously, and Congressional committees are carrying on their own investigations. Similar activity is going on at state and local levels, and many educational bodies and private enterprises are also acting in the field.

All these measures and proposed measures should be given critical, constructive, and public consideration by the Bar to help our people and the authorities involved determine whether they are reasonable and practical methods of maintaining security or whether their potentialities in terms of stifling freedom of expression outweigh their utility as security measures. Searching scrutiny of this character by able and fair-minded lawyers will greatly contribute toward enlightening the whole nation as to how we can best strike the difficult balance between security and individual rights in these trying times. Your contributions will be all the greater if you give the matter continuous and detailed attention and make your conclusions widely known.

A second contribution which I think the Bar may make relates to fair administrative and legislative hearings for persons under investigation and fair trials for persons accused of crime involving security. The Bar has a notable tradition of willingness to protect the rights of the accused. It seems to me that if this tradition is to be meaningful today it must extend to all defendants, including persons accused of such abhorrent crimes as conspiracy to overthrow the government by force, espionage, and sabotage. Undoubtedly, some uninformed persons will always identify the lawyer with the client. But I believe that most Americans recognize how important it is to our tradition of fair trial that there be adequate representation by competent counsel.

Lawyers in the past have risked the obloquy of the uninformed to protect the rights of the most degraded. Unless they continue to do so in the future, an important part of our rights will be gone. In addition to defense of those indicted in court, participation in and study of administrative and legislative hearings by the Bar with a view to the formulation of procedures which will reconcile the rights of individuals with the needs of security should be a source of real help to the bodies conducting such hearings in the resolution of their problems.

What I have said adds up to this: I believe the Bar has a profound contribution to make in this vital area of national policy and practice, and, morever, has a moral responsibility to make that contribution. I am confident that it will measure up to that responsibility.

Very sincerely yours,

HARRY S. TRUMAN

§ *Mr. Truman, in defense of his ideas of freedom and of Americanism, did not shrink from head-on collisions with their assailants. Like many, he found one of their principal assailants in what had come to be widely known as McCarthyism. To it he paid his respects in the last speech that he made in the 1952 presidential campaign, in St. Louis on November 1.*

. . . And then there is another element in the Republican campaign, and this is really a shocking and terrifying thing.

Americans have no more precious possession than the Bill of Rights. Those few paragraphs in the Constitution of the United States were the product of centuries of struggle by mankind against tyranny. They are a code of conduct for men in public life everywhere to assure that, no matter what happens, America will remain a land of freedom, of liberty, and justice.

But eternal vigilance is still the price of liberty. There is no assurance that the ideals embodied in our Bill of Rights will survive if there is a determined effort by men in positions of leadership to snuff them out.

A powerful group of men in the Republican party is now determined to rise to power through a method of conduct as hostile to American ideals as anything we have ever seen. This method has come to be known as McCarthyism.

This method tries people by accusation and slander instead of by evidence and proof.

It destroys reputations by repeated utterances of gigantic falsehoods. It spares neither the lowly government clerk nor men of the towering stature of General George C. Marshall.

This new method of American politics has already been used with a terrifying degree of success. It defeated a distinguished Senator, Tydings of Maryland, in 1950, and helped to defeat several others.

Now, for the first time, it is being used in a presidential election. The Republican candidate for Vice-President has made it his stock in trade in this campaign. Senator McCarthy himself was a featured speaker at the Republican convention—and was provided a national radio and television hook-up in this campaign, to see if he could do to Governor Stevenson what was done to Senator Tydings.

I would have expected the Republican candidate for President to be against this kind of thing. I would have expected him to defend the name of his old friend and benefactor, George Marshall, against those detractors.

But he did not do it. Instead, he just uttered a few generalities about the American tradition of justice. And he went on to say that Senators McCarthy and Jenner were on his team and should be re-elected. And he himself has been using the same kind of innuendo and distortion in his own speeches.

We must get rid of McCarthyism in our public life.

§ *President Truman's first involvement with civil rights occurred less than a month after he had taken office, when he plunged into the fight to establish a permanent Fair Employment Practices Commission. Since January 20, 1945, a bill to accomplish this end had lan-*

guished in committee. The Congress had meanwhile failed to appropriate funds for the existing F.E.P.C. for the fiscal year 1946. Mr. Truman wrote to Representative Adolf J. Sabath of Illinois, the committee chairman, urging that the permanent F.E.P.C. bill come to the floor.

"To abandon at this time the fundamental principle upon which the fair employment practice committee was established is unthinkable," he wrote. "Even if the war were over, or nearly over, the question of fair employment practices during the reconversion period and thereafter would be of paramount importance. Discrimination in the matter of employment against any properly qualified persons because of their race, creed, or color is not only un-American in nature, but will lead eventually to industrial strife and unrest."

§ In 1946 the President appointed a committee of prominent citizens, known as the President's Committee on Civil Rights, to study the entire field and make recommendations. It issued a historic report, "To Secure These Rights." After thoroughly reviewing both the favorable and the unfavorable aspects of civil rights in American society, the committee went on to make a number of proposals, among which were (1) reorganization and strengthening of the Civil Rights Section of the Department of Justice; (2) creation by the states of divisions similar to the federal Civil Rights Section; (3) special training for federal and state police in the handling of cases involving civil rights; (4) establishment of federal and state permanent commissions on civil rights to maintain constant surveillance; (5) clarification and strengthening of federal statutes to make clear what is and what is not a federal crime; (6) federal legislation outlawing police brutality, lynching, and all forms of peonage; (7) federal legislation outlawing the poll tax and other impediments to voting; (8) self-government for the District of Columbia; (9) citizenship for the people of Guam and Samoa; (10) repeal of state laws discriminating against aliens; (11) federal and state laws ending Jim Crow laws and other forms of racial segregation and discrimination; (12) withholding federal grants-in-aid from public and private agencies that practice discrimination and segregation.

The President adopted some of these proposals in his recommendations for legislative action to reinforce civil rights, stated in a special message to Congress on February 2, 1948.

To the Congress of the United States: In the State of the Union message on January 7, 1948, I spoke of five great goals toward which we should strive in our constant effort to strengthen our democracy and improve the welfare of our people. The first of these is to secure fully our essential human rights. I am now presenting to the Congress my recommendations for legislation to carry us forward toward that goal.

This nation was founded by men and women who sought these shores that they might enjoy greater freedom and greater opportunity than they had known before. The founders of the United States proclaimed to the world the American belief that all men are created equal, and that governments are instituted to secure the inalienable rights with which all men are endowed. In the Declaration of Independence and the Constitution of the United States, they eloquently expressed the aspirations of all mankind for equality and freedom.

These ideals inspired the peoples of other lands, and their practical fulfillment made the United States the hope of the oppressed everywhere. Throughout our history men and women of all colors and creeds, of all races and religions, have come to this country to escape tyranny and discrimination. Millions strong, they have helped build this democratic nation and have constantly reinforced our devotion to the great ideals of liberty and equality. With those who preceded them, they have helped to fashion and strengthen our American faith—a faith that can be simply stated:

We believe that all men are created equal and that they have the right to equal justice under law.

We believe that all men have the right to freedom of thought and of expression and the right to worship as they please.

We believe that all men are entitled to equal opportunities for jobs, for homes, for good health, and for education.

We believe that all men should have a voice in their government and that government should protect, not usurp, the rights of the people.

These are the basic civil rights which are the source and the support of our democracy.

Today, the American people enjoy more freedom and opportunity than ever before. Never in our history has there been better reason to hope for the complete realization of the ideals of liberty and equality.

We shall not, however, finally achieve the ideals for which this nation was founded so long as any American suffers discrimination as a result of his race, or religion, or color, or the land of origin of his forefathers.

Unfortunately, there are still examples—flagrant examples—of discrimination which are utterly contrary to our ideals. Not all groups of our population are free from the fear of violence. Not all groups are free to live and work where they please or to improve their conditions of life by their own efforts. Not all groups enjoy the full privileges of citizenship and participation in the government under which they live.

We cannot be satisfied until all our people have equal opportunities for jobs, for homes, for education, for health, and for political expression, and until all our people have equal protection under the law.

One year ago I appointed a committee of fifteen distinguished Americans and asked them to appraise the condition of our civil rights and to recommend appropriate action by federal, state, and local governments.

The committee's appraisal has resulted in a frank and revealing report. This report emphasizes that our basic human freedoms are better cared for and more vigilantly defended than ever before. But it also makes clear that there is a serious gap between our ideals and some of our practices. This gap must be closed.

This will take the strong efforts of each of us individually and all of us acting together through voluntary organizations and our governments.

The protection of civil rights begins with the mutual respect for the rights of others which all of us should practice in our daily lives. Through organizations in every community—in all parts of the country—we must continue to develop practical, workable arrangements for achieving greater tolerance and brotherhood.

The protection of civil rights is the duty of every government which derives its powers from the consent of the people. This is equally true of local, state, and national governments. There is much that the states can and should do at this time to extend their protection of civil rights. Wherever the law-enforcement measures of state and local governments are inadequate to discharge this primary function of government, these measures should be strengthened and improved.

The federal government has a clear duty to see that constitutional guarantees of individual liberties and of equal protection under the laws are not denied or abridged anywhere in our union. That duty is shared by all three branches of the government, but it can be fulfilled only if the Congress enacts modern, comprehensive civil rights laws, adequate to the needs of the day, and demonstrating our continuing faith in the free way of life.

I recommend, therefore, that the Congress enact legislation at this session directed toward the following specific objectives:

1. Establishing a permanent commission on civil rights, a joint Congressional committee on civil rights, and a Civil Rights Division in the Department of Justice.

2. Strengthening existing civil rights statutes.

3. Providing federal protection against lynching.

4. Protecting more adequately the right to vote.

5. Establishing a Fair Employment Practice Commission to prevent unfair discrimination in employment.

6. Prohibiting discrimination in interstate transportation facilities.

7. Providing home rule and suffrage in presidential elections for the residents of the District of Columbia.

8. Providing statehood for Hawaii and Alaska and a greater measure of self-government for our island possessions.

9. Equalizing the opportunities for residents of the United States to become naturalized citizens.

10. Settling the evacuation claims of Japanese-Americans.

As a first step, we must strengthen the organization of the federal government in order to enforce civil-rights legislation more adequately and to watch over the state of our traditional liberties.

I recommend that the Congress establish a permanent commission on civil rights reporting to the President. The commission should continuously review our civil-rights policies and practices, study specific problems, and make recommendations to the President at frequent intervals. It should work with other agencies of the federal government, with state and local governments, and with private organizations.

I also suggest that the Congress establish a joint Congressional committee on civil rights. This committee should make a continuing study of legislative matters relating to civil rights and should consider means of improving respect for and enforcement of those rights.

These two bodies together should keep all of us continuously aware of the condition of civil rights in the United States and keep us alert to opportunities to improve their protection.

To provide for better enforcement of federal civil rights laws, there will be established a division of civil rights in the Department of Justice. I recommend that the Congress provide for an additional Assistant Attorney General to supervise this division.

I recommend that the Congress amend and strengthen the existing provisions of federal law which safeguard the right to vote and the right to safety and security of person and property. These provisions are the basis for our present civil rights enforcement program.

Section 51 of Title 18 of the United States Code, which now gives protection to citizens in the enjoyment of rights secured by the Constitution or federal laws, needs to be strengthened in two respects. In its present form this section protects persons only if they are citizens, and it affords protection only against conspiracies by two or more persons. This protection should be extended to all inhabitants of the United States, whether or not they are citizens, and should be afforded against infringement by persons acting individually as well as in conspiracy.

Section 52 of Title 18 of the United States Code, which now gives general protection to individuals against the deprivation of federally secured rights by public officers, has proved to be inadequate in some cases because of the generality of its language. An enumeration of the principal rights protected under this section is needed to make more definite and certain the protection which the section affords.

A specific federal measure is needed to deal with the crime of lynching—against which I cannot speak too strongly. It is a principle of our democracy, written into our Constitution, that every person accused of an offense against the law shall have a fair, orderly trial in an impartial court. We have made great progress towards this end, but I regret to say that lynching has not yet finally disappeared from our land. So long as one person walks in fear of lynching, we shall not have achieved equal justice under law. I call upon the Congress to take decisive action against this crime.

Under the Constitution the right of all properly qualified citizens to vote is beyond question. Yet the exercise of this right is still subject to interference. Some individuals are prevented from voting by isolated acts of intimidation. Some whole groups are prevented by outmoded policies prevailing in certain states or communities.

We need stronger statutory protection of the right to vote. I urge the Congress to enact legislation forbidding interference by public officers or private persons with the right of qualified citizens to participate in primary, special, and general elections in which federal officers are to be chosen. This legislation should extend to elections for state as well as federal officers insofar as interference with the right to vote results from discriminatory action by public officers based on race, color, or other unreasonable classification.

Requirements for the payment of poll taxes also interfere with the right to vote. There are still seven states which, by their constitutions, place this barrier between their citizens and the ballot box. The American people would welcome voluntary action on the part of these states to remove this barrier. Nevertheless, I believe the Congress should enact measures insuring that the right to vote in elections for federal officers shall not be contingent upon the payment of taxes.

I wish to make it clear that the enactment of the measures I have recommended will in no sense result in federal conduct of elections. They are designed to give qualified citizens federal protection of their right to vote. The actual conduct of elections, as always, will remain the responsibility of state governments.

We in the United States believe that all men are entitled to equality of opportunity. Racial, religious, and other invidious forms of discrimination deprive the individual of an equal chance to develop and utilize his talents and to enjoy the rewards of his efforts.

Once more I repeat my request that the Congress enact fair employment practice legislation prohibiting discrimination in employment based on race, color, religion, or national origin. The legislation should create a Fair Employment Practice Commission with authority to prevent discrimination by employers and labor unions, trade and professional associations, and government agencies and employment bureaus. The degree of effectiveness which the wartime Fair Employment Practice Committee attained shows that it is possible to equalize job opportunity by government action and thus to eliminate the influence of prejudice in employment.

The channels of interstate commerce should be open to all Americans on a basis of complete equality. The Supreme Court has recently declared unconstitutional state laws requiring segregation on public carriers in interstate travel. Company regulations must not be allowed to replace unconstitutional state laws. I urge the Congress to prohibit discrimination and segregation, in the use of interstate transportation facilities, by both public officers and the employees of private companies.

I am in full accord with the principle of local self-government for residents of the District of Columbia. In addition, I believe that the Constitution should be amended to extend suffrage in presidential elections to the residents of the District.

The District of Columbia should be a true symbol of American freedom and democracy for our own people and for the people of the world. It is my earnest hope that the Congress will promptly give the citizens of the District of Columbia their own local elective government. They themselves can then deal with the inequalities arising from segregation in the schools and other public facilities, and from racial barriers to places of public accommodation which now exist for one third of the District's population.

The present inequalities in essential services are primarily a problem for the District itself, but they are also of great concern to the whole nation. Failing local corrective action in the near future, the Congress should enact a model civil rights law for the nation's capital.

The present political status of our territories and possessions impairs the enjoyment of civil rights by their residents. I have in the past recommended legislation granting statehood to Alaska and Hawaii, and organic acts for Guam and American Samoa, including a grant of citizenship to the people of these Pacific islands. I repeat these recommendations.

Furthermore, the residents of the Virgin Islands should be granted an increasing measure of self-government, and the people of Puerto Rico should be allowed to choose their form of government and their ultimate status with respect to the United States.

All properly qualified legal residents of the United States should be allowed to become citizens without regard to race, color, religion, or national origin. The Congress has recently removed the bars which formerly prevented persons from China, India, and the Philippines from becoming naturalized citizens. I urge the Congress to remove the remaining racial or nationality barriers which stand in the way of citizenship for some residents of our country.

During the last war more than 100,000 Japanese-Americans were evacuated from their homes in the Pacific states solely because of their racial origin. Many of these people suffered property and business losses as a result of this forced evacuation and through no fault of their own. The Congress has before it legislation establishing a procedure by which claims based upon these losses can be promptly considered and settled. I trust that favorable action on this legislation will soon be taken.

The legislation I have recommended for enactment by the Congress at the present session is a minimum program if the federal government is to fulfill its obligation of insuring the Constitutional guarantees of individual liberties and of equal protection under the law.

Under the authority of existing law, the executive branch is taking every possible action to improve the enforcement of the civil rights statutes and to eliminate discrimination in federal employment, in providing federal services and facilities, and in the armed forces.

I have already referred to the establishment of the Civil Rights Division of the Department of Justice. The Federal Bureau of Investigation will work closely with this new division in the investigation of federal civil rights cases. Specialized training is being given to the bureau's agents so that they may render more effective service in this difficult field of law enforcement.

It is the settled policy of the United States government that there shall be no discrimination in federal employment or in providing federal services and facilities. Steady progress has been made toward this objective in recent years. I shall shortly issue an executive order containing a comprehensive restatement of the federal nondiscrimination policy, together with appropriate measures to ensure compliance.

During the recent war and in the years since its close we have made such progress toward equality of opportunity in our armed forces without regard to race, color, religion, or national origin. I have instructed the Secretary of Defense to take steps to have the remaining instances of discrimination in the armed services eliminated as rapidly as possible. The personnel policies and practices of all the services in this regard will be made consistent.

I have instructed the Secretary of the Army to investigate the status of civil rights in the Panama Canal Zone with a view to eliminating such discrimination as may exist there. If legislation is necessary, I shall make appropriate recommendations to the Congress.

The position of the United States in the world today makes it especially urgent that we adopt these measures to secure for all our people their essential rights.

The peoples of the world are faced with the choice of freedom or enslavement, a choice between a form of government which harnesses the state in the service of the individual and a form of government which chains the individual to the needs of the state.

We in the United States are working in company with other nations who share our desire for enduring world peace and who believe with us that, above all else, men must be free. We are striving to build a world family of nations—a world where men may live under governments of their own choosing and under laws of their own making.

As part of that endeavor the Commission on Human Rights of the United Nations is now engaged in preparing an international bill of human rights by which the nations of the world may bind themselves by international covenant to give effect to basic human rights and fundamental freedoms. We have played a leading role in this undertaking designed to create a world order of law and justice fully protective of the rights and the dignity of the individual.

To be effective in these efforts we must protect our civil rights so that by providing all our people with the maximum enjoyment of personal freedom and personal opportunity we shall be a stronger nation—stronger in our leadership, stronger in our moral position, stronger in the deeper satisfactions of a united citizenry.

We know that our democracy is not perfect. But we do know that it offers a fuller, freer, happier life to our people than any totalitarian nation has ever offered.

If we wish to inspire the peoples of the world whose freedom is in jeopardy, if we wish to restore hope to those who have already lost their civil liberties, if we wish to fulfill the promise that is ours, we must correct the remaining imperfections in our practice of democracy.

We know the way. We need only the will.

§ As was to be expected, the President's vigorous and comprehensive proposals were the genesis of bitter controversy both in Congress and at the Democratic national convention at Philadelphia in 1948. Mr. Truman, after his nomination, came before the convention and in his acceptance speech announced that he would call Congress into special session that very month to take action on, among other things, civil rights. Congress reconvened, and on July 27 Mr. Truman said to it:

Finally, I again urge upon the Congress the measures I recommended last February to protect and extend basic civil rights of citizenship and human liberty. A number of bills to carry out my recommendations have been introduced into Congress. Many of them have already received careful consideration by Congressional committees. Only one bill, however, has been enacted, a bill relating to the rights of Americans of Japanese origin.

I believe that it is necessary to enact the laws I have recommended in order to make the guarantees of the Constitution real and vital.

§ In the wake of the 1948 victory Mr. Truman launched a determined drive to get a civil rights program through Congress, and immediately focused on the chief source of obstruction, the Senate filibuster. Soon after Congress convened in January 1949 Democratic leaders in the Senate, at Mr. Truman's request, proposed to reconsider the Senate rules in order to limit the filibuster. But the upshot was that the Senate adopted a new cloture rule despite assertions of administration Democrats that it would strengthen rather than weaken the Southern filibuster against the civil rights program. And the pattern of Congressional response for the remainder of the Truman administration followed a well-rutted negative. The House occasionally passed requested measures—an anti-poll tax bill got through it at least four times during Mr. Truman's incumbency—but the Senate habitually blocked action by filibuster, by threat of filibuster, or by committee bottleneck.

Although faced with virtually unremitting legislative defeat, the President made substantial strides toward civil rights by executive action. Some of these advances he summarized near the close of his administration in a 1952 campaign speech in Harlem.

Now many people have wondered how I came to have such a deep interest in civil rights. I want to tell you about that. Right after World War II, religious and racial intolerance began to show up just as it did in 1919. There were a good many incidents of violence and friction, but two of them in particular made a very deep impression on me. One was when a Negro veteran, still wearing his country's uniform, was arrested and beaten and blinded. And not long after that two Negro veterans with their wives lost their lives at the hands of a mob.

It is the duty of the state and local government to prevent such tragedies. But as President of the United States I felt I ought to do everything in my power to find what caused such crimes and to root out the causes. It was for that reason that I created the President's Committee on Civil Rights. I asked its members to study the situation and recommend to the whole country what we should do.

Their report is one of our great American documents. When it was handed to me, I said that it was a new charter of human freedom. Five years have passed, but I have never seen anything to make me change my mind.

Those five years have seen some hard fighting by those who believe in civil rights for all our people. . . . Those five years have seen a lot of progress—progress in spite of obstacles that have been placed in our way.

I want to review that progress for you today.

Right after the Committee on Civil Rights made its report to me, I sent to the Congress a special message making ten recommendations for new legislation. Only two of these ten recommendations have been approved by Congress. The opponents of civil rights in the Congress have blocked every effort to enact such important legislation as a fair employment practices law, an anti-poll tax law, an anti-lynch law. Not only that, they have succeeded in changing the rules under which Congress operates so as to make it impossible to stop a filibuster.

Who are the opponents—who are the opponents of civil rights? All you'll have to do is look at the record. Read the Congressional Record and you'll find them. I sent a good F.E.P.C. bill to Congress; but the Republicans introduced the McConnell Amendment—a toothless substitute for F.E.P.C.—and the Republicans in the House voted two to one for that amendment, beating the Democratic majority that wanted F.E.P.C. The Republicans also introduced and got passed in the Senate the Wherry rule making it next to impossible to stop these filibusters. . . .

When Congress refused to act I went ahead to do what I could within the executive branch itself. This fight of ours cannot stop just because we've been blocked in the United States Congress.

First, I acted to stop racial discrimination in the armed services. The Navy and the Air Force have now eliminated all racial distinctions. And for over two years every soldier coming into an Army training unit in this country has been assigned on the basis of his individual merit—regardless of race or color. All troops in Korea are now integrated, and integration is going forward elsewhere overseas.

I also had a Fair Employment Board set up in the Civil Service Commission. Today, every federal agency has a fair employment practice program that is working. Any federal employee or applicant for federal employment who feels he has been discriminated against because of race can now ask for and receive justice.

At my request the Solicitor General of the United States went before the Supreme Court to argue that Negro citizens have the right to enter state colleges and universities on exactly the same basis as any other citizens. And we won that fight. And more than a thousand Negro graduate and professional students have been accepted by ten state universities that had barred their doors to Negroes before.

At my request the Solicitor General again went before the Supreme Court and argued against the vicious restrictive covenants that had prevented houses in many places from being sold to Negroes and to Jews. It was a great day in the history of civil rights when we won that case also before the Supreme Court.

As one result of that decision, more Negroes are home owners today than ever before in American history.

Our locally operated public housing projects are increasingly open to families of all races and creeds. The number of integrated projects has increased eightfold in eight years. In the last few years nine states and eight cities have forbidden discrimination or segregation in public housing.

In the last few years eleven states and twenty cities have enacted fair employment practice laws. This is where the greatest gap exists in our federal laws on civil rights, and I have repeatedly urged the Congress to pass the kind of law we need.

Such a statute must have enforcement powers if it is to mean anything. To talk about voluntary compliance with fair employment practice is just plain nonsense. Federal fair employment legislation with enforcement power is greatly needed and it ought to be on the books, and I'm going to keep fighting for it, come hell or high water.

Progress has been made in assuring Negroes the opportunity to exercise their right to vote as citizens. The courts have made the infamous "white primary" a thing of the past. Thank God for that!

And there are only five poll tax states left in this Union. Nevertheless, we still need laws to abolish the poll tax and otherwise protect the right to vote where intimidation or restrictions still exist.

In the last five years two states have enacted anti-lynch laws. Five states and forty-five cities have passed laws against wearing masks in public—which will strip the hoods off the Ku Klux Klan. One of the finest things that have happened recently was the conviction and prosecution of those Ku Kluxers down in North Carolina and Southern States.

This is splendid progress in the fight to guarantee our citizens protection against mob violence, but it's not enough. It is the clear duty of the federal government to stand behind local law enforcement agencies and to step in if they fail to control mob action. That is exactly what we have been doing through the F.B.I. and through the Civil Rights Section of the Department of Justice.

Last year, a mob formed in Cicero, Illinois, and prevented a Negro veteran and his family from moving into an apartment house. Fortunately, Illinois was blessed with a great governor who is now your Democratic candidate for President.

Governor Stevenson, who believes in action in these matters, restored law and order with the National Guard. But a local grand jury did the incredible thing of indicting—not the ringleaders of the mob—but the Negro veteran's lawyer and the property owner.

At this point the federal government stepped in to prevent a gross miscarriage of justice. It obtained an indictment of the city officials who had failed in their duty to assure equal justice under law, and the officials who abetted the mob were tried and convicted in the federal court.

It was also last year that this nation was shocked by the bomb murder in Florida of Harry T. Moore and his wife. These tragic deaths came shortly after the bombings of synagogues and Catholic churches and of the housing project at Carver Village. For several months the F.B.I. have been gathering evidence on the mobs responsible for these outrages. And, this week, the United States government began to present that evidence to a federal grand jury at Miami.

These are examples how your federal government—under a Democratic President—stands behind the Constitutional guarantees of human rights. The federal government could do a better job if we had stronger civil rights laws—and we must never let down in fighting for those laws.

Now, the progress we have been making in the field of human rights is in grave danger. Make no mistake about that.

One person in this country has to think of all the people all the time. That person is the President of the United States. If you want this civil rights program to continue, you must make the right man President this year.

Now every special interest in the United States has a highly paid lobby at Washington who spend their time banqueting the legislators and trying to force legislation through for their special interest. And the only lobbyist that the 150,000,000 people have who can't afford to hire one is the President of the United States.

§ *The President might have listed still other executive actions taken in behalf of civil rights. On December 2, 1949, in a meeting of State Committees on Discrimination in Housing Administration, United States Solicitor General Philip B. Perlman announced that Federal Housing Administration financing would be refused for any new houses or apartments whose occupancy or use was restricted on the basis of race, creed, or color. In commenting on this policy he said: "President Truman has been working on this matter for some time, and is most happy over the results of his efforts."*

In the face of repeated failures to secure legislation for a Fair Employment Practices Commission Mr. Truman on December 3, 1951 sought to establish something of an approximation of it by executive action. He set up a top-level interdepartmental committee to police compliance with clauses in government contracts against racial or religious discrimination in employment. With Korean mobilization at its peak, the contracts involved covered one fifth of the economy.

Finally, the President gave consistent support to the Universal Declaration of Human Rights adopted by a resolution of the United Nations General Assembly on December 10, 1948. The United States proposal for a Declaration of Human Rights was submitted by Mrs. Franklin D. Roosevelt, U.S. Representative on the United Nations Commission on Human Rights, at its second session in Geneva December 1–19, 1947. Typical of Truman's support of these efforts remarks in the course of a speech in Washington on June 29,

...en past difficulties faced our nation, we met the challenge with ...., ng charters of human rights—the Declaration of Independence, the Constitution, the Bill of Rights, and the Emancipation Proclamation. Today our representatives and those of other liberty-loving countries on the United Nations Commission on Human Rights are preparing an International Bill of Rights. We can be confident that it will be a great landmark in man's long search for freedom.

2. ATOMIC ENERGY

Mr. Truman, when he announced that the atomic bomb had been dropped on Hiroshima, also declared that he would recommend that "Congress consider promptly the establishment of an appropriate commission to control the production and use of atomic energy." On October 3, 1945, he sent a message to Congress in keeping with his original intentions.

Almost two months have passed since the atomic bomb was used against Japan. That bomb did not win the war, but it certainly shortened the war. We know that it saved the lives of untold thousands of American and Allied soldiers who would otherwise have been killed in battle.

The discovery of the means of releasing atomic energy began a new era in the history of civilization. The scientific and industrial knowledge on which this discovery rests does not relate merely to another weapon. It may some day prove to be more revolutionary in the development of human society than the invention of the wheel, the use of metals, or the steam or internal-combustion engine.

Never in history has society been confronted with a power so full of potential danger and at the same time so full of promise for the future of man and for the peace of the world. I think I express the faith of the American people when I say that we can use the knowledge we have won not for the devastation of war but for the future welfare of humanity.

To accomplish the objective we must proceed along two fronts— the domestic and the international.

The first and most urgent step is the determination of our domestic policy for the control, use, and development of atomic energy within the United States.

We cannot postpone decisions in this field. The enormous investment which we made to produce the bomb has given us the two vast industrial plants in Washington and Tennessee, the many associated works throughout the country. It has brought together a vast organization of scientists, executives, industrial engineers, and skilled workers—a national asset of inestimable value.

The powers which the Congress wisely gave to the government to wage war were adequate to permit the creation and development of this enterprise as a war project. Now that our enemies have surrendered, we should take immediate action to provide for the future use of this huge investment in brains and plant.

I am informed that many of the people on whom depend the continued successful operation of the plants and the further development of atomic knowledge are getting ready to return to their normal pursuits. In many cases these people are considering leaving the project largely because of uncertainty concerning future national policy in this field. Prompt action to establish national policy will go a long way toward keeping a strong organization intact.

It is equally necessary to direct future research and to establish control of the basic raw materials essential to the development of this power whether it is to be used for purposes of peace or war. Atomic force in ignorant or evil hands could inflict untold disaster upon the nation and the world. Society cannot hope even to protect itself— much less to realize the benefits of the discovery—unless prompt action is taken to guard against the hazards of misuse.

I therefore urge, as a first measure in a program of utilizing our knowledge for the benefit of society, that the Congress enact legislation to fix a policy with respect to our existing plants and to control all sources of atomic energy and all activities connected with its development and use in the United States.

The legislation should give jurisdiction for these purposes to an atomic energy commission with members appointed by the President with the advice and consent of the Senate.

The Congress should lay down the basic principles for all the activities of the commission, the objectives of which should be the promotion of the national welfare, securing the national defense, safeguarding world peace, and the acquisition of further knowledge concerning atomic energy.

The people of the United States know that the overwhelming power we have developed in this war is due in large measure to American science and American industry, consisting of management and labor. We believe that our science and industry owe their strength to the spirit of free inquiry and the spirit of free enterprise that characterize our country.

The commission, therefore, in carrying out its functions should interfere as little as possible with private research and private enterprise, and should use as much as possible existing institutions and agencies. The observance of this policy is our best guarantee of maintaining the pre-eminence in science and industry upon which our national well-being depends.

All land and mineral deposits owned by the United States which constitute sources of atomic energy, and all stock piles of materials from which such energy may be derived, and all plants or other property of the United States connected with its development and use should be transferred to the supervision and control of the commission.

The commission should be authorized to acquire at a fair price, by purchase or by condemnation, any minerals or other materials from which the sources of atomic energy can be derived, and also any land containing such minerals or materials which are not already owned by the United States.

The power to purchase should include real and personal property outside the limits of the United States.

The commission should also be authorized to conduct all necessary research, experimentation, and operations for the further development and use of atomic energy for military, industrial, scientific, or medical purposes. In these activities it should, of course, use existing private and public institutions and agencies to the fullest practicable extent.

Under appropriate safeguards the commission should also be permitted to license any property available to the commission for research, development, and exploitation in the field of atomic energy. Among other things, such licensing should be conditioned, of course, upon a policy of widespread distribution of peacetime products on equitable terms which will prevent monopoly.

In order to establish effective control and security, it should be declared unlawful to produce or use the substances comprising the sources of atomic energy or to import or export them except under conditions prescribed by the commission.

Finally, the commission should be authorized to establish security regulations governing the handling of all information, material, and equipment under its jurisdiction. Suitable penalties should be prescribed for violating the security regulations of the commission or any of the other terms of the act.

The measures which I have suggested may seem drastic and far-reaching. But the discovery with which we are dealing involves forces of nature too dangerous to fit into any of our usual concepts.

The other phase of the problem is the question of the international control and development of this newly discovered energy.

In international relations, as in domestic affairs, the release of atomic energy constitutes a new force too revolutionary to consider in the framework of old ideas. We can no longer rely on the slow progress of time to develop a program of control among nations. Civilization demands that we shall reach at the earliest possible date a satisfactory arrangement for the control of this discovery, in order that it may become a powerful and forceful influence toward the maintenance of world peace instead of an instrument of destruction.

Scientific opinion appears to be practically unanimous that the essential theoretical knowledge upon which the discovery is based is already widely known. There is also substantial agreement that foreign research can come abreast of our present theoretical knowledge in time.

The hope of civilization lies in international arrangements looking, if possible, to the renunciation of the use and development of the atomic bomb, and directing and encouraging the use of atomic energy and all future scientific information toward peaceful and humanitarian ends. The difficulties in working out such arrangements are great.

The alternative to overcoming these difficulties, however, may be a desperate armament race which might well end in disaster. Discussion of the international problem cannot be safely delayed until the United Nations Organization is functioning and in a position adequately to deal with it.

I therefore propose that these discussions will not be concerned with disclosures relating to the manufacturing processes leading to the production of the atomic bomb itself. They will constitute an effort to work out arrangements covering the terms under which international collaboration and exchange of scientific information might safely proceed.

The outcome of the discussions will be reported to the Congress as soon as possible, and any resulting agreements requiring Congressional action will be submitted to the Congress.

But regardless of the course of discussions in the international field, I believe it is essential that legislation along the lines I have indicated be adopted as promptly as possible to insure the necessary research in, and development and control of, the production and use of atomic energy.

§ *The administration provided no draft of legislation embodying the President's recommendations. The leaders of both houses of Congress, however, obtained from what the New York Times called "other sources" a twenty-one-page detailed presentation of the broad outline of policy that the President's message suggested.*

In the months that followed, the attention of Congress centered on two rival pieces of legislation. One was the McMahon bill, offered by Senator Brien McMahon, Democrat of Connecticut. In a letter of February 2, 1946 Mr. Truman went on record as supporting the bill because it reflected his desire for civilian control of atomic energy and for government ownership of all atomic energy patents. The alternative was the May-Johnson bill, which had the support of Secretary of War Patterson although the President had given the McMahon bill his official blessing. The May bill came under attack of a number of scientists who contended that it would give military men control of atomic energy and discourage research because of its harsh security provisions.

Midway in the controversy Senator Vandenberg introduced an amendment to the McMahon bill that would put the military in an advisory relationship to a controlling civilian board, with powers to keep in close touch with all activities and to make direct appeal to the President to change commission policy or nullify commission acts. The Vandenberg amendment was passed by Congress in modified form.

Mr. Truman's own views on civilian versus military control of atomic energy were expounded in a campaign speech in Milwaukee on October 14, 1948:

I believe from the bottom of my heart that we are engaged in a great crusade to determine whether the powers of government will be used for the benefit of all the people or for the benefit of a privileged few.

Tonight I'm going to talk about something that ought not to be in politics at all, but the Republican candidate has brought it in. When he did this he displayed a dangerous lack of understanding of the subject. At the same time he clearly implied a belief that there should be private exploitation of a tremendous asset which belongs to the people of the United States. He blundered into a subject which is of immediate concern to every person in the United States and in the whole world.

That is atomic energy.

This is a force which holds great danger of catastrophe in the wrong hands. At the same time it holds great promise of a better life in the right hands. Everyone must understand clearly what is involved.

Atomic power is so overwhelming that most people have difficulty in seeing how it affects their daily lives. But the fact is, the future of every one of us depends in large measure on whether atomic energy is used for good or evil.

There are three fundamental facts about atomic energy that each of us should understand.

First of all, the atomic bomb is the most terrible weapon that man has ever contrived.

Second, because atomic energy is capable of destroying civilization, it must be controlled by international authority.

And third, if properly controlled, atomic energy can enrich human life for all the generations to come. . . .

A free society requires the supremacy of civil rather than military authority. This is in no sense a reflection upon our armed services. It is part of the spirit of our free institutions that military specialists must always be under the direction of civilians.

Because of the power and world significance of atomic energy, I was convinced that it had to be placed under civilian control. The Democratic Seventy-ninth Congress enacted a law which made civilian control possible. The wisdom of that decision has been proved again and again during the past two years.

§ *In the same speech he dealt with another issue that was coming to the fore: the role of private enterprise in the development and use of atomic energy. The President had this to say:*

We are steadily making advances in the field of atomic science.

I can assure you that the civilian Atomic Energy Commission has maintained the leadership and readiness of the United States in atomic weapons—despite the presence of what the Republican candidate for President is pleased to call the "dead hand" of government.

The progress we are making in developing atomic energy for peaceful uses may at first seem less dramatic than the creation of the atomic bomb. But, in fact, it promises the world a whole new age of creative abundance.

The Atomic Energy Commission has begun work on the first experimental plant intended to supply atomic power for industrial purposes.

Great progress is being made in the use of atomic materials for research in biology and medicine. Here, we are warring against cancer and the other diseases which take their terrible toll of lives.

Atomic materials are also opening up tremendous new possibilities in agriculture and industrial research. And these same radioactive materials are among our most important research tools in the field of fundamental physical science. Fifty years from now, the world will be a vastly different place because the power of the atom is being harnessed. It is our job to see that atomic energy makes the world not a wasteland of destruction but a vastly better place in which to live.

Atomic energy is not just a new form of power, like coal or oil. It is a force which can be compared only with the cosmic energies of the sun itself. The fission of a single pound of uranium releases as much energy as the burning of three million pounds of coal. A force like this cannot be handled on a business-as-usual basis.

The Republican candidate for Presidency made a speech on

atomic energy at Phoenix, Arizona, on September 23. The obvious implication in that speech is that the Republican candidate feels that the peacetime uses of atomic energy should be taken from the government and turned over to private corporations. Here again is the basic conflict between the Democratic and Republican parties. Here again is the vital issue between the people and the selfish interest.

I believe that atomic energy should not be used to fatten the profits of big business. I believe that it should be used to benefit all the people. The largest private corporation in the world is far too small to be entrusted with such power, least of all for its own profit.

Most responsible businessmen know this. Men who know what atomic energy means do not talk about the "dead hand of government." For our own protection and to insure our national security, we must continue to develop atomic energy as a public trust. Our atomic materials are very precious, and must be guarded closely. Atomic energy cannot and must not be another Teapot Dome for private exploitation—any more than it can be allowed to enter into competitive armaments.

Our atomic plants cost billions of dollars of public money to build, and millions more to operate each year. They belong to all the people.

The use of atomic material presents technical hazards which require very careful safety measures.

And here is the most important point of all. You cannot separate the peacetime use of atomic materials from their potential military use.

Atomic material in a power station is not far from being an atomic arsenal. This is the blunt fact that requires an international control that will really work. The same fact makes it absolutely necessary to insist upon public ownership and control in the United States.

At the same time, we must make full use of the skill and initiative of private business. Business concerns have had and will continue to have an indispensable part in this great venture. This is a basic principle of the McMahon Atomic Energy Act of 1946—one of the wisest laws ever to be put on our statute books.

The success of our whole atomic energy program, military as

well as peaceful, has been based on constant and effective teamwork between government and private enterprise. Today, over three thousand private contractors and suppliers are participating in our atomic energy program. Today, the great atomic plants at Oak Ridge, at Hanford, and elsewhere are operated by private industrial organizations under government supervision. Today, scores of college and university laboratories are carrying out important atomic research.

Everything possible is being done to find legitimate opportunities for ever greater participation by private enterprise, consistent with the public interest. But we must not put profit-making above the national welfare.

The platform of the Republican party upon which my opponent is running for election fails to mention atomic energy. I assumed at first that this was merely an oversight. It is clear now, however, that this omission was deliberate. It is clear from the comments of the Republican candidate that powerful, selfish groups within the Republican party are determined to exploit the atom for private profit.

I shall fight this effort with all my strength.

The government is the indispensable trustee of the people for the development of atomic energy. Some day it may be possible to fit atomic energy more closely into the normal pattern of American business. But I cannot tell you that this is just around the corner. I will make no light promises of that sort. Our national policy has been that atomic energy is such a vast new force in our lives that it must be kept under public control as long as safety and the people's interest require. We must continue to follow that policy. That is the only way we can assure the development of atomic energy for the benefit of humanity. That is the only way we can assure that it will be used not for death but for a more abundant life.

This great discovery belongs to the people and must be used for the people. There has been no more vital issue before the American people in this century. The existence of civilization itself depends upon the wisdom and prudence of the American people in choosing the course we are to follow.

I pray that your decision may be the right one.

§ *Curiously and out of chronology, it remained for the administration of Mr. Truman's successor to turn up a proposal connected* with atomic energy that also involved the control of the nation's natural resources, a subject important to Mr. Truman from long before his presidency. This proposal was the highly controversial Dixon-Yates contract.

It grew out of the Atomic Energy Commission's increasing demands on the Tennessee Valley Authority for power, coupled with the reluctance of the Eisenhower administration to meet the exigency by expansion of the T.V.A. Instead, private utilities were to feed energy to the Authority to replace the quota of power fed by it to the A.E.C. Edgar Dixon, president of Middle South Utilities, Inc., and Eugene Yates, chairman of the Southern Company, negotiated with the A.E.C. and with the Bureau of the Budget, and in April 1954 the so-called Dixon-Yates contract coalesced.

In the Congressional elections of that year it was attacked by Democrats as "nefarious," "worse than Teapot Dome," and so on. Mr. Truman, actively participating in the campaign, spearheaded the attack in a Kansas City speech of October 16.

In the 1952 campaign the Republicans kept talking about the so-called creeping socialism of the Democratic program and that when they came to power they would restore to this nation the benefits of free competitive enterprise. The Republicans certainly could not have been too serious about restoring a free competitive enterprise which we already had. Free competitive enterprise was doing very well under Democratic management, bringing prosperous times to agriculture, to business, and to labor. But now look at what has happened. Let's look at the mysterious Dixon-Yates contract award by the administration. Surely this Dixon-Yates award cannot be said to be competitive—since competitive bidding was not permitted. I wonder if we can even regard it as any kind of private enterprise, since all the risks are assumed and underwritten by the government and the profits are guaranteed by the government. In fact, it is a public subsidy at public expense for the benefit of a private monopoly. The Dixon-Yates award consequently is a good example of what Republicans mean when they campaign for free competitive enterprise.

It is not competitive. This is certainly not what we mean by enterprise, since no venture by pioneering private individuals is involved and all the risks are assumed by the public.

Since it is neither competitive nor is it enterprise, there is no doubt about its being free. It is just a plain give-away of public money and national resources.

I am afraid of the effect this transaction may have on the future of our atomic energy program.

The Atomic Energy Commission is one of the most sensitive and is the most important agency in our government.

The Atomic Energy Commission has enjoyed the respect and confidence of the public and the Congress since it was established. Atomic energy today is our greatest public resource. Its effect on the future development of the nation is unlimited. Extreme care and vigilance must be exercised to make sure that the people get the full benefit of this revolutionary new source of power.

The people have paid for it—and the people own it.

The Commission should not be subjected to influences that would impair its standing with the public or the Congress by raising doubts concerning its dealings with private industry.

There is another vast resource owned by the people about which I am equally concerned, and that is the T.V.A. Bad as the Dixon-Yates contract is, it would be tragic if it were the opening wedge to destroy the T.V.A., one of our greatest public assets.

I personally believe there is a brazen attempt in the making to wreck it. The T.V.A. has shown the way to open up vast areas of this country by the harnessing and utilization of water power. And by its efficient management, the T.V.A. has become a yardstick which keeps the big utility combines of the country from over-charging the consumer for power and light.

In the past, right-thinking Republicans as well as Democrats took part in the development and conservation of our natural resources.

Many important public power developments have been built where private utility companies were unable or unwilling to provide electric power and light. Millions of rural homes and farms today would lag in the progress and comfort of the rest of the country if they had to depend upon private utility monopolists.

But now that the government-sponsored electrification program has reached such successful development and operation, the big utility monopolies are trying to take over control.

Apparently they are being encouraged by this Republican administration in their attempted raids.

Within twenty months this administration has confronted the country with a historic and dangerous program to give away the resources and rights carefully developed by Republicans as well as Democrats over thirty years. Unless we do something about it, these precious rights are in grave danger of being given away to special monopolistic interests in the West, the Northwest, the South, and wherever else the people own great assets.

§ *On July 11, 1955, President Eisenhower canceled the Dixon-Yates contract.*

3. NATURAL RESOURCES

Mr. Truman's philosophy of how our natural resources should be developed and used is rather fully set forth in his several State of the Union messages. In that of January 7, 1948, he said:

The resources given by nature to this country are rich and extensive. The material foundations of our growth and economic development are the bounty of our fields, the wealth of our mines and forests, and the energy of our waters. As a nation, we are coming to appreciate more each day the close relationship between the conservation of these resources and the preservation of our national strength.

Yet we are doing far less than we know how to do to make use of our resources without destroying them. Both the public and private use of these resources must have the primary objective of maintaining and increasing these basic supports for an expanding future.

We must continue to take specific steps toward this goal. We must vigorously defend our natural wealth against those who would misuse it for selfish gain.

We need accurate and comprehensive knowledge of our mineral resources and must intensify our efforts to develop new supplies and to acquire stock piles of scarce materials.

We need to protect and restore our land—public and private— through combating erosion and rebuilding the fertility of the soil.

We must expand our reclamation program to bring millions of acres of arid land into production and to improve water supplies for additional millions of acres. This will provide new opportunities for veterans and others, particularly in the West, and aid in providing a rising living standard for a growing population.

We must protect and restore our forests by sustained-yield forestry and by planting new trees in areas now slashed and barren.

We must continue to erect multiple-purpose dams on our great rivers—not only to reclaim land, but also to prevent floods, to extend our inland waterways, and to provide hydroelectric power. This public power must not be monopolized for private gain. Only through well established policies of transmitting power directly to its market and thus encouraging widespread use of low rates can the federal government assure the people of their full share of its benefits. Additional power—public and private—is needed to raise the ceilings now imposed by power shortages on industrial and agricultural development.

We should achieve the wise use of resources through the integrated development of our great river basins. We can learn much from our Tennessee Valley experience. We should no longer delay in applying the lessons of that vast undertaking to our other great river basins.

§ *The President's State of the Union message of January 5, 1949, returned to the subject.*

Our growing population and the expansion of our economy depend upon the wise management of our land, water, forest, and mineral wealth. In our present dynamic economy, the task of conservation is not to lock up our resources but to develop and improve them. Failure, today, to make the investments which are necessary to support our progress in the future would be false economy.

We must push forward with the development of our rivers for power, irrigation, navigation, and flood control. We should apply the lessons of our Tennessee Valley experience to our other great river basins.

I again recommend that action be taken by the Congress to approve the St. Lawrence Seaway and power project. This is about the fifth time I have recommended it.

We must adopt a program for the planned use of the petroleum reserves under the sea, which are—and must remain—vested in the federal government. We must extend our programs of soil conservation. We must place our forests on a sustained-yield basis and encourage the development of new sources of vital minerals.

In all this we must make sure that the benefits of these public undertakings are directly available to the people. Public power should be carried to consuming areas by public transmission lines where necessary to provide electricity at the lowest possible rates. Irrigation waters should serve family farms and not land speculators.

§ *The Truman administration, partly through the heritage of previous administrations and partly by its own initiative, was a good deal involved in the construction of new river valley projects and the expansion of old ones. The first Hoover Commission had found that by June 30, 1947, federal electric power commitments had reached gigantic proportions. Forty-seven hydroelectric and ten steam power plants had been built or purchased, thirty-seven additional plants were under construction, and seventy-nine more had been authorized by Congress. The Hoover Commission estimated that by 1960 these various undertakings would result in 172 public power plants with a capacity of about 20,233,637 kilowatts.*

Two general plans have been followed in the administration of river valley projects. One is the valley authority plan, represented by T.V.A., with a single independent federal corporation operating within a region. The valley authority, headed by a board of directors, is responsible for planning, constructing, and operating various public works to conserve and use the natural resources of the region. Other government agencies continue to operate in the region, but their activities are affected by the plans and policies of the valley authority.

A second approach, illustrated by the Missouri Valley Authority, is based on co-ordinated action by several federal agencies, including the Army Corps of Engineers, the Bureau of Reclamation, and the Soil Conservation Service.

President Truman points to his own preferences in a speech at the dedication of the Tennessee Valley Authority's Kentucky Dam on October 10, 1945.

Nine years ago the first dam of the Tennessee Valley Authority —the Norris Dam on the Clinch River—was dedicated by my illustrious predecessor, Franklin D. Roosevelt. At the very start of his presidency he had the great vision and foresight to recommend and encourage the comprehensive development of this entire great valley.

It is now a matter of great pride to me to dedicate the sixteenth great structure built by the T.V.A.—the Kentucky Dam. The system of dams across the Tennessee now puts under the control of man a whole vast river and harnesses it to do his work. This has not yet happened on any other river. The completion of this dam marks a new high point in modern pioneering in America.

Nine years ago T.V.A. was a highly controversial subject. Today, it is no longer an experiment, but a demonstration. By all except a small minority it is now regarded as a great American accomplishment, of which all of us are proud.

Here in this great valley, American enterprise and courage and skill have come through again with a genuine achievement. The T.V.A. does not belong to the people of the Tennessee Valley alone. It belongs to all the United States. And, indeed, it has inspired regional resource development all over the world. Distinguished observers from more than fifty countries have come to this historic American valley. They came here to study what has been done. They went away to try to adapt to their own regions the lessons that have been learned here from actual experience.

As a Senator I was always a strong supporter of the T.V.A. And I can say to you that I have never had occasion to regret my support of the T.V.A. and of the idea it represents. Its record has fully justified the hopes and the confidence of its old friends.

But it is more than dams and locks and chemical plants and power lines. It is an important experiment in democracy. In it administrative methods have been devised which bring the people and their federal government closer together—not in Washington, but right where the people live. Here in this valley there has been firmly established the basic principle of development of resources on an autonomous regional basis.

Why has T.V.A. succeeded so well? Why does it have the esteem of the people of the valley and attract the attention of other regions of America and of the entire world? To me the answer is clear— T.V.A. is just plain common sense. It is common sense hitched up to modern science and good management. And that's about all there is to it.

Instead of going at the river piecemeal, with a dam here and a dam there, the river was treated as a whole. The dams were all designed so that they would fit together as a unit and in that way get the most service out of the river for mankind.

Consider Kentucky Dam itself. This dam will hold back 4,000,000 acre-feet of flood water from the lower Ohio and Mississippi Rivers.

The people behind the levees on those rivers know how much that will mean to them in protection from disaster. When the danger of flood is past, those flood waters are not to be wasted. They will be put through the water wheels here at the dam to produce great quantities of electricity. That electricity will rush to serve the people of the valley, their homes and farms and industries.

Kentucky Dam also provides a deepwater navigable channel 183 miles long. The other T.V.A. dams carry that reliable deepwater channel all the way to Knoxville in east Tennessee, 650 miles away. As a result, the South and the Middle West of this nation are now connected by water transportation. The benefits of this dam go not only to the Tennessee Valley; they go to St. Paul and Minneapolis, to New Orleans and Memphis, to St. Louis and Kansas City, to Omaha and Sioux City—to all the communities in the great Mississippi Valley that are served by our inland waterways.

In addition to power and flood control and navigation, there is recreation. T.V.A. has joined with the various states and local communities in the development of great lakes here in the South. Here we have boating, fishing, and hunting, where thousands upon thousands of people in the Tennesseee Valley and the Middle West may enjoy themselves. As President Roosevelt said when he first recommended the creation of the Tennessee Valley Authority in April of 1933: "The usefulness of the entire Tennessee River . . . transcends mere power development; it enters the wide fields of flood control, soil erosion, afforestation, elimination from agricultural use of marginal lands, and distribution and diversification of industry."

His prophecy has been fulfilled, for in the T.V.A. the Congress has provided for a tying together of all the things that go to make up a well rounded economic development.

It is easy to see that most of these common-sense principles can be applied to other valleys, and I have already recommended to the Congress that a start be made in that direction. Careful planning and common-sense development can convert the idle and wasting resources of other valleys into jobs and better living.

No two valleys are exactly alike, of course. For that reason the details of just how this region or that region should be developed are matters that require study and judgment in each particular case. The procedure in each valley will have to be a little different. The details of administration and control may have to be different. But the underlying common-sense principles of this development here in the Tennessee Valley can provide guidance and counsel to the people in other regions who likewise aspire to put their resources to the greatest use.

Let me emphasize that in the last analysis such development is a matter for the people themselves to decide. Here in this valley, state and local agencies, public and private, have joined with T.V.A. in a two-way partnership. This was a natural result of the policy of regional decentralization. That same policy ought to be followed in the other river valleys as regional agencies are created by the Congress and set to work.

We must continue all over the United States to wage war against flood and drought. Our vast store of natural resources can be made to serve us in peace with the same efficiency as they did in war. We should exercise our common sense, go ahead, and continue to get the job done.

Much has already been done in the last twelve years on river development in other parts of the country—on the Columbia and Colorado, on the Missouri, on the rivers of the central valley of California. They are all designed to make the rivers and their generous bounty serve instead of injuring mankind.

Waters are now being harnessed and changed into electricity— electricity which has helped supply the weapons of victory in war, electricity which can be used to improve the standards of living and comfort and efficiency in the farms and homes of thousands of American families. Waters are now making crops grow on land where recently there was only desert dust.

The valleys of America await their full development. The time has come, now that materials and manpower are more plentiful, to press forward. The days of the pioneer are not dead. The development of our natural resources calls for men of courage, of vision, of endurance, just as in the pioneering days of old.

The nation, I am sure, is determined to march forward. We will not listen to the whispers of the timid, that dreams like those of the Tennessee Valley are impossible to accomplish. In the great valleys of America there is a challenge to all that is best in our tradition. Ahead of us lies a great adventure in building even stronger the foundations of our beloved country. America will not hesitate to meet that challenge.

I hope that the development of this great valley here will result in the development of our other river valleys along the same line. You know, our resources have barely been touched. . . . This great development has proven conclusively that a free people can do anything that is necessary for the welfare of the human race as a whole.

We created the greatest production machine in the history of the world. We made that machine operate to the disaster of the dictators. Now then, we want to keep that machine operating.

We have just discovered the source of the sun's power—atomic energy; that is, we have found out how to turn it loose. We had to turn it loose in the beginning for destruction. We are not going to use it for destruction any more, I hope. But that tremendous source of energy can create for us the greatest age in the history of the world, if we are sensible enough to put it to that use and to no other. I think we are going to do just that.

§ But the President's conservation policies encountered a formidable opposition. A conspicuously successful weapon of the opposition was to block the appointment or continued tenure of administrative officers the most intimately identified with objectives of the Fair Deal; e.g. the rejection by the Senate Interstate Commerce Committee of the nomination of Leland Olds for a third term on the Federal Power Commission. In a letter to Vice-President Barkley, read in the Senate, Mr. Truman charged that powerful corporations were blocking Olds's appointment. "We cannot allow great corporations to dominate the commissions which have been created to regulate them," the President said.

Another method used to strike at the Truman conservation program was embedded among the numerous provisions of the Interior Department Appropriation Bill of 1948. The bill had a rider providing that the commissioner of the Reclamation Bureau of the Interior Department and all regional directors of the Bureau should have had at least ten years of engineering experience. Neither the incumbent commissioner, Michael W. Straus, nor the regional director in California was an engineer. "This rider is designed to effect the removal of two men," Truman commented on the bill, "who have supported the public power policy of the government and the 160-acre law which assures that Western lands reclaimed at public expense shall be used for the development of family-size farms."

Mr. Truman condemned the rider as being in effect a bill of attainder and a violation of the Constitution's separation of legislative and executive functions. Particularly ominous, in the President's judgment, was the implication for other executive officials: "the risk of being legislated out of office if they incur the wrath of the special interests as a result of vigorous enforcement of the law."

He signed the appropriation bill. He had to. Congress had already adjourned, and a veto would have closed down the Department of the Interior.

Flood control was a subject on which President Truman, throughout his administration, was pleading for more effective measures, as he did in his special message to Congress on July 16, 1947.

The major opportunity of our generation to increase the wealth of the nation lies in the development of our great river systems. I urged in the State of the Union Message on January 6, 1947, that the program for improvement of our rivers be pushed with full vigor.

Since that time the urgency of one phase of our water resources control program has been demonstrated forcefully and tragically. Vast areas of the most productive sections of the Missouri and upper Mississippi River Valleys have been subjected to a series of the most destructive floods in our history. Too frequently within our memory, as well as in earlier years, the Mississippi River basin has been similarly stricken. This continued threat and the recurring and accumulative damage to the national economy and well-being call strongly for the prompt use of more effective countermeasures. Prudence requires that adequate measures be taken for protection against these devastating floods.

Measures for flood control should be integrated with plans for the use and conservation of water resources for other purposes. This will insure maximum control of floods at the least cost and will permit the full utilization of water resources in the development of this vast region.

The drainage basin of the Mississippi River and its tributaries comprises nearly half of the nation in area and population. It is a rich central core from which stem goods and services vital to the entire country. A large proportion of the people in this great central basin, their homes and businesses, their fertile farmlands, and their transportation and communication systems are concentrated in the flood plains and lowlands immediately adjacent to the rivers. Nature also requires the use of these flood plains for drainage. Consequently, we must pay the price for occupancy of these lands, either in the form of continued flood damage or in preventive measures.

The economy of controlling floods as compared with the cost of continuing under the handicap of their disruptive force has been amply demonstrated.

In the short ten-year period from 1937 through 1946 a total of more than a billion dollars in flood damage has been suffered in the Mississippi basin. The real cost to the nation, of course, has been much greater. Dollars are not adequate to measure the toll in the hundreds of lives lost and the suffering of millions of persons affected. The cost of rehabilitation and repair of flood damage, though staggering, is but the initial burden. Extended effects, both in distance and time, are reflected throughout the nation as a result of the disruption of lives and activities in the flood zone. These more remote inroads on our health and prosperity are not so obvious, but they may total many times the more apparent losses in the flood area.

In the light of the accumulative burden of our flood problem in the decade just past, the impact of this year's floods in the Missouri and upper Mississippi Valleys is even more appalling. Again, unprecedented flood stages have been experienced at many points on these rivers, and the total damages will approach and may exceed the half-billion-dollar loss suffered in 1937. Again thousands of our people have been forced to leave their homes and their normal pursuits. All or a large part of the year's income has been ruthlessly taken from thousands of farmers. The loss of their crops is not only a personal calamity to these farmers, but is a staggering blow to the nation and to other countries where many additional thousands will be deprived of essential foods.

The recurrent floods in the Mississippi basin constitute a national problem which demands immediate attention. The means for solution are available to us and will permit us, at the same time, to prevent destruction and waste of productive soils, to improve the utility of the rivers for transportation, to conserve water that would otherwise be wasted with destructive force, and to use this water constructively for domestic purposes, for irrigation, for development of needed electric power, for the abatement of pollution, and for the enjoyment of recreational activities.

After the destructive floods of 1927 in the lower valley of the Mississippi, the Congress charged the Corps of Engineers of the War Department with the preparation of plans for control of floods in that valley and with the making of surveys of tributary rivers for their development for flood control and allied purposes. Since that time, surveys, studies, and preparation of plans have gone forward hand in hand with urgently needed construction. As a result we now have available comprehensive and detailed plans for most of the work needed to eliminate destructive floods and provide for the beneficial use of water in the Mississippi River basin.

The Congress has also provided legislative authority to proceed with these plans.

The flood control act of May 15, 1928, authorized a plan for the protection of the lower Mississippi Valley. Subsequent legislation has permitted the extension and development of that plan to a high degree of completion. The flood control act of 1938 approved comprehensive flood control plans for each of the five major tributary basins of the Mississippi River and authorized the expenditure of funds for the initiation and partial accomplishment of those plans. Subsequent general flood control acts have authorized expenditure of additional sums to continue this work. These acts provided that federal investigations and improvements for flood control and allied purposes should be prosecuted by the War Department, under the direction of the Secretary of War and the supervision of the chief of engineers.

The flood control act of 1936 provided for federal investigation of watersheds and for measures of runoff and water flow retardation and soil erosion prevention on watersheds, to be prosecuted by the Department of Agriculture. The reclamation laws authorize irrigation programs and the prosecution of such programs by the Bureau of Reclamation of the Department of the Interior, in co-ordination with plans for flood control. The federal water power acts and appropriate parts of the flood control acts provide for participation of the Federal Power Commission when hydroelectric power is involved in these programs.

A comprehensive program for flood control in the entire Mississippi River basin is essential. The lower Mississippi River, as it flows through its alluvial valley, must carry the flood discharge from every tributary river basin from the Appalachians to the Rocky Mountains. Fortunately we have never had a simultaneous occurrence of major floods on all the great tributaries: the Missouri, Ohio, upper Mississippi, Arkansas, and Red Rivers. Such a coincidence of flood crests is highly improbable, but if it did occur under present conditions the floods would overflow the entire lower Mississippi Valley from Cairo, Illinois, to the Gulf of Mexico and would cause untold damage to one of the richest areas in the world. It would not be feasible to build levees high enough and floodways wide enough to pass such a flood safely to the Gulf. Therefore, it is necessary to prevent the concurrence of tributary floods by a co-ordinated system of storage reservoirs in the major tributary basins. In these same tributary basins, levees, flood walls, and diversion channels are necessary to protect cities, towns, and farms. Farther up on the headwater tributaries of each major basin, and throughout their watersheds, soil conservation measures are needed to retard the flow and runoff and reduce the loss of topsoil which is impoverishing our farm lands and clogging our reservoirs and river channels.

Corollary to the control of floods is the harnessing of flood waters for productive uses which will return to the government a large share of the initial investment. Fortunately, the means available to us for control of floods in many cases furnish the oppportunity for use of water for irrigation, navigation, and development of hydroelectric power. Multiple-use reservoirs produce these and other benefits, including the improvement of municipal and industrial water supplies, new recreational areas and opportunities, the preservation of fish and wildlife, and the abatement of pollution.

The problem confronting us is of prime importance in our national life. During the war it was unavoidably necessary to defer in large part works of this character. In the immediate postwar period conflicting needs for other government programs caused further deferment. These conflicting needs are now diminishing, and the experience of the last few months has presented convincing evidence that we must press forward vigorously toward a solution of this problem.

In the execution of a comprehensive program for the development of the Mississippi River basin, protection from floods is of such urgency that it should be given first attention. We already have plans for the projects which will largely provide this protection. The construction agencies of the Departments of War, Interior, and Agriculture are ready to proceed with these projects when funds are provided.

I therefore urge that this Congress undertake a program which will provide for the substantial completion within ten years of the flood control projects necessary for the protection of the Mississippi River basin. Most of these necessary projects have already been authorized by the Congress. This ten-year program should also contain a smaller group of projects which have not yet been authorized by the Congress but are now being planned and investigated. As rapidly as the plans are completed these projects will be submitted for approval by the Congress in accordance with present law and procedure.

An orderly program of appropriations for prosecution of this work on a sustained and comprehensive basis is essential. Any plan of this magnitude can be accomplished in an efficient manner only if the planning and constructing agencies have advance knowledge of the funds that they may expect over a period of years. If construction schedules and contracts are extended over long periods because of limited and varying appropriations, excessive costs to the federal government are the result. An orderly program of appropriations will get the job done efficiently and economically.

I recommend that this ten-year program be initiated during this fiscal year.

This plan does not change the desirability of the ultimate establishment of valley authorities, but the urgency of the flood problem is such that we must take necessary steps to expedite this program without awaiting determination of the administrative pattern for the various regional valley development programs.

In addition to the program aimed primarily at flood control, there are many valuable projects for navigation, irrigation, hydroelectric power development, and other utilization of water resources which are essential to a complete and well rounded valley development program. These projects will be included in their proper place in the regular annual budget program and consequently are not specifically within the scope of this message.

We must never forget that the conservation of our natural resources and their wise use are essential to our very existence as a nation. The choice is ours. We can sit idly by—or, almost as bad, resort to the false economy of feeble and inadequate measures—while these precious assets waste away. On the other hand, we can, if we act in time, put into effect a realistic and practical plan which will preserve these basic essentials of our national economy and make this a better and a richer land.

§ Mr. Truman's flood control program developed an additional facet late in 1951 when he asked Congress to adopt a $1,500,000,000 plan for flood damage insurance. One of the grimmest facts of flood disasters is that in a few hours' time the lifetime savings of home owners, businessmen, and farmers can be wiped out. Since private insurance companies are unwilling to underwrite these risks, the President proposed that the government do so. But even in the wake of the great Missouri flood of 1951 Congress was indisposed to act. He repeated his request in 1952, but it got nowhere.

◇

§ All the Presidents since Woodrow Wilson had proposed that the St. Lawrence River be developed by construction of canals and hydroelectric facilities. The project had always been successfully blocked by interests in Atlantic seaboard cities that feared a decline of business in their ports. Mr. Truman's views were incorporated in a speech before a joint session of the Canadian Parliament at Ottawa on June 11, 1947.

Gratifying as the volume of our trade now is, it is capable of even further expansion to our mutual benefit [i.e., the benefit of Canada and the United States]. Some of our greatest assets are still to be developed to the maximum. I am thinking of one particularly that holds tremendous possibilities, the magnificent St. Lawrence-Great Lakes system, which we share and which we must develop together.

The St. Lawrence project stirs the imagination of men long accustomed to majestic distances and epic undertakings. The proposal for taking electric power from the river and bringing ocean shipping 2,400 miles inland, to tap the fertile heart of our continent, is economically sound and strategically important.

When this program is carried out, the waterway that is a part of our boundary will more than ever unite our two countries. It will stimulate our economies to new growth and will spread the flow of trade.

§ *Mr. Truman pressed the St. Lawrence project on numerous occasions in messages on the State of the Union, in election campaigns, and in letters to the presiding officers of the two houses of Congress, but always without result.*

◇

§ *The President expressed his conviction of the importance of our national parks in general in his speech at the dedication of one of them, the Everglades National Park, on December 6, 1947.*

These are the people's parks, owned by young and old, by those in the cities and those on the farms. Most of them are ours today because there were Americans many years ago who exercised vision, patience, and unselfish devotion in the battle for conservation. . . .

Public lands and parks, our forests and our mineral reserves, are subject to many destructive influences. We have to remain constantly vigilant to prevent raids by those who would selfishly exploit our common heritage for their own private gain. Such raids on our natural resources are not examples of enterprise and initiative. They are attempts to take from all the people just for the benefit of a few.

As always in the past when the people's property has been threatened, men and women whose primary concern has been their country's welfare have risen to oppose these selfish attacks. . . .

For conservation of the human spirit, we need places such as Everglades National Park, where we may be more keenly aware of our Creator's infinitely varied, infinitely beautiful, and infinitely bountiful handiwork. Here we may draw strength and peace of mind from our surroundings.

§ *In 1947 the Supreme Court, in United States v. California, held that the federal government, not the states, has "paramount rights" in all natural resources lying under the marginal sea, i.e. from the coast line out to a three-mile limit. The littoral states, led by California, Texas, and Louisiana, which for years had been leasing under-*

water areas to private concerns for oil-producing operations, succeeded in getting through Congress in 1952 legislation that gave the states control. Mr. Truman's opinion of this development is stated in a speech delivered in Washington on May 17, 1952.

The minerals that lie under the sea off the coasts of this country belong to the federal government—that is, to all the people of this country. That ownership has been affirmed and reaffirmed in the Supreme Court of the United States. Those rights may be worth as much as somewhere between $40,000,000,000 and $100,000,000,000.

If we back down on our determination to hold these rights for all the people, we will act to rob them of this great national asset. That is just what the oil lobby wants. They want us to turn the vast treasure over to a handful of states, where the powerful private oil interests hope to exploit it to suit themselves.

Talk about corruption. Talk about stealing from the people. That would be robbery in broad daylight—and on a colossal scale. It would make Teapot Dome look like small change.

I got a letter from a fellow down in Texas today who is a friend of mine, and he was weeping over what the school children of Texas were going to lose if Texas didn't get the oil land nine miles out from the shore. And I composed a letter to him and then didn't send it. I said, What about the school children in Missouri and Colorado and North Dakota and Minnesota and Tennessee and Kentucky and Illinois? Do they have any interest in this at all? Evidently not. It should all go to Texas. Well, it's not going there if I can help it.

I can see how the members of Congress from Texas and California and Louisiana might like to have all the offshore oil for their states. But I certainly can't understand how the members of Congress from the other forty-five states can vote to give away the interest the people of their states have in this tremendous asset. It's just over my head and beyond me how any interior Senator or Congressman could vote to give that asset away. I'm still puzzled about it. As far as I am concerned, I intend to stand up and fight to protect the people's interest in this matter.

§ *He did stand up and fight, by uncompromising veto (May 29) of the offshore oil bill, which he characterized as "a free gift of immensely valuable resources—to the states which happen to be located nearest to them."*

4. POSTWAR RECOVERY AND RECONVERSION

Mr. Truman's early months in office produced endless speculation about how far and how energetically he would continue the New Deal. To many he had seemed excessively deferential to Congress— an intimation that he would hardly assert bold programs of legislative policy. Some New Dealers were wondering if he were not at heart a conservative and would not pursue a conservative course. President Truman put a quietus on these doubts in his message to Congress of September 6, 1945. This message, in addition to outlining the postwar reconversion program, is the first comprehensive statement of what later became known as the Fair Deal. As that, it is one of the key documents of his presidential career.

The sudden surrender of the Japanese has not caught us unawares. President Roosevelt, as early as the fall of 1943, began to set up machinery which he foresaw would become necessary to meet the reconversion period. The Congress in its wisdom has adopted some of that machinery by statute, and has improved and added to it. As a result, government agencies for some time have been able to plan for the immediate and long-range steps which now have to be taken. . . .

The general line of approach to the problem is to achieve as full peacetime production and employment as possible in the most efficient and speedy manner. The following policies have been laid down and will be followed:

(1) Demobilize as soon as possible the armed forces no longer needed.

(2) Cancel and settle war contracts as quickly as possible.

(3) Clear the war plants so as to permit contractors to proceed with peacetime production.

(4) Hold the line on prices and rents until fair competition can operate to prevent inflation and undue hardship on consumers.

(5) Hold wages in line where their increase would cause inflationary price rises. Where price ceiling would not be endangered, collective bargaining should be restored.

(6) Remove all possible wartime government controls in order to speed and encourage reconversion and expansion.

(7) Keep only those controls which are necessary to help reconversion and expansion by preventing bottlenecks, shortages of material, and inflation.

(8) Prevent rapid decrease of wage incomes or purchasing power.

The major objective, of course, is to re-establish an expanded peacetime industry, trade, and agriculture, and to do it as quickly as possible.

The end of the war came more swiftly than most of us anticipated. Widespread cutbacks in war orders followed promptly. As a result, there has already been a considerable number of workers who are between jobs as war industries convert to peace. Other workers are returning to a forty-hour week and are faced with a corresponding reduction in take-home pay.

This has led to a natural feeling of uneasiness among the rank and file of our people. Let me emphasize that there will be no reason for undue timidity. A vast backlog of orders may soon make possible the greatest peacetime industrial activity that we have ever seen. But this can happen only if the Congress and the administration move vigorously and courageously to deal with the economic problems which peace has created. Then there need be no reason to fear either the immediate future or the years that lie ahead of us.

Determined action now will create the atmosphere of confidence which is so vital to a rapid reconversion with a minimum of unemployment and hardship.

No matter how rapidly reconversion proceeds, however, no amount of effort or planning will be able immediately to provide a job for everyone displaced from war work. Obviously, displaced war workers cannot find jobs until industry has been regeared and made ready to produce peacetime goods. During this lag the government should provide help. The cost of this transition from war to peace is as much a part of the cost of war as the transition from peace to war—and we should so consider it.

This course is recommended not only as a matter of justice and humanity, but also as a matter of sound business. Nothing would be more harmful to our economy than to have every displaced war worker stop buying consumer goods. And nothing would be more conducive to a large-scale cessation of buying than the feeling on the part of displaced war workers that all their income had stopped and that their remaining financial resources had to be hoarded.

For one group of those who may become unemployed in the near future—the demobilized veterans—the Congress has already made special provision.

By contrast, there are more than 15,000,000 workers not protected under our present unemployment insurance laws. There are many millions more for whom protection is inadequate. Many of these have been unable to accumulate adequate savings. . . .

Specifically, coverage should be extended to include federal employees, maritime workers, and other workers not now insured. This additional compensation during the present emergency will have to be financed entirely by the federal government, but the benefits should appropriately be administered by the states.

I also recommend . . . that the Congress provide, through supplementary federal emergency benefit payments, additional unemployment benefits so as to bring them up to adequate standards in all the states. All payments, however, should be made through the existing unemployment compensation machinery of the several states.

During this emergency every eligible worker should be entitled to twenty-six weeks of unemployment benefits in any one year. The maximum weekly payment for those workers whose previous earnings were high enough should be not less than $25 per week.

If the Congress decides to take this very necessary step, it will also wish to reconsider and increase the unemployment allowance provided for veterans.

There has been so much misrepresentation about this temporary proposal that I think I should categorically state what the bill does not do.

It does not give everyone $25 a week. Under it an applicant must be ready, willing, and able to work and must have earned wages high enough so that the percentage rate will yield this maximum figure.

It does not federalize the unemployment compensation system. It leaves it with the states.

It is not intended to take the place of the permanent amendments to the unemployment compensation system which are now being studied by the Congress. It is an emergency measure designed to expand the present system without changing its principles. It is designed only to meet the immediate pressing human problems of reconversion.

In addition to those workers who will temporarily lose their jobs, there will be millions of others whose incomes will fall sharply with the end of war production. These will be added to the several million wage earners who even now have hourly earnings much below what is necessary for a decent standard of living.

The inadequacy of these wages, in many cases, has been temporarily concealed by wartime increases in take-home pay resulting from overtime work. As these props to income are removed, however, low-wage earners will be hard pressed to feed, clothe, and house their families. This flies in the face of a sound public policy. Failure to correct this situation will slow down, if it will not actually stop, our drive toward an expanding market for business and agriculture.

The foundations of a healthy national economy cannot be secure so long as any large section of our working people receive substandard wages. The existence of substandard wage levels sharply curtails the national purchasing power and narrows the market for the products of our farms and factories.

In the Fair Labor Standards Act of 1938 the Congress adopted a program intended to provide a minimum wage standard for a large number of American workers. In that statute, the Congress declared it to be our national policy to eliminate from interstate industry wage levels detrimental to the maintenance of minimum standards of living. The establishment then of a minimum wage of 25 cents per hour represented a first step toward the realization of that policy. The goal of 40 cents per hour, which under the act was to be made effective by 1945, was actually made fully effective more than a year ago by the voluntary action of the industry committees.

I believed that the goal of a 40-cent minimum was inadequate when established. It has now become obsolete.

Increases in the cost of living since 1938 and changes in our national wage structure require an immediate and substantial upward revision of this minimum. Only in that way can the objectives of the Fair Labor Standards Act be realized, the national purchasing power protected, and an economy of full production and abundance preserved and maintained for the American people.

The high prosperity which we seek in the postwar years will not be meaningful for all our people if any large proportion of our industrial wage earners receive wages as low as the minimum now sanctioned by the Fair Labor Standards Act.

I therefore recommend that the Congress amend the Fair Labor Standards Act by substantially increasing the minimum wage specified therein to a level which will eliminate substandards of living and assure the maintenance of the health, efficiency, and general well-being of workers.

The scope of the Fair Labor Standards Act also should be clarified and extended. In view of changes which have occurred since 1938, I believe it is no longer necessary to exclude from the minimum wage program the large number of workers engaged in agricultural processing who are now excluded. There now exists a twilight zone in which some workers are covered, and others doing similar work are not. Extension of coverage would benefit both workers and employers by removing competitive inequities.

Our achievements in this field during the last seven years of establishing minimum wages have been gratifying; but we must continue to move forward, step by step.

I urge that the Congress act promptly. The wage structure on which businessmen may make future plans should be settled quickly.

Wartime Controls

One of the outstanding achievements of the war has been the success of the government in holding the line against inflation. This is the first time in any major war that the United States has been able substantially to stabilize its economy.

That fact now permits us to enter into the difficult period of readjustment without the threat of a disastrous price collapse.

For this result much credit is due to the Congress, which in the face of great insistence from many interested pressure groups refused steadfastly to take the easy way.

Great credit is due to the Office of Economic Stabilization, the War Labor Board, the Office of Price Administration, the War Food Administration, the War Production Board, and the other stabilization agencies. Despite great pressure and often unjust abuse, they continued to hold the line for the benefit of the great mass of Americans.

And, above all, great credit is due to the people of the United

States, the great body of average citizens, who, for four difficult years and with only a few exceptions, subordinated their personal interest to the long-range interest of the nation as a whole.

We must keep in mind the experience of the period immediately after the First World War. After a lull of a few months following the Armistice of 1918, prices turned upward, scrambling for inventories started, and prices soon got completely out of hand. We found ourselves in one of the worst inflations in our history, culminating in the crash of 1920 and the disastrous inflation of 1920 and 1921. . . .

Prices must be held firmly on reconversion items as well as on cost-of-living items during the coming months.

I request the Congress, therefore, to extend the provisions of the second War Powers Act, either in its present form or with appropriate limitations, preserving the powers necessary to achieve the objectives I have outlined.

The Congress has my definite assurance that none of these war powers will be exercised by the executive branch of the government unless they are deemed essential to the attainment of the objective of an orderly stabilized reconversion. The Congress should, of course, if it extends the statute, reserve the right to terminate it by legislation at any time it deems necessary.

I hope that the Congress will not delay the extension of this authority. Delay would retard reconversion by creating uncertainty on the part of business as to whether necessary controls will be retained or not. Businessmen, in planning for next year's activities, will be assisted greatly by knowing in advance whether or not the government is going to keep a firm hand at the brakes to prevent inflation.

The termination of the wartime food subsidies, for which a total of $1,798,000,000 has been authorized for the current year, is one of the important problems in reconversion. Agencies dealing directly with this problem are now meeting jointly to determine in what order and at what time these food subsidies may be eliminated without an undue disturbance to farm income or living costs.

Subsidies for purposes other than food are also being reviewed by the agencies concerned, who are collecting the necessary data for an orderly liquidation at the earliest date compatible with the stabilization program.

Those subsidies which were designed originally to stimulate

increased production should not be removed at a time or in a manner to incite inflation and upset our economy.

I have directed that early reports be made on this important problem.

War Powers and Executive Agencies Reorganization

I should like to bring to the attention of the Congress the legal difficulties that will arise unless care is taken in the drafting of legislation terminating wartime controls and wartime agencies.

Certain of the wartime statutes which have been made effective "in time of war," "during the present war," or "for the duration of the war" continue to be effective until a formal state of peace has been restored, or until some earlier termination date is made applicable by appropriate governmental action.

Another group of statutes which by their provisions terminate "upon the cessation of hostilities" or "upon termination of the war," will in fact and in law terminate only by a formal proclamation to that effect by the President or by appropriate Congressional action.

From time to time action will be taken with respect to these agencies, with the general objective of streamlining the government into a peacetime organization as quickly as possible.

The time has not yet arrived, however, for the proclamation of the cessation of hostilities, much less the termination of the war. Needless to say, such proclamations will be made as soon as circumstances permit.

It has been necessary during the course of the war to make numerous important redistributions of functions among executive agencies.

This has been accomplished by the President under the authority of Title I of the first War Powers Act. This act expires six months after the termination of the war or at such earlier time as may be designated by appropriate governmental action.

If the Congress or the President were formally to declare the present war terminated, it would automatically cause all the steps taken under the first War Powers Act with respect to the war agencies to expire and would have the government revert automatically to its pre-existing status six months after the declaration.

If this were to occur, it would cause great confusion and chaos in the government. It is the policy of this administration not to exercise wartime powers beyond the point at which it is necessary to exercise them.

Those functions of the wartime agencies which must be retained during part or all of the period of reconversion should be transferred as promptly as practicable to the permanent departments and agencies of the government. The remaining functions, appropriate only to the crisis through which we have passed, should be terminated in an orderly, systematic fashion as soon as possible.

A program of winding up wartime agencies and distributing their functions on a peacetime basis is now being pursued under the powers vested in the President by Title I of the first War Powers Act.

Therefore, I urge that the Congress do not yet adopt a resolution proclaiming the termination of the war or the termination of the emergency or the cessation of hostilities. Such a resolution would automatically cause the death of many war powers and wartime agencies before we are ready.

At the same time I recognize that the Congress may wish to repeal certain specific wartime statutes. If this is to be done, the repeal should be on a selective basis, through the adoption of specific statutes dealing with each wartime power which the Congress decides should be terminated.

In my message dated May 24, 1945, it was recommended that permanent legislation be enacted which would authorize the President to submit to the Congress, from time to time, plans providing for the reorganization of executive agencies, each such plan to become effective unless the Congress should reject it by concurrent resolution.

This type of joint action by the Congress and the President has produced, and will produce, far better results than can be achieved by the usual legislative process in the field of executive reorganization.

If proper progress is to be made, it is necessary to permit the President to lay out the machinery for carrying out his responsibility for the conduct of the executive branch, subject to rejection by the two houses of Congress. Executive initiative, subject to Congressional veto, is an effective approach to governmental reorganization.

The responsibility of conducting the executive branch rests upon the President. It is fair and efficient to permit him to lay out the machinery for carrying out that responsibility.

The means for doing this should be generally along the lines of the Reorganization Act of 1939, which gives the initiative to the President, but reserves power to the Congress by a majority vote to nullify any action of the President which does not meet with its approval.

Considerable progress was made in efficiency of government under this Reorganization Act of 1939. I recommend that such powers be made of permanent duration and that the legislation be sufficiently flexible to permit any kind of adjustment for which necessity may arise.

It is clear to all of us that the government has a difficult and important task in the years which lie ahead. Our government belongs to the people, and the people have a right to expect from their government the greatest possible efficiency in carrying out its tasks.

Our government has never been as efficient as we should like to see it. To some degree this may be charged to the size of some of the tasks assigned to it. To some extent it is also due to the lack of trained government personnel and the low salaries paid to government officials.

There is no question that the war has taught us a great deal about government administration. There is still, however, much room for improvement.

I have undertaken directly through the members of the Cabinet and also through the directors of the Office of War Mobilization and Reconversion and the Bureau of the Budget to emphasize the need for more efficient operation in all the executive branches of the government. I have requested them to examine administrative procedures and to speed up and simplify their operations to the maximum practical degree.

I have also requested the Bureau of the Budget to examine closely with each department and agency head the actual needs of his office following the surrender of Japan. They have been asked to reduce budgets promptly and fully wherever cuts are indicated. The Bureau of the Budget is now completing studies which will result in reductions of millions of dollars in the expense of operating our government.

We must continue relentlessly this program for increased government efficiency. The Congress can depend upon the Executive to push this program with the utmost vigor.

Full Employment

I am confident that, with the co-operation of American industry, labor, and agriculture, we can bridge the gap between war and peace.

When we have reconverted our economy to a peacetime basis, however, we shall not be satisfied with merely our prewar economy. The American people have set high goals for their own future. They have set these goals high because they have seen how great can be the productive capacity of our country.

The levels of production and income reached during the war years have given our citizens an appreciation of what a full production peacetime economy can be.

They are not interested in boom prosperity—for that only too often leads to panic and depression. But they are interested in providing opportunity for work and for ultimate security. Government must do its part and assist industry and labor to get over the line from war to peace.

That is why I have asked for unemployment compensation legislation.

That is why I now ask for full-employment legislation.

The objectives for our domestic economy which we seek in our long-range plans were summarized by the late President Franklin D. Roosevelt over a year and a half ago in the form of an economic Bill of Rights. Let us make the attainment of those rights the essence of postwar American economic life.

I repeat the statement of President Roosevelt:

"In our day these economic truths have become accepted as self-evident. We have accepted, so to speak, a second Bill of Rights under which a new basis of security and prosperity can be established for all—regardless of station, race, or creed.

"Among these are:

"The right to a useful and remunerative job in the industries or shops or farms or mines of the nation.

"The right to earn enough to provide adequate food and clothing and recreation.

"The right of every farmer to raise and sell his products at a return which will give him and his family a decent living.

"The right of every businessman, large and small, to trade in an atmosphere of freedom from unfair competition and domination by monopolies at home or abroad.

"The right of every family to a decent home.

"The right to adequate medical care and the opportunity to achieve and enjoy good health.

"The right to adequate protection from the economic fears of old age, sickness, accident, and unemployment.

"The right to a good education.

"All of these rights spell security. And after this war is won we must be prepared to move forward, in the implementation of these rights, to new goals of human happiness and well-being.

"America's own rightful place in the world depends in large part upon how fully these and similar rights have been carried into practice for our citizens. For unless there is security here at home there cannot be lasting peace in the world."

I shall from time to time communicate with the Congress on some of the subjects included in this enumeration of economic rights.

Most of them, in the last analysis, depend upon full production and full employment at decent wages.

A national reassertion of the right to work for every American citizen able and willing to work—a declaration of the ultimate duty of government to use its own resources if all other methods should fail to prevent prolonged unemployment—these will help to avert fear and establish full employment. The prompt and firm acceptance of this bedrock public responsibility will reduce the need for its exercise.

I ask that full employment legislation to provide these vital assurances be speedily enacted. Such legislation should also provide machinery for a continuous full-employment policy—to be developed and pursued in co-operation among industry, agriculture, and labor, between the Congress and the Chief Executive, between the people and their government.

Full employment means full opportunity for all under the American economic system—nothing more and nothing less. In human terms, full employment means opportunity to get a good peacetime job for every worker who is ready, able, and willing to take one. It does not mean made work, or making people work.

In economic terms, full employment means full production and the opportunity to sell goods—all the goods that industry and agriculture can produce.

In government terms, full employment means opportunity to reduce the ratio of public spending to private investment without sacrificing essential services.

In worldwide terms, full employment in America means greater economic security and more opportunity for lasting peace throughout the world.

These goals and the machinery to carry them out are set forth in legislation now pending before the Congress on which extensive public hearings have been held. The country justifiably expects early action along these lines.

Fair Employment Practice Committee

During the years of war production we made substantial progress in overcoming many of the prejudices which had resulted in discriminations against minority groups.

Many of the injustices based upon considerations of race, religion, and color were removed. Many were prevented. Perfection was not reached, of course, but substantial progress was made.

In the reconversion period and thereafter, we should make every effort to continue this American ideal. It is one of the fundamentals of our political philosophy, and it should be an integral part of our economy.

The fair employment practice committee is continuing during the transition period. I have already requested that legislation be enacted placing the fair employment practice committee on a permanent basis. I repeat that recommendation.

Labor Disputes and Wage Stabilization

Our national welfare requires that during the reconversion period production of civilian goods and services—as full production as possible—go forward without interruption, and that labor and industry co-operate to keep strikes and lockouts at a minimum.

Those who have the responsibility of labor relations must recognize that responsibility. This is not the time for shortsighted management to seize upon the chance to reduce wages and try to injure labor unions. Equally it is not the time for labor leaders to shirk their responsibility and permit widespread industrial strife.

With this objective in view, I shall shortly convene a conference of representatives of organized labor and industry for the purpose of working out by agreement means to minimize labor disputes.

In the interim period, pending the convening of the conference, I have called upon the representatives of organized labor and industry to continue their adherence to the no-strike, no-lockout policy. During this interim period labor disputes which threaten a substantial interference with the transition to a peacetime economy should be submitted to the War Labor Board. They would there be handled by the board under existing procedures. The country will expect parties to any such disputes to comply voluntarily with the determinations of the War Labor Board.

*   *   *

I have conferred upon the War Labor Board adequate authority to correct maladjustments and inequities in wage rates arising in the reconversion period which will tend to interfere with the effective transition to a peacetime economy.

The Board should be terminated as soon after the conclusion of the forthcoming industry-labor conference as the orderly disposition of the work of the Board and the provisions of the War Labor Disputes Act permit, and after facilities have been provided to take care of the wage stabilization functions under the Act of October 2, 1942.

Meanwhile, plans for strengthening the Department of Labor and bringing under it functions properly belonging to it are going forward. With the return to a peacetime economy and the elimination of the present temporary wartime agencies and procedures, we must look to collective bargaining, aided and supplemented by a truly effective system of conciliation and voluntary arbitration, as the best and most democratic method of maintaining sound industrial relations.

United States Employment Service Extension

Placing demobilized veterans and displaced war workers in new peacetime jobs is the major human problem of our country's reconversion to a peacetime economy. It is imperative that this work be done swiftly and efficiently, and that men and women lose a minimum amount of time between jobs. The next few months are crucial. What we do now will affect our American way of life for decades to come.

The United States Employment Service has an important responsibility in the performance of this task.

At present this agency operates as a national and centralized system with a free flow of information among its offices. Under the 1946 Appropriation Act the offices are to be turned back to the forty-eight states within ninety days after the cessation of hostilities.

Shortly after the declaration of war the government realized that the manpower of the nation could be mobilized more efficiently if the United States Employment Service were centralized under federal control. Hundreds of thousands of workers had to be recruited from all parts of the country. Often they were wanted in regions far from their homes. Certain areas had surpluses of labor; others were desperately in need of more workers. This situation could be met only through a centrally operated employment service that covered the entire nation.

Now we are faced with this problem in reverse. Hundreds of thousands of men and women will want to seek jobs in towns and cities other than those in which they worked during the war. They may want to return home, or they may want to strike out in search of new opportunities in new surroundings.

Millions of veterans also will be coming back in search of peacetime jobs. They will want to know where such jobs can be found, not only in their own areas, but also in other parts of the land.

The task of helping this vast army of job seekers to fit themselves into a peacetime economy is fully as difficult as the mobilization of manpower for war. To make any decided change in the machinery to handle this problem now would cause unnecessary hardship to workers and veterans. It would slow down the entire process of reconversion.

I urgently recommend that the Congress do not yet return the employment service to the states. Ultimately it should be so returned. However, it should be continued under federal control at least until the expiration of the War Mobilization Act—June 30, 1947.

Agriculture

The government now must be prepared to carry out the nation's responsibility to aid farmers in making their necessary readjustments from a wartime to a peacetime basis. The Congress already has provided postwar supports against price collapse for many farm products. This was a provision of wisdom and foresight.

After the First World War farm prices dropped more than fifty per cent from the spring of 1920 to the spring of 1921. We do not intend to permit a repetition of the disaster that followed the First World War. The Secretary of Agriculture has assured me that he will use all means now authorized by the Congress to carry out the price support commitments.

But there is need for additional measures to strengthen the machinery for carrying out price support commitments and for laying the basis for broader peacetime markets for agricultural products.

The Congress already has provided for one such postwar measure that needs now to be adapted to our changed situation. Recognizing that the lend-lease program required greatly increased production and that this increase could not be suddenly discontinued when the program stopped, the Congress wisely set aside $500,000,000 of lend-lease funds for price support of farm commodities.

This money is now available for the purpose for which it was intended, but in order that it may be used most effectively whenever the need arises, I recommend early legislation which would make those funds available to the Commodity Credit Corporation on a continuing basis. Such action would reaffirm the specific intent of the Congress as to the use of this money for safeguarding farm prices.

Strengthening the machinery for carrying out price support commitments is one measure necessary to safeguard farm prices. Stimulation of the export of farm commodities is another. More food is needed in the war-ravaged areas of the world. In the process of meeting relief requirements abroad we have the opportunity of developing export markets for the future.

The farmer has always faced certain specific problems which are peculiar to his occupation. His crops are at the mercy of the weather.

The factory owner and the worker at the machine have available to them insurance programs which protect them from losses. Our farmers have the right to the same kind of protection. Strengthening and further development of crop insurance for farmers, organized and backed by the federal government, can give them this protection. A well rounded crop insurance program, together with the assurance of reasonable and stable farm prices, will go a long way toward meeting basic problems which have plagued farmers in the past.

Much that has been accomplished ‘during the war was made

possible by the wise national program in support of scientific research in agriculture and forestry and by the program for the conservation and improvement of our soil and forest resources. These policies have paid large dividends during the war. We ought to continue and strengthen them.

Within recent years the Congress has enacted various measures which have done much to improve the economic status of this country's farmers and to make rural living more attractive. In enacting individual pieces of legislation it has not been possible to make adjustments in existing measures in keeping with the changing pattern of needs. The Secretary of Agriculture is now re-examining existing agricultural programs in the light of peacetime needs in order that they may make the fullest contribution to the welfare of farmers and the people as a whole. I hope that the Congress, also, through its appropriate committees, will give careful consideration to this problem with a view to making such adjustments as are necessary to strengthen the effectiveness of these various measures.

Selective Service

While the cruel lessons of war are fresh in every mind, it is fitting that we now undertake appropriate measures for the future security of the United States.

To meet . . . immediate obligations will require the maintenance for some time of a real measure of our present land, sea, and air power.

And in this first year after victory our people have another obligation, one which is felt in almost every American home. We owe it to those now in the armed forces that they be returned to civilian life with all possible speed.

To provide the personnel necessary to meet these immediate obligations we must obtain replacements for those veterans who have already rendered long and arduous service.

We shall make every effort to raise these replacements by recruiting volunteers. To that end I ask that the Congress consider ways and means to assure the maximum success of the recruiting campaigns which have already been authorized. I suggest that legislation be enacted to remove the present restriction on eligibility for voluntary enlistment and to allow the armed forces to enlist a larger number of volunteers than is now authorized. It is further recommended that, in order to enable the armed forces satisfactorily to compete in the procurement of personnel, the Congress provide suitable inducements for volunteer service in the Army and Navy.

However, in view of our extensive national commitments, I am certain, as are the War and Navy Departments, that we cannot rely on voluntary recruitment as the sole method of procuring the necessary replacements. I therefore urge that the Congress continue inductions to assure replacements for these veterans, in such numbers as are not supplied by volunteers.

An unforgivable discrimination would result if, by suspending inductions now, we should favor those who have had no military service at the cost of requiring continued sacrifice from those who have already done their part.

Our first concern should be for those who have been in the armed forces for several years. They have been separated from their homes and from their loved ones. Many of them have been under constant fire and continuous danger for months and even years. We should try to avoid imposing further service upon them.

The only way that this can be done is to continue the induction of young men who as yet have not served a tour of active duty in the armed services. Only when we find that we are able to obtain a sufficient number of volunteers to fill the necessary quotas for our occupational needs can we discontinue the Selective Service system.

Of course it is entirely up to the Congress to choose the means by which we will provide and maintain the necessary strength to meet our commitments. The alternatives presented are very simple. There are no others. Either we retain men now in the service for a further indefinite period, or we provide replacements by further inductions.

As you know, I have already directed the Selective Service to cut down the number of inductions from 80,000 to 50,000 per month, and to limit them to the age group of 18 through 25. It would seem reasonable to limit inductions hereafter to men between the ages of 18 and 25, inclusive, and fix their maximum term of service at two years.

Under the existing statute, inductees can be legally retained only for the duration of the war and a period of six months thereafter. I trust that, in any event, the Congress will not pass a resolution to the effect that the war has terminated for the purpose of this statute. To do so would give to all inducted men and temporary officers of the Army now on active duty the right to civilian status, and would create an impossible demobilization situation.

These are the military steps which it is apparent must be taken at once to meet the needs of the transition from war to peace. First things necessarily come first.

But the full needs of our national security run far beyond this immediate period of transition. We should make timely preparation for the nation's long-range security, while we are still mindful of what it has cost us in this war to have been unprepared.

Housing

The largest single opportunity for the rapid postwar expansion of private investment and employment lies in the field of housing, both urban and rural. The present shortage of decent homes and the enforced widespread use of substandard housing indicate vital unfilled needs of the nation. These needs will become more marked as veterans begin to come back and look for places to live.

I urgently recommend that the Congress, at an early date, enact broad and comprehensive housing legislation.

The cardinal principle underlying such legislation should be that house construction and financing for the overwhelming majority of our citizens should be done by private enterprise.

We should retain and improve upon the present excellent government facilities which permit the savings of the people to be channeled voluntarily into private house construction on financing terms that will serve the needs of home owners of moderate income.

The present principles of insurance of housing investment—now tested by years of experience—should be retained and extended, so as to encourage direct investment in housing by private financing institutions.

The government, in addition to providing these facilities to help private enterprise and private capital build homes, should take effective measures to stimulate research in methods and materials of housing construction. In this way better and cheaper methods may be developed to build homes.

In addition to this type of research the government might well undertake to assist communities in making recurrent community studies in matters relating to housing and real estate generally. Such a program would contribute in great degree to the progress of private initiative and private capital investment in housing.

We must go on. We must widen our horizon even further. We must consider the redevelopment of large areas of the blighted and slum sections of our cities so that in the truly American way they may be remade to accommodate families not only of low-income groups as heretofore, but of every income group. We must make it possible for private enterprise to do the major part of this job. In most cases it is now impossible for private enterprise to contemplate rebuilding slum areas without public assistance. The land cost generally is too high.

The time has come for the government to begin to undertake a program of federal aid to stimulate and promote the redevelopment of these deteriorating areas. Such federal aid should be extended only to those communities which are willing to bear a fair part of the cost of clearing their blighted city areas and preparing them for redevelopment and rebuilding.

A decent standard of housing for all is one of the irreducible obligations of modern civilization. The housing challenge is now squarely before us. The people of the United States, so far ahead in wealth and productive capacity, deserve to be the best-housed people in the world. We must begin to meet that challenge at once.

Research

Progress in scientific research and development is an indispensable condition to the future welfare and security of the nation. The events of the past few years are both proof and prophecy of what science can do.

Science in this war has worked through thousands of men and women who labored selflessly and, for the most part, anonymously in the laboratories, pilot plants, and proving grounds of the nation. Through them science, always pushing forward the frontiers of knowledge, forged the new weapons that shortened the war.

Progress in science cannot depend alone upon brilliant inspiration or sudden flights of genius. We have recently had a dramatic demonstration of this truth. In peace and in war, progress comes slowly in small new bits, from the unremitting day-by-day labors of thousands of men and women.

No nation can maintain a position of leadership in the world of today unless it develops to the full its scientific and technological resources. No government adequately meets its responsibilities unless it generously and intelligently supports and encourages the work of science in university, industry, and in its own laboratories.

The development of atomic energy is a clear-cut indication of what can be accomplished by our universities, industry, and government working together. Vast scientific fields remain to be conquered in the same way.

In order to derive the full profit in the future from what we have learned, I urge upon the Congress the early adoption of legislation for the establishment of a single federal research agency which would discharge the following functions:

1. Promote and support fundamental research and development projects in all matters pertaining to the defense and security of the nation.

2. Promote and support research in the basic sciences and in the social sciences.

3. Promote and support research in medicine, public health, and allied fields.

4. Provide financial assistance in the form of scholarships and grants for young men and women of proved scientific ability.

5. Co-ordinate and control diverse scientific activities now conducted by the several departments and agencies of the federal government.

6. Make fully, freely, and publicly available to commerce, industry, agriculture, and academic institutions the fruits of research financed by federal funds.

Scientific knowledge and scientific research are a complex and interrelated structure. Technological advances in one field may have great significance for another apparently unrelated. Accordingly, I urge upon the Congress the desirability of centralizing these functions in a single agency.

Although science can be co-ordinated and encouraged, it cannot be dictated to or regimented. Science cannot progress unless founded on the free intelligence of the scientist. I stress the fact that the Federal Research Agency here proposed should in no way impair that freedom.

Transition Tax Revision

I recommend that a transitional tax bill be enacted as soon as possible to provide limited tax reductions for the calendar year 1946.

This matter has been under study jointly by Congressional and Treasury tax staffs. I am assured that a program will be ready for early consideration by the Congress.

We must reconcile ourselves to the fact that room for tax reduction at this time is limited. A total war effort cannot be liquidated overnight.

After passage of the transitional bill, I hope that the Congress will give careful consideration to the modernization of the federal tax structure. A major objective to this modernization should be the encouragement of business incentives and expansion, and of consumer purchasing power. In this connection consideration of further tax reductions should have due regard to the level of governmental expenditures and the health and stability of our economy.

Small Business

During the war special attention was paid to small business. The American small business is the backbone of our free enterprise system. The efforts of the Congress in protecting small business during the war paid high dividends, not only in protecting small business enterprise, but also in speeding victory. In spite of the fact, however, that many businesses were helped and saved, it is true that many thousands of them were obliged to close up because of lack of materials or manpower or inability to get into war production.

It is very important to the economy of the United States that these small businesses and many more of them be given opportunity to become a part of American trade and industry. To do this, assistance should be given to small businesses to enable them to obtain adequate materials, private financing, technological improvements, and surplus property.

While some special facilities for small business are required, the greatest help to it will come from the maintenance of general prosperity and full employment. It is much more difficult for small business to survive the hazards which come from trade recessions and widespread unemployment. What small business needs chiefly is a steady supply of customers with stable purchasing power.

I am sure that the Congress will see to it that in its legislation adequate protection and encouragement will be given to the small business of the nation.

Veterans

It has been a fundamental objective of the Congress and of the administration to make generous provision for those who have served the nation in its armed forces, and for the dependents of those who have died in their country's cause.

Although a full list of what has been done toward this objective would be entirely too long to enumerate here, it might be well to list some of the major steps already taken:

(1) Adoption of a National Service Life Insurance Act, under which about 17,500,000 insurance applications have been approved, resulting in insurance coverage of more than $135,000,000,000.

(2) Provision of increased compensation or pension for disabled veterans.

(3) Extension and expansion of hospital benefits.

(4) Vocational education and training for veterans having a service-connected disability constituting a vocational handicap.

(5) Mustering-out pay ranging from $100 to $300, dependent upon length of service and rate of pay.

(6) Education or training for any veteran whose education or training was interrupted by entrance into the service.

(7) Guarantee of loans to veterans for the purchase of a home, a farm, or a business.

(8) Legislation to protect the veteran's right to re-employment in his preservice job, if desired.

(9) Provision of unemployment allowances for veterans who become unemployed at any time within two years after discharge, of $20 per week for not to exceed fifty-two weeks.

(10) Civil service laws to insure preference to veterans in governmental service.

(11) There has also been instituted in each state pursuant to law an efficient system whereby the counseling and placement needs of veterans will be the responsibility of veterans appointed for that special work.

The transition of veterans from military to civilian activities cannot be accomplished satisfactorily by the federal government alone or the states alone, or, indeed, by both. Government can help chiefly through organization and over-all planning. But the real work must be done in each community through co-operation of the industrial, labor, and civic organizations interested in the welfare of the community and of the veterans.

Broad and generous as . . . legislation for veterans has been, there will be need of amendments and improvements. I recommend that the Congress give prompt consideration to the recommendations which have been made by the Veterans Administration for the purpose of clarifying and liberalizing the provisions relative to hospital and medical care, to vocational training under the Vocational Rehabilitation Act, and to education and training under the Servicemen's Readjustment Act.

I also urge consideration of the suggestions made by the Veterans Administration with respect to the loan guarantee features of the latter act, to amendments clarifying and liberalizing the National Service Life Insurance Act, and those which would increase the rates of compensation for specific injuries, including multiple amputations.

I have recommended that the Selective Training and Service Act be continued; but if the Congress determines to the contrary, I urgently recommend that it clarify the provisions thereof which specifically deal with the right of re-employment.

Favorable consideration should be given by the Congress to federal reclamation projects as outstanding opportunities for returning veterans. The great Columbia basin project in the Northwest, the projects in the Missouri River basin, and others of equal significance will bring into existence many thousands of new family-size farms upon which returning veterans can secure a livelihood for themselves and their families and create new wealth for the nation.

A number of farms can be made ready for veterans rapidly if legislation now pending is enacted without delay. This legislation would authorize necessary and proper assistance to veterans who seek to develop farm homes on irrigated lands in federal reclamation project areas.

I also recommend that the Congress expedite legislation giving veterans social security coverage credit for the period of their service in the armed services.

In the last analysis, if we can insure the proper economic conditions we may be sure that the genius and initiative of Americans who met successfully all demands of the greatest war in history, both on the fighting front and on the production front, will make certain the reintegration of veterans into an expanding civilian economy. Anything less would not meet the country's obligations to its veterans.

Public Works and National Resources

We have torn from the earth copper, petroleum, iron ore, tungsten, and every other mineral required to fight a war, without regard to our future supplies. At the same time our splendid prewar program to build up our national resources was sharply halted. The diligent and constant search for additional deposits of minerals was almost abandoned in favor of a frantic effort to discover and make possible the production of the materials of war.

The long-range programs to conserve the previous inches of topsoil which, in many parts of the country, lie between plenty and poverty, were necessarily interrupted. We had neither the manpower nor the materials to spare for projects to prevent the ravages of floods which constantly despoil our land. We had neither the men nor the facilities to continue a large-scale program of reclaiming land or bringing new land into cultivation.

With a few exceptions we were forced to suspend the program to which this nation is committed of harnessing the waters of our great rivers so that they may become vehicles of commerce, beneficent producers of cheap electric power, and servants of the nation instead of instruments of destruction.

In brief, although during this war this nation has reached the apex of its power—a peak of greatness and might which the world had never seen—our national capital account has greatly suffered. We must proceed with all possible diligence not merely to restore these depleted resources to their prewar standards but to make them greater and richer than ever before. We must make a diligent effort to discover new deposits of the precious and indispensable minerals upon which our national life is founded. We must develop for the use of industry new technologies so that the vast deposits of low-grade ores that have not heretofore been considered usable may be put to work for the good of all of us. We should build and improve our roads—the arteries of commerce; we must harness our streams for the general welfare; we must rebuild and reclaim our land; we must protect and restore our forests.

This is not only to provide men and women with work; it is to assure to the nation the very basis of its life. It is to play the part of a good businessman who insists carefully on maintaining and rebuilding his plant and machinery.

We know that by the investment of federal funds we can, within the limits of our own nation, provide for our citizens new frontiers—new territories for the development of industry, agriculture, and commerce.

We have before us the example of the Tennessee Valley Authority, which has inspired regional resource development throughout the entire world.

We know that we have programs, carefully considered and extensively debated, for regional development of the Columbia River in the great Northwest, the Missouri River, the Central Valley of California, and the Arkansas River.

In the Columbia Valley the first major step has been completed for the reclamation of barren land and the production of enormous quantities of power. The waters of the Missouri and the Arkansas and the rivers of California can be put to work to serve the national interest in a similar fashion.

If these rivers remain scourges of our nation, it is only because we do not have the prudence to harness them for the benefit of our people. If there are among us for any period of time farmers who do not farm because there is no suitable land available to them, workers who do not work because there is no labor for their hands, we have only ourselves to blame so long as we fail to make available to them the opportunities before our very eyes.

I hope that the Congress will proceed as rapidly as possible to authorize regional development of the natural resources of our great river valleys.

It should be unnecessary to say that the conservation and development of the national plant must proceed according to an intelligent and co-ordinated design. The watersheds of this nation are not utterly independent, one of the other; our irreplaceable wealth of minerals, land, and timber is not composed of segments which can effectively be dealt with separately. Any program of public works must have as its unifying purpose the greatest possible contribution to the wealth of the nation and to the wealth-producing capability of the nation.

It is necessary that we proceed as speedily as possible to set up machinery to make an inventory of our national wealth and our basic resources and to test the suitability of plans and proposals for public works in light of this purpose. An agency of this sort could provide us with consistent direction toward the goal of rehabilitation and improvement of our basic national resources.

Shortages of materials and manpower made it necessary in the interest of the war effort to suspend many public works which might otherwise have been undertaken. Now that materials and manpower will become more plentiful we should be prepared to undertake a program of useful public works, not only to improve the physical plant of the United States but to provide employment to great masses of our citizens when private industry cannot do so. Only such public works should now be undertaken, however, as will not compete with the use of materials and manpower by private industry. Plans for other public works should be perfected and put in reserve.

In this connection I have several recommendations:

(1) During the war the construction of federal public works has been restricted to those necessary for national defense and the prosecution of the war. Projects which normally would have been constructed were deferred and a large backlog of needed construction has accumulated. Plans for some of these projects—specifically those relating to reclamation, rivers and harbors, flood control, and conservation of our natural resources—are now ready, and their construction can go forward when funds are provided and materials and manpower are available without competing with private industry. Plans for other federal projects are being prepared through the use of funds wisely appropriated by the Congress for advance preparation. Additional funds are needed for this purpose, and I urge that the Congress provide them.

(2) I recommend that the Congress enact legislation authorizing additional construction of certain federal buildings. A portion of this program has already been authorized, but has been held up by reason of cost limits imposed upon the buildings which cannot now be met because of increased needs and costs.

(3) I recommend that the Congress release the funds for the highway program authorized under the federal aid highway act of 1944 (Public Law 521, Seventy-eighth Congress). Under this act $500,000,000 has been authorized for the first year and $500,000,000 for each of the two succeeding years, making a total authorization of $1,500,000,000. With the states' share of the cost included, this would provide a total highway construction program of $3,000,000,000 for a three-year period.

(4) I recommend that the Congress appropriate $25,000,000 to continue the construction of the Inter-American Highway through the Central American republics to the Canal Zone.

(5) I recommend that the Congress enact legislation to provide the necessary airports and airport facilities to serve the great needs of an expanded postwar air transportation and commerce. A well planned airport program would improve transportation, amplify the usefulness of the airplane, and contribute to a healthy aircraft manufacturing industry.

The Congress now has before it a survey of the present and future needs for airports in the United States, prepared by the Secretary of Commerce. This report indicates the necessity for approximately 3,000 new airports and for improvements to more than half of the existing 3,000 airports. The report recommends that the program be spread over a period of ten years and that the cost be shared equally between federal and nonfederal governmental agencies. I recommend passage of appropriate legislation to implement this program.

(6) States and local governments should be encouraged to construct useful public works of the types that must necessarily supplement and go along with the private construction of homes and industrial facilities. If private construction is to move forward at a rapid rate, it is vitally important that local governments promptly proceed with the construction of such facilities as streets, sewers, water supply, hospitals, airports, schools, and other necessary public facilities. Such projects should be undertaken at this time where they supplement and encourage private construction, not where they compete with it for manpower and materials.

The Congress has already authorized under Title V of the war mobilization and reconversion act of 1944 appropriations for advances of federal funds to state and local governments to assist them in the preparation of detailed drawings and specifications for their public works. The appropriation thus far made is entirely inadequate, and I shall request additional funds in order to speed up this important activity during the reconversion period.

The majority of state and local governments are awaiting a decision concerning federal assistance. In order to get needed public facilities started promptly which do not compete with private construction, I recommend that the Congress give early consideration to grants for such public works under conditions that will insure that each level of government, federal, state, and local, shall make its appropriate contribution.

(7) The Congress has also been giving consideration to legislation with respect to the construction of hospitals and health centers throughout the country. During the war the government, through the Federal Works Agency and the Public Health Service, has assisted state and local governments and nonprofit organizations in the construction of such facilities. The beneficial results of this program are well known. The federal government must continue to recognize its obligation to maintain and improve the health of the nation by providing federal grants where necessary for the construction of hospital and health centers.

Programs of internal improvements of a public character—federal, state, and local—must preserve competitive bidding, guarantee collective bargaining and good wages for labor, utilize the skills of our returned veterans to the fullest extent, and effectively prevent discrimination because of race, creed, or color.

Congressional Salaries

Now that restrictions on voluntary salary increases have been removed, I hope that the Congress will take action soon on the salaries of its members.

My experience as a member of the Senate has given me a very keen appreciation of the quantity and quality of the work of the members of the Congress. They are called upon to carry great responsibility and make important decisions in a multiple of matters involving the welfare of the nation and of the world. Their tasks continue day in and day out. They have increased in number and in importance year by year.

There is no doubt in the mind of any thinking American that members of the Congress are grossly underpaid and have been for many years. I think that they are entitled—and have already so expressed myself—to a salary anywhere from fifteen to twenty-five thousand dollars a year. I recommend that the Congress enact legislation providing that the salaries of its members be increased to $20,000 per year.

At the same time I recommend the repeal of the provision now applicable to the House of Representatives for an additional expense allowance. There should be a straight, out-and-out salary increase for all members. We should make service in the Congress of the United States available without hardship to ordinary citizens who have to look to the salary for their sole support. I also recommend that an adequate retirement system should be provided for the members of the Congress who have served for a long period of years.

§ *The action taken on various points of Mr. Truman's ambitious program is summarized under the several topics of the section. It is of profit at this juncture to retrace the results of his recommendations in three areas: social security, housing, and agriculture.*

Social Security. *Three weeks after the President had submitted his reconversion program the House Ways and Means Committee voted to postpone "indefinitely" the administration's unemployment compensation bill. Even more comprehensive proposals for social security revision were made in his message to Congress of May 24, 1948. He called for the addition of 20,000,000 workers not covered and an increase in benefits for the aged and dependents. The limit on earnings taxable under the law was to be increased from $3,000 to $4,800, and the date for the increase in the tax rate from 1 per cent to 1½ per cent was to be advanced from January 1, 1950 to January 1, 1949. He proposed that workers be insured against loss of earnings due to temporary or extended disability. In the old age assistance program he proposed that women be eligible for benefits at sixty instead of sixty-five, and that all beneficiaries, male or female, be permitted to earn up to $40 a month through part-time employment. (The limit at this time was $15 a month.)*

After his election in 1948 he repeated his requests to Congress for improvements in the social security program. In addition to the extensions of coverage previously requested he asked that farmers, self-employed businessmen and professional men, domestic help, and workers in nonprofit institutions be covered. He asked that taxes and benefits be approximately doubled for workers making more than $3,000 and that the maximum insurance benefits be raised from $85 to $150 a month. He repeated his request for disability insurance and proposed direct federal contributions to the states with established programs to aid the needy.

The chief fruits of these efforts were the amendments of 1950 extending old age insurance to 10,000,000 more persons. The larger categories represented in this number were the nonagricultural self-employed and state and local government employees who might come into the program voluntarily.

Housing. One of Mr. Truman's chief accomplishments in the field of housing was to bring order to the chaotic multiplicity of government agencies operating in it. In 1947 government housing activities were scattered among thirteen agencies in seven regular departments. Congress approved the President's request for a new housing and home finance agency to co-ordinate and supervise existing activities. Following his 1948 victory he wrote a 5,000-word letter to Speaker Rayburn making a vehement attack on the "real estate lobby" and listing nine "false" propaganda contentions of "this little group of ruthless men." There was a brief intense struggle in Congress that focused on the public housing provision of the bill, endorsed jointly by Mr. Truman and Senator Taft, and on June 30 the House passed the entire bill in a major Fair Deal victory. Ironically, in the light of the President's severe castigation of the Republican party, the victory was possible only because twenty-four liberal Republicans gave administration forces the necessary votes to get public housing into the housing bill. The Senate also approved, and on July 5 Mr. Truman ordered prompt implementation of his housing program.

Agriculture. The chief innovation of the Truman administration in agricultural policy was the Brannan plan. This plan would permit farm prices to find their natural level through the operation of supply and demand, thus giving the consumer the benefit of any fall in the farm commodity market. The farmer would be aided by a direct subsidy payment, representing the difference between the price received and the parity price. Mr. Truman's first public observations on the Brannan plan were made at a press conference on April 7, 1949 when he said that the plan spoke for itself, that he knew what was in it, and that it was all right.

Although the Brannan plan was decisively defeated in the House, in

April of the following year Mr. Truman urged the enactment of a farm program tied to the plan, as "more efficient, less costly, and more conducive to the abundant production of farm crops, yielding a fair return to farmers, and selling at prices consumers can afford." Although he did not refer to the Brannan plan by name, it was clearly involved. A general belief in Congress was that the Brannan plan was a dead duck, that the President knew it, and that he had probably sent the message primarily for the record and for use in the 1950 campaign. The 81st Congress never permitted the plan to come to a vote.

5. THE PRESIDENT'S ECONOMIC REPORTS

One of the most important of the several staff services created during the Truman administration was the Council of Economic Advisers established by the Employment Act of 1946. The Council assists the President in the preparation of the annual Economic Report to Congress, required each January, and with such other studies and reports related to federal economic policy and legislation as the President may request.

A passage from the first Economic Report contains Mr. Truman's general tribute to the value of the new Council.

The Congress passed the Employment Act of 1946 by an overwhelming bipartisan vote. This act wisely provided for a council of economic advisers to the President, men who as a result of training, experience, and attainments are exceptionally qualified to analyze and interpret economic developments, to appraise programs and activities of the government, and to formulate and recommend national economic policy.

The Congress also provided for a permanent joint committee to receive and analyze this annual economic report of the President and to submit recommendations concerning it to both Houses.

In transmitting this first economic report I am conscious of its significance as the beginning of a series of reports that will serve the Executive and the Congress as the basis for an orderly and continuing review of the economic state of the union and for integrated and comprehensive steps to ensure the permanent economic health of the nation.

The economic report is an opportunity for national self-examination and self-criticism. It is a challenge to the President and the Congress to determine the causes of whatever problems we face in our economic life and to find the solutions of those problems. It provides an opportunity for all our citizens to judge the merits of the analysis and proposed action. It is a new and splendid tool to help us in our tasks. And like all governmental tools, its effectiveness will increase year by year as we learn by doing.

§ *President Truman's last annual Economic Report, made to Congress on January 15, 1953, is an important document of retrospect and summary, here reproduced in extenso.*

ECONOMIC AND SOCIAL GAINS, 1945–1953

In this, my seventh and final Annual Economic Report to the Congress under the Employment Act of 1946, I think it appropriate to review the period of which the Act is both product and symbol.

Early in the past quarter century the United States fell from good times into a period of great economic adversity. Out of this experience there arose the compelling demand which finally produced the declaration of national economic policy contained in the Employment Act—that our great resources were pledged to the maintenance of maximum production, employment, and purchasing power.

Later within this quarter century we achieved in great measure the kind of economic society of which the Act is a symbol—a prosperous and growing economy of free men, with increasing opportunity for all. In this accomplishment we have testimony that we can hold fast to our gains and add to them in the years ahead.

During this past quarter century the strength and vigor of the American economy have been severely tested. Since 1929 the nation has suffered its most disastrous depression, fought its most costly war, and moved through a difficult postwar readjustment. Most recently it has devoted a large portion of its output in the effort of the free world to overcome the menace of aggression.

Now, despite the wastage of depression and the heavy but necessary expenditures for war and national security, the nation is far stronger economically than it was a quarter century ago. Its people are enjoying a much higher standard of living. Its farms and factories are far more productive. And it is displaying in remarkable fashion the capacity for economic growth on which its future welfare and security so largely depend.

The nation's progress during this past quarter century is evident in the figures which sum up total economic activity.

In 1929 the output of all goods and services was 172 billion dollars; in 1952, total output amounted to 345 billion dollars—measured in both cases in uniform 1952 prices. Industrial production has doubled, and agricultural output has risen about fifty per cent.

Last year, on the average, more than 61,000,000 workers had civilian jobs, compared with almost 48,000,000 in 1929. Both were good years for employment. In 1952, however, the average individual worked fewer hours—and produced more goods. From 1929 to 1952 the length of the work week for all types of activity dropped from about forty-eight to forty hours, but each worker turned out on the average eighty per cent more goods and services.

This greater yield reflects more and better equipment and higher skills than existed twenty-five years ago. Invention and business initiative have more than kept up with the rise in the number of men and women seeking work and have made it possible for them to find better jobs.

While we have been producing more for consumers, we have at the same time been adding to equipment on farms and in factories. In 1952, for example, we spent about $26,000,000,000 for machines and other kinds of durable equipment, compared with a little more than $11,000,000,000 in 1929, both measured in 1952 prices.

Vast resource development projects and conservation programs have been undertaken in the past quarter century, some public, some private, and many a mixture of the two. Public construction expenditures for flood control, navigation improvements, agricultural land reclamation, hydroelectric power facilities, and soil and forest conservation have increased more than three hundred per cent in real terms.

Multiple-purpose development of the Tennessee, Columbia, and other rivers has been far advanced. Huge additional amounts are being invested in atomic energy. Private mining, timber, and other concerns have increasingly adopted conservation practices and have invested heavily in research and development.

Individual farmers, frequently aided by the government, have greatly enlarged their investment in their own land. Production and consumption of nearly all raw materials have increased since 1929. These developments have enormously enlarged the productive power of our factories and farms, helped to power and equip the American home with the most modern conveniences, and correspondingly lifted the standard of living.

The nation's progress is shown also in greatly increased earnings and improved living standards. In 1929 average annual income after taxes was a little more than $1,000 per capita, while last year the average was about $1,500—again measured in 1952 prices. It should be noted that, while the real buying power of individuals was rising, the population of the United States increased by about 35,000,000. Our economy now provides much more for many more people.

The greatly improved living standards which have been achieved during the past quarter century are evident in more tangible data than the number of dollars earned or spent. In 1929 there were 23,000,000 automobiles in use, and in 1952 there were 44,000,000. In the same span of time the number of homes with a mechanical refrigerator increased from about 10 to 80 per cent. The number with radios increased from 40 to 96 per cent, and 40 per cent now have television sets. Compared with 10 per cent in 1929, nearly 90 per cent of all farms are now electrified.

During the era as a whole we have built 12,000,000 new nonfarm homes, most of them since World War II. Home ownership increased from 48 per cent of all families in 1930 to 55 per cent in 1950. Terms of housing finance have improved greatly, bringing home ownership within the reach of lower income groups, and also facilitating construction of apartments and other houses for rent. In the blighted sections of cities a hopeful number of slum clearance and redevelopment projects, both public and private, have been undertaken, though far from enough.

And the record has not been written in total quantities alone, whether of dollars, automobiles, or houses. The products of our economy are now far better distributed than they used to be. Adequate statistics do not go back to 1929. But since 1935–36 the real incomes of families and single persons in the lowest two fifths of the income range have increased 90 per cent, while the increase in the top fifth has been about 40 per cent. This improved distribution is not only a mark of social progress and increasing human contentment;

it is also a vital underpinning of sustained and advancing general prosperity for all sectors of the economy.

Improved and more widely available education, medical care, and economic security are among the cherished features of the American way of life. So are the basic freedoms, full enjoyment of which depends upon progressive removal of discriminatory practices in the market place and elsewhere.

These are higher values in the sense that they are abiding objectives of policy and action. But they also undergird the economic and moral strength of the country. They provide the source of a strong, healthy, and skilled labor force and an imaginative and responsible management. They provide a motivation for economic growth.

Although the pursuit of these values during the past quarter century has been interrupted by depression, world-wide war and depression, world-wide war and the necessities of the defense build-up, considerable headway has none the less been made.

Total educational expenditures, in constant prices, have about doubled since 1929. Capital outlays for public schools, again in constant prices, have gone up 63 per cent in the same period. Teachers are better trained, curriculums have improved, and schools are designed for more effective learning.

Total per capita expenditures for health and medical services have nearly doubled during this era, after adjusting for price change. Outlays for hospital construction, both public and private, have risen about 83 per cent. There is one doctor for every 740 persons now, compared with one for every 800 in 1929. Expenditures for medical research mounted to nearly $200,000,000 in 1952. The quality of medical care has improved with the development of new drugs, better techniques of surgery and hospital treatment, and the extension of preventive medicine.

It has been essential to do justice to those who have fought to defend us against enemies. Since 1929 the number of veterans has increased from 4,700,000 to 19,700,000. Veterans and their families now comprise 40 per cent of the total civilian population. Some 7,800,000 veterans have received education and training aid since World War II, and an additional 600,000 have received vocational rehabilitation training. Increasing numbers of Korean war veterans will be receiving similar help. Unemployment insurance has been paid to about 9,000,000 veterans. Farm and business loans and housing mortgage guarantees and loans have also helped veterans.

Progress in social security has been significant, with the advent in the mid-1930's of old age insurance, unemployment insurance, and new and improved public assistance programs. The federal old age and survivors insurance program covers 45,000,000 persons, while federal-state public assistance is available for dependent children, the blind, needy old persons, and the permanently and totally disabled. The federal-state unemployment insurance system now covers about 35,000,000 jobs.

The eventual elimination of discrimination based on race, religion, economic status, or section of the country is a continuing objective of national policy. Discrimination is in part economic in origin, and can be reduced by economic measures. Throughout the past quarter century, particularly as part of the economic and social reforms of the '30's, great though insufficient gains have been made.

Workers have been guaranteed the right to organize and bargain collectively. The Fair Labor Standards Act established the principle of minimum wages and maximum hours. Fair employment practices acts have been passed in some twelve states.

Economic justice for American agriculture has advanced tremendously since the period just before the great depression. Vast conservation programs, intensified agricultural research, loans and assistance to farm families, especially low-income families, price supports to reduce instability, and rural electrification have combined to improve rural life.

Since 1929 per capita farm income in constant dollars has increased about 80 per cent. The gain here has been relatively large, because the farmer had been left so far behind during the uneven prosperity of the late 1920's.

Opportunities for business have also widened, particularly as a result of the unprecedented period of prosperity since around 1940. There were only a third as many business failures in 1952 as in 1929, even though the number of business firms in operation has increased by one third. In this quarter century, while wholesale prices rose 80 per cent and consumers' prices 55 per cent, corporate profits rose more than 300 per cent before taxes and more than 100 per cent after taxes.

Working conditions have benefited enormously under the joint impact of union efforts, business policies of sharing productivity gains, and government programs. For factory workers with three dependents the increase in average weekly take-home pay (after allowing for the taxes paid by a family of this size) has been from $39 to about $63, measured in 1952 prices.

During recent weeks a variety of commentators far and wide have noted the profoundly protective and stabilizing elements which have been built into our economic system during the past quarter century.

There is now a rather prevalent view that the danger of any economic setback getting out of hand during the next few years is minimized by broader and fairer distribution of income among individuals and economic groups; a more progressive tax system which automatically adjusts in part to changes in business conditions; a level of public expenditures which, while we all want to see it lower as soon as world conditions permit, stabilizes demand and stimulates private investment; unemployment compensation and the rest of the social security system; farm price supports; a far more shockproof system of banks and securities exchanges; the greater firmness of wage rates due in part to strong unions; and more enlightened business practices with respect to pricing, marketing, collective bargaining, and investment planning.

And not the least of the stabilizing effects of these programs is the increasing confidence in the maintenance of prosperity which they inspire.

Despite these great gains, many of our domestic economic problems have not been solved, some things should have been done better, many inadequacies still exist, and above all the task of maintaining and advancing the rate of progress and forging new tools to meet new needs is always with us.

In addition, while the current defense build-up is near its peak, the new problem of America's role in the world economy presses for solution. This problem will long endure, and it will call for many further changes in our thought and action.

Here at home the recent period of economic growth has been accompanied by periodic inflation. Such periods of inflation not only threaten the continuance of growth but also prevent the benefits of growth from being enjoyed equitably by all the people in all sectors of the economy. We can still observe, despite unparalleled prosperity, deprivation of one kind or another among American families to be counted in the millions.

We may face in the future, particularly when defense spending can safely be reduced, more serious tests of our ability to avoid depression than those which have occurred since World War II. And as we continue to build safeguards against such a test it would be imprudent to rely excessively upon the stabilizing factors already in being which have been set forth above. They are not of themselves sufficiently strong to check inflation when it threatens or to safeguard us from depression and maintain continuous prosperity and growth. While much has been accomplished, much remains to be done.

The basic legislation which calls for this Economic Report—the Employment Act of 1946—is the framework within which we should strive to develop the further improvement of our economic condition. In the remainder of this message I shall endeavor to evaluate this framework and to set within it some of the problems we face and some of the promises that lie ahead if we meet these problems effectively.

The Employment Act of 1946 is one of the most fundamental compacts in domestic affairs which the people through their government have made during my tenure as President. It represents the refusal of Americans in all pursuits—in business, labor, agriculture, and government—to accept recurrent depression as a way of life. It voices a profound conviction that all of us, working together, can maintain and enlarge prosperity, not only during or as an aftermath of war, but enduringly for all time.

The Act is more than an essay in wishful thinking. It represents the closely reasoned conclusion of economic minds, both scholarly and practical, that its objectives are obtainable by sensible private and public policies and can best be sought within the framework of our established political and economic institutions.

There were historical roots for this endeavor. The lessons of the past had been particularly compelling in the decade and a half which preceded 1946. These had been years of unprecedented contrast, so far as economic abundance was concerned. On the one hand there was the stark tragedy of the early '30's, and then the seemingly boundless energies of the early '40's.

The period had been rich in careful social experimentation and legislative reform; the economic role and responsibilities of the federal government had increased enormously. Many of the experiments had been temporary in character to meet the emergencies of the depression or the extraordinary demands of war. But many of them were developed and improved to become permanent additions to our economic and social fabric.

Yet the Employment Act was not written in a spirit of conflict. It was not focused on the interests of any one group, whether powerful or downtrodden, but was addressed explicitly to the general welfare. And to an amazing degree, when one considers the thinking which it marked, it was noncontroversial. The subcommittees of the Senate and the House which skillfully ushered it into the legislative world worked to a large extent as bipartisan teams, and the final bill commanded overwhelming majorities of both parties in both houses of Congress.

There are those who have suggested from time to time that, because the act was relatively noncontroversial, it cannot have been very consequential. This is erroneous. Near-unanimity, in this instance, was not a mark of the unimportant or the hackneyed; it was evidence that a legislative proposal of the greatest moment was extraordinarily well timed. It wrote into the codes of the nation a great new area of agreement about the essential functions and responsibilities of the federal government almost as soon as that agreement existed.

It is likewise a mistake to underestimate the importance of the Employment Act, as some have done, because it did not set down a specific prescription of economic policies for solving future economic problems. The decision of its framers in this respect was deliberate and did not represent simply an inability to get agreement on more technical or specific provisions.

Instead, the decision was that such basic legislation should not attempt to prejudge the exact character, causes, and remedies of all of the future's general economic problems, but rather to define the general spirit and provide the general method for meeting these problems as they arise. With these problems in view, the Act has three specific purposes.

First, it is the purpose of the Act to achieve, within the Congress and the Executive Branch, and also between private enterprise and all levels of government, better economic policy co-ordination. In the '30's, and again during World War II, the economic programs of the government had become increasingly diverse and complex, and any realistic appraisal indicated than they would remain so. The special pressures which were brought to bear upon public economic policy-making had become more powerful, more numerous, and more confusing.

But this growth of complexity had not been matched, especially within the permanent institutions of the government, by the development of adequate means for gauging whether our farm programs, developmental programs, international trade policies, tax policies, credit policies, business regulatory policies, industrial relations laws, and the rest, were consistent with one another and fitted together into a sensible economic policy for the over-all economy. In the thinking of Congressmen from particular sections and on particular committees, and of leading administrators with specialized responsibilities, the whole too often was lost in preoccupation with the parts.

The governmental reforms in the Employment Act have sought to meet this problem by strengthening the President's facilities for economic policy co-ordination within the executive branch, by supplying the Congress with a similar facility, and by providing in the Economic Report a regular method for improved co-ordination between the two branches. Thus the Act meets the problem squarely within the framework of our constitutional system of separated powers.

Instead of attempting to circumvent the system with a hybrid agency which would be clearly responsible neither to the Congress nor the President, it installs a mechanism intended to make the traditional system work better. And it provides also, by requiring consultation with business, farm, labor, consumer, and other groups, for co-operation and co-ordination between private and public economic thought and action.

Second, it is the purpose of the Employment Act—the one most widely recognized at the time of its passage—to prevent depressions. As World War II drew to a close, recollections of the shocking costs of the great depression were much sharper than they are today after a dozen years of uninterrupted high prosperity.

The minds of most of us in 1946 were still deeply etched with the memory of the winter of 1932–33, when about 15,000,000 American workers, or about thirty per cent of the total civilian labor force, had no jobs; when industrial production was only half of what it had been in 1929 and the total output of the economy only about two thirds; when business was deep in the red; when farm prices and incomes had dropped out of sight; and when banks were collapsing by the hundreds. It has been calculated that the depressions cost us some $600,000,000,000 of output, measured in 1952 prices, or three and one half times everything we produced in 1929.

The Employment Act stands as a pledge on the part of the people, voiced through their laws, that never again shall such sacrifice be laid on the altar of "natural economic forces." In the bigger economy we now have, a disaster of anywhere near the same proportions could mean some 20,000,000 of our workers walking the streets.

Moreover, the cost of another serious depression would not stop at our own borders. What was becoming apparent in 1946 is now a reality: the strength and stability of the whole free world depend on the avoidance of economic collapse in this country.

Third, the Employment Act had still another clear purpose even more profound and challenging than those of improving economic policy co-ordination and preventing depressions. It is one which carries beyond the essentially negative and intermittent objective of counteracting slumps. It is the positive resolution of a great people, not simply to avoid pitfalls, but to maintain as a matter of continuing policy a full, bountiful, and growing economy for themselves, for their children, and as a standard and inspiration toward the freedom and welfare of all peoples—and to do this in full peace no less than in limited war.

This is a purpose of which we must never lose track. The Act is not meant simply for salvage operations; it does not set up a stand-by mechanism to be brought onto the scene only on those extreme occasions when the economy needs to be dredged out of a hole. It symbolizes the marshaling of the forces of private and public policy in support of a full and growing economy.

In such an economy performance is not measured in the dimension of employment alone; instead, a dynamic, growing productive potential enables us to provide a steady expansion of output as well as full employment. In such an economy expansion facilitates the spread of economic justice, and the quality of the expansion is measured in terms of justice as well as efficiency. In such an economy there is abundance and stability enough to permit an increasing devotion of energies to the higher values. More and more people, being able to take the needs of their stomachs for granted, can devote increasing attention to the needs of their minds and hearts.

Such are the purposes of the Employment Act. And after seven years it may be fairly said that we have made a start toward fulfilling these purposes. The job of course has not been finished. Indeed, since the purposes are perennially fresh, it will never be finished. But the start has been good.

The progress has been tangible in the matter of policy co-ordination. These last seven years have been extraordinarily eventful ones in the realm of economic policy. We have negotiated a transition from major war to substantial peace with unprecedented economic success. We have experienced a relatively peaceful period of restocking and retooling in the civilian economy, while at the same time bringing the United States' economic role in international affairs into line with its newly expanded international responsibilities.

And then, most recently, we have been executing the build-up of a preparedness defense mobilization of a character which has no forerunner in American history and which has been managed in a fashion not to weaken the civilian economy but rather to strengthen it.

I submit that in no previous period have the economic programs of government shown so high a degree of internal consistency or so clear a relationship to the needs of the over-all economy. This achievement I credit in large measure to the existence of the Employment Act, to the facilities for policy co-ordination with which it provides the President, and to the greater concern for systematic and inter-related programming which the Act has inspired in most executive branch officials. And it has been accomplished in a government conducting economic programs far more extensive and complex than ever before.

Correspondingly, there has been greater coherence and clearer attention to the needs of the total economy in the economic legislation of the Congress within the last few years. Outstanding in this respect has been the tax legislation since the Korean outbreak, which has evidenced an unprecedented sense of fiscal responsibility on the part of the Congress. And this was implemented by the alert and emphatic insistence of the Congressional Joint Economic Committee, immediately after the Korean outbreak, on the need for a pay-as-we-go anti-inflationary tax program.

Besides the improvements in policy co-ordination which the Employment Act has assisted in both the legislative and executive branches, it has been useful in reinforcing the channels for communication between them. It would be foolish to deny that many difficulties in legislative-executive co-ordination have persisted. But these are a reflection of broad political problems in our governmental process; they are no indictment of the mechanism of the Employment Act itself. As the basic obstacles to legislative-executive policy-making are progressively overcome, that mechanism will prove increasingly useful.

More commonly overlooked but equally significant, the machinery under the Employment Act has helped to bring to private enterprise a better understanding of the problems of government, to bring to government a better understanding of the problems of private enterprise, and to help both to integrate their actions more effectively for the benefit of the whole economy.

This is the most realistic way—the American way—to avoid excessive centralization of authority. The continuous consultation among the Council of Economic Advisers, other agencies concerned with economic affairs, and representatives of workers, farmers, businessmen, and consumers has brought improved results over the years and should be continued. It has helped greatly in the development of national economic policies and in the preparation of these Economic Reports.

The Employment Act's second great purpose, that of preventing depression, has been served well since 1946. The nation has thus far traversed its first aftermath of a major war without a major depression. This record as a whole cannot be attributed to the Employment Act. But at the very least, the Act symbolizes the related operation of many public programs, the longer-viewed character of business, labor, and agricultural decision-making, and the better co-ordination of private and public policies, which have featured this period. And these things together have vastly assisted in the maintenance of high prosperity.

In 1947 and again in 1948, reporting under the Employment Act was an important device for calling the attention of the Congress and the nation to the inflationary danger then in process. It was pointed out that excessively rising prices, if unchecked, would ultimately result in an economic downturn. Specific actions, both private and public, were suggested to meet this threat. Where these actions were taken, they proved valuable. To the extent they were not taken, in private action or in legislation, the inflation was not sufficiently arrested.

Because inflation was not sufficiently arrested, the postwar economy encountered its first recessionary test in 1949. When this occurred the various reports under the Employment Act measurably helped the government and the business community to understand that episode and to meet it successfully. In much the same fashion the Council of Economic Advisers, in its current Economic Review, the Joint Economic Committee, and other government agencies are now laying foundations for successful transition to a more civilian-oriented economy in the years ahead.

And, finally, there has been a strengthening in practice of the Employment Act's third great purpose, that of positive, continuing maintenance of an economy operating at maximum—which means growing—levels of employment, production, and purchasing power. In some ways this has been the most significant accomplishment under the Act, sometimes lost sight of by those who believe that the Act has not yet been tested because we have not had a depression to challenge its effectiveness.

The periodic reports under the Employment Act have helped to express in a practical way the possibility and promise of an expanding economy. In 1948, when there was some sentiment that employment and production were at abnormally high levels and that there must be a serious downturn before progress could be resumed, the reports under the Act pointed out that an economy like ours must move forward to remain healthy.

By mid-1950, despite the slight recession of 1949, and before the Korean outbreak led to increasing defense outlays, the economy was registering levels of production and employment higher than in the boom year 1948.

Immediately after the Korean outbreak, when there was some doubt as to whether we could greatly accelerate our security efforts without imperiling the civilian economy or without great and prolonged shortages of civilian goods, the work under the Employment Act was fundamental to the program of over-all economic expansion which the government adopted.

What has happened since is in some respects even more striking than what happened during World War II. Starting with productive resources not nearly so slack as they were in 1939, and without the extreme pressure of total war, our national output has risen from about 285 billion dollars in 1948 (the peak before Korea) to an annual rate in excess of 350 billion dollars at the end of 1952, both measured in 1952 prices.

The difference between these two figures is far greater than the increase in total security efforts, and consequently per capita civilian supplies and per capita incomes after taxes and adjusted for price change are higher now than in 1948.

This is a remarkable record. It reflects the practical application of the philosophy of the Employment Act, and it opens up limitless prospects for the years ahead if the same approach is maintained and further improved.

While the details of action must change with the times, I believe it worth while now to set forth a few economic principles for the future—principles arising out of experience, and already justified by what their application has achieved.

Under the Employment Act full employment means more than jobs. It means full utilization of our natural resources, our technology and science, our farms and factories, our business brains and our labor skills.

The concept of full employment values ends as well as means; it values leisure as well as work; it values self-development as well as dedication to a common purpose; it values individual initiative as well as group co-operation. In the broadest sense full employment means maximum opportunity under the American system of responsible freedom.

And it is a concept which must grow as our capacities grow. Full employment tomorrow is something different from full employment today. The growth of opportunity, with a growing technology, requires a constantly expanding economy.

This is needed to abolish poverty and to remove insecurity from substantial portions of our population. It offers the prospect of transforming class or group conflict into co-operation and mutual trust, because the achievement of more for all reduces the struggle of some to get more at the expense of others.

Although our dedication to full employment has made great strides within recent memory, we cannot afford to be complacent. We cannot assume that henceforth what needs to be done to promote the maintenance of full employment will be done. None of us—regardless of party—should let the idea of full employment degenerate into a slogan bandied about for narrow political advantage. Like freedom, it needs to be guarded zealously and translated into action on a continuing basis. Moreover, if we fail in this, our very freedom may be placed in jeopardy.

The enemies of our free system say that, in the long run, we cannot succeed in this task. They point to history and to the false conclusions which Marx drew from the defect of nineteenth-century industrialism. They point also to the calamity of the great depression of the early '30's. They argue that general economic insecurity must grow remorselessly in our society, leading ultimately to collapse and revolution. These enemies say that time and history are on their side. But history and time are on our side if we use our opportunities wisely.

This does not mean that we know enough to avoid economic fluctuations completely, or that we would want to even if we could. In a dynamic free economy the consumer is sovereign. Business is always seeking to anticipate the nature and intensity of consumer demand. In response to anticipated or actual changes, the economy is marked by a ceaseless shifting of resources from areas of lesser to areas of greater demand; existing industries are growing or contracting; new industries and products make their appearance, requiring new skills; prices and employment are being accommodated to the ebb and flow of demand; investment decisions are adjusted to changing conditions.

This process requires the flexibility which is so characteristic of our economy. Some errors of anticipation are inevitable. The expansion of capacity may appear temporarily excessive, inventories may have been overbought, and waves of excessive optimism and pessimism may appear in the economy. These factors must lead to some fluctuations in the general level of business. This is the price we pay for a dynamic economy, and it is not too high for what we gain.

But while some economic fluctuations may remain necessary or even desirable, it does not follow that we should not try our best to maintain full employment, or that we should wait until small recessions begin to spiral before seeking to reverse their course or to prevent them from growing into large depressions. Such a passive attitude is fraught with danger.

For all experience has taught us that when the economy starts to roll downhill it becomes progressively more difficult to check the decline. It is far easier, and a far more rewarding task, to maintain the momentum of a growing economy than to reverse a downward spiral. Thus the essence of sound economic policy is constant vigilance and prompt action.

The Employment Act is not an antidepression measure; it is a proprosperity measure. It does not call for quiescence until hard times; it calls for daily vigor, in the American tradition, to make tomorrow even better than today.

Expansion is vital, because our population is growing, the number of those seeking jobs is growing, and their individual productivity is growing. But expansion cannot continue smoothly unless it is based on a sound and fair distribution of the increasing product. Our economy is built upon mass markets.

Unless each important sector receives a workable share of the expanding output, the expansion will come to an end because the market demand will be lacking. Growing capacity to produce requires growing ability to buy.

I have already cited the great gains we have made in bringing about better balance in our economy during the past quarter century. But while our economy now seems to be in fairly good balance, there are signs of some trends in the opposite direction. It is none too early to note these.

While agriculture is highly prosperous, the most recent period has witnessed a relative inability of agriculture to join in the gains which other groups have registered. Even in absolute terms, there has been for a year or so an adverse trend in farm incomes. This may be looked upon with favor by those who believe that the farmer's prices have been relatively too high, or that he has received more than his fair share of the national income during recent years. But it will not be looked upon favorably by those who know that, even at the peak, the farm population as a whole did not attain real parity of income with other major sectors of the population. Nor will it be looked upon with favor by those who realize from bitter experience that any decline in relative farm prosperity is not a good omen for the economy as a whole. This is a problem of economic balance which requires active attention and far-reaching efforts.

A second area in which we should strive for even better economic balance is in the wage structure. While the gains made by the strongly positioned wage earners have undoubtedly tended to lift labor standards generally, and while most of the working population has made real gains, there is now need for relatively more stress upon helping those at the bottom of the wage structure.

This places a large responsibility upon public programs, not only such programs as minimum wage laws, but also those which, by developing natural resources, facilitating private industrial growth, and improving the level of education and health, raise the productivity of these types of workers.

There is also need for even better balance between the opportunities open to large and to small business through the further encouragement of competition and the strengthening of those laws designed to prevent unfair competition and to restrain monopoly; and also through more positive programs to make the benefits of ample credit and full access to the new products of science and research and invention available to business regardless of size or financial power.

And finally, there is need to work toward even better economic balance in and among the different geographical regions of the country, through improved protection against discriminatory practices, and through federal programs designed toward the strengthening and further equalization of opportunity for human and material development. Top priority on this list, of course, should be accorded to the broader extension of adequate health services, housing and educational facilities, and to the further development of natural resources and industrial potentialities.

While the Employment Act calls for an appraisal of recent economic trends and foreseeable future trends, it places main emphasis upon future needs and how these needs may best be satisfied. It imposes the responsibility to define what maximum levels of employment, production, and purchasing power we should seek to attain in the year or years immediately ahead. It requires also that we state the policies, both private and public, best suited to reach these goals.

Thus the Act rejects the idea that we are the victims of unchangeable economic laws, that we are powerless to do more than forecast what will happen to us under the operation of such laws. Instead, the Act correctly asserts that our economy within reasonable limits will be what we make it, and that intelligent human action will shape our future.

In accord with this faith in human progress through human endeavor, the reports under the Employment Act several years ago began to estimate what levels of employment and production should be our goals for the years ahead, taking into account the material and human resources at our disposal.

These estimates were then used to analyze what kind of purchasing power, what relative flows of income to investors and consumers, to businessmen and workers and farmers, would be most conducive to the achievement of these employment and production goals.

This was primarily an effort in economic education and not a blueprint for central planning in the manner of the totalitarian states. It was in the American tradition of planning—which means the co-operative effort to look ahead and to work together toward making the future better than the present. The idea has been that, if our private and public policies are geared to planning for economic growth, we can achieve this growth.

If businessmen and farmers plan their investment programs with the realization that a steadily expanding economy will provide markets for more food and more industrial products, these regularized investment programs in themselves will contribute to a high and stable rate of growth. If business and labor plan their price and wage policies to encourage the balanced expansion of production and consumption, of jobs and markets, then our economic growth can be steady.

And government, because it is the most powerful single force in the economy, has the clearest responsibility to plan its operations so that they will make the greatest contribution in the long run to economic stability and growth. Under current world conditions this problem of government is complicated. Government must now give prime consideration to our national security, which is even more vital than absolute economic stability or a uniform rate of economic growth.

The more effectively all of these forces within the American economy work together in this kind of planning for the future, the greater the likelihood that economic fluctuations will be ironed out and a steadier rate of growth maintained. The less effectively this is done, for example if important groups in the economy assume that the traditional business cycle is inevitable and conform their actions to this belief, the more difficult it will be to maintain steady growth.

It is noteworthy that efforts to encourage this kind of action have met with increasing response in recent months. Not only governmental agencies, but many planning organizations supported by business, and many business organizations themselves, are now following this same approach with hearty enthusiasm. They are studying future markets and how to serve them. This is one of the most concrete signs of progress. But it is only the first taste of what may be accomplished as this process continues in the American tradition.

Private enterprise, under our free system, bears the major responsibility for full employment. This report has already set forth the basic features of that responsibility and how much its exercise is contributing to the well-being of the American people. The role of responsible government, while vital, is in a sense supplemental.

It is the duty of government to help improve the environment in which private enterprise works. In normal times this means the minimum use of direct control over materials, prices, and wages. As soon as we safely can, in view of the world situation and our own increasing productive ability, we should suspend operation of these controls. To aid in maintaining stability in the longer run, the government should place principal reliance upon the careful use of fiscal and credit policy, along with the well established regulatory and protective programs.

But in addition to encouraging an environment favorable to enterprise and exerting a stabilizing influence, responsible government has an even more general task. This is to enable the people to develop together those resources which in their very nature cannot be developed otherwise. Public spending, as determined by the Congress and other legislative bodies throughout the nation, represents a continuing determination by the people as to what part of their total productive power they wish to devote to the things which they must do together instead of doing separately.

While there should be true economy in public spending no less than in private spending, it is obviously superficial to regard public spending as unworthy by definition. Throughout our history the American people have recognized that their public programs represent a high order of national priority and are undertaken for this very reason.

These services under current conditions include defense, foreign aid, benefits to veterans, social security, public education, and the like. And they include long-term resource developmental programs, aid to agriculture, aid to housing, and other efforts which, while clearly desirable in themselves, are also necessary to improve and to support the functioning of the free enterprise system.

All of these programs, like those of private industry, should be geared primarily to the long-run needs of the nation. The pace and timing, however, are partly dependent upon changing conditions. For example, the speed-up of our defense efforts has caused us to cut back some other programs to avoid undue strain. If and when we can relax our defense efforts, we shall be able to push ahead with the other programs which serve the long-term peaceful needs of the people.

Since public spending diverts resources from private use, except in times of depression, the burden of this diversion is borne by the people whether or not taxes are imposed. But taxation serves to impose the burden more equitably and in a manner least detrimental to the whole economy. For otherwise, particularly when the economy is running at very high levels, spending in excess of taxation aggravates inflation—the most unfair and damaging way of imposing the burden.

Under present conditions of very high defense spending we have made a good record of keeping close to a balanced budget, although we should have done even better. In times of very high prosperity but a lower level of defense spending, we should accumulate a budget surplus for the independently desirable purpose of reducing the large national debt.

If we should run into periods of declining economic activity, on the other hand, we should expect some decline in revenues. But this should not frighten us into cutting back those programs which the nation needs, and which in fact would help to cushion the decline and to restore full employment. If a substantial part of our productive resources were lying idle because private enterprise could not utilize them, it would do good rather than harm to utilize them through public action even though this occasioned some deficit.

It is not true that the goal of maintaining full employment must be sacrificed in order to avoid inflation. The postwar inflation was not a continuing process; most of it came in two major spurts. The first followed shortly after the war, when controls were prematurely abandoned before supply could come into balance with demand. The second took place in late 1950 and early 1951, under the impact of the Korean outbreak followed by the large-scale Chinese intervention.

The fact that these two inflationary spurts came under the peculiar conditions of an immediately postwar period or the first stages of preparation for defense against the possibility of future war is no reason to neglect the lessons of this experience. We live in a world where peace is neither complete nor certain, and where changes in the international situation could rapidly occur.

It was a mistake to abandon controls too rapidly in 1946, and we should not abandon them too rapidly now, although the outlook for stability is better now than it was at that time. Similarly, we would have been much better off if price and wage controls could have been imposed more quickly after the Korean outbreak and especially after the Chinese intervention in late 1950, instead of early in 1951.

But we were handicapped not only by the inadequacy of legislative authorization, but also by the absence of a stand-by organization ready to cope with the first wave of inflation. The sharp price increases between the Chinese attack and early 1951 were a dramatic illustration of the importance of adequate economic preparedness in a cold war period—a lesson we should not forget.

Nonetheless, this peculiar problem of dealing with near-war situations should not be confused with the more general and enduring problem of maintaining full employment without inflation. Since early 1951, despite the pressure of the defense program, we have achieved a reasonably stable price level while enjoying full employment, and the prospect is that we will continue to do so this year.

This does not mean that we have thus far learned fully how to reconcile enduring full employment with adequate price stability. Much more work needs to be done in this direction, in the field of fiscal policy, monetary and credit policy, and other public policies which are not limited to use in emergency periods.

Even more important, we must learn more about the value of individual and group self-restraints, about the general economy and its interrelationships, and about those private price and wage policies which may contribute most to a stable and growing economy.

But we should guard against the dangerous solution of trying to avoid the problem of preventing inflation by abandoning the pursuit of full employment. Stable prices do not outweigh the disadvantages of a sluggish or static economy; and downward-spiraling prices are certainly no blessing in a declining economy.

While striving vigorously to avoid inflationary movements we must realize that our primary purpose is full production and employment and the fair distribution of this abundance among all people in all groups. Price policy, like all other economic policy, should be constantly tested against these objectives; it should not be allowed to obscure them.

These comments apply to monetary policy. That policy can contribute to economic stability. For example, during the inflationary period, as part of a comprehensive program to combat inflation, I made recommendations to the Congress, which were not accepted, to restrain inflationary bank credit through changes in reserve requirements.

More recently, some changes in monetary policy have occurred, affecting bank credit, the bond market, and interest rates. This is one weapon in the anti-inflation armory, but price stability since early 1951 has been the product of many economic forces and government programs in the field of taxation, credit restraints, and material and price-wage controls, and has resulted largely from increased production.

Monetary policy is a tool which must be used with great wisdom and skill. It is the function of monetary policy to control the expansion of credit, so that the total money supply will be commensurate with the needs of the economy, avoiding on the one hand contractions in the money supply which would interfere with production, employment, and investment. A money supply which is in balance with the level of economic activity, adequate credit at reasonable rates of interest, and, above all, the distribution of the money supply on a fair and workable basis among individuals and groups have been essential to our growing prosperity.

Just as a money supply which is redundant can have unfortunate inflationary consequences, so an inadequate supply of money, or of credit, can push backward the business man who must borrow to operate, the farmer who traditionally depends upon credit to produce and market his crops, the home owner who wants a decent house that he can afford to live in, and the worker who is not willing to accept lower production and more unemployment in exchange for lower prices.

We must and can find ways to price stability which do not threaten to bring on the very hardships they are intended to prevent. Excessively tight money, which means higher cost of capital, may reduce prices, but it does so by depressing productive efforts. The sound method to stabilize prices is not to reduce incomes, but to expand productive effort and the output of goods.

Big business, big labor, and big farm organizations are permanent parts of the American economy. Few of us would change this if we could, for much of the economy's dynamism and productiveness depends upon this very circumstance. Nonetheless, thoughtful and continuing efforts are required to keep an economy of large groups from damaging conflicts of interest.

There is the problem, first, of maintaining fair and peaceful bargaining among the powerfully organized private groups. The government can help in this by protecting the development and encouraging the maintenance of balanced bargaining power.

Beyond this, however, there is the problem of reconciling the interest of particular groups with the general interest. The net bargains of the organized groups—as is sometimes the case, for example, with a "price-wage spiral"—do not always add up to the public interest. Nor do they protect the broad interest of weakly organized consumers.

Government intervention into such situations should proceed cautiously and be more inclined to wield the instruments of persuasion than those of authority. Above all, the effort, in both public and private quarters, should be to set the particular problem in an economy-wide framework.

It is essential, for instance, that the best available thinking of farmers and farm experts be brought to bear on the farm policy problem. But this is not enough; the needs of consumers, of industry, of national security—to name but a few—must also be weighed carefully in the process of developing a farm program. This, indeed, is the theme of the Employment Act, and why utilization of its machinery is essential to the treatment of economic matters affecting the whole nation.

Finally, there is the fundamental problem of reconciling the effective operation of an economy of large groups with the maintenance of effective competition. For competition is the shield of the often inarticulate consumer; and by opening doors to new ideas, new enterprises, and new successes it is a prime source of economic progress.

The government has a long record of concern with this problem. That concern must not be allowed to flag; the cutting edge of competitive markets must not be allowed to dull. At the same time there is no need to stimulate those speculative excesses of competition which stampede markets into violent upward and downward fluctuations.

Moreover, our action in this sphere must not be the creature of stereotype. We must be quick to recognize and encourage new forms of competition, so long as they work to the advantage of the public.

Some people say that full employment is possible only during war, or only while meeting the shortages caused by war, or only while building defenses to fight another war if it should come. This idea is fallacious, although it may have some utility if it warns us to prepare for the new economic problems of a more peaceful world. The two depressions which we suffered after World War I came when the country had no substantial economic policies to prevent them and no commitment to a policy of full employment.

It is true that the economic recovery between 1933 and the outbreak of World War II in 1939, while very substantial, was not complete. This proves how difficult it is to recover completely from a great depression once it has been allowed to occur; it does not prove that prosperity cannot be sustained once it is achieved.

Moreover, the task between 1933 and 1939 was to achieve recovery and reform at the same time, which is a peculiarly difficult undertaking which we should never again be faced with in the same degree. The real test of the economic reforms then enacted came, not during the period when they were first put into effect, but in the period following World War II. It is against this later history that we must test the adequacy of these measures to avoid depression and maintain prosperity without war.

After World War II the level of defense spending was reduced by an annual rate of well over a hundred billion dollars, expressed in the price level of today. While there were important war-created backlogs, the support for the very high levels of economic activity which prevailed from 1946 to mid-1950 was increasingly found in the satisfaction of the peacetime needs of our industries and our people.

I have already cited the high significance of the quick rebound of the economy from the minor fluctuation of 1949, a rebound which was fully manifest before the new defense program was foreseeable.

By mid-1950 only a relatively small portion of our economic activity could be attributed to the shortages created during World War II, and out of our total annual output of about 310 billion dollars (measured in the prices of today) only about 20 billion dollars, or less than 7 per cent, was being devoted to national defense and related international purposes. This was prosperity without war.

Since our response to the Communist aggression in mid-1950 our prosperity has of course been accompanied and stimulated by high and rising defense spending. But it is erroneous to say that this spending has been the main prop for our economy, because taxes have been correspondingly increased so that the defense program thus far has been on a pay-as-we-go basis and consequently has not added the amount of inflationary stimulus which would otherwise have been the case.

In this respect the situation is very different from that during World War II, when only about half the cost of the war was being paid out of taxes. It should also be noted that defense spending draws resources away from production for civilian use; and in this sense the increase in civilian supplies since mid-1950 has not been because of defense spending but despite it.

We have not only been paying as we go for the defense program measured by taxes; we have also been paying for it as we go measured by the expansion of production.

Despite this vastly increased production, which has exceeded the expansion of the defense program, full employment has been maintained during recent months, when a decreasing portion of our total national output has gone to defense spending and an increasing portion has been supported by civilian demand despite very high taxation.

This trend is now continuing and, according to the accompanying appraisal by the Council of Economic Advisers, it is likely to continue throughout 1953. Here we have a strong indication, once again, that prosperity need not depend upon war.

The reductions in defense spending in the years ahead, no matter how estimated, will be only a fraction of the reductions which we took in our stride after World War II. Meanwhile, we must continue to improve further our economic knowledge and understanding and maintain and advance those policies which have stood so well the test of critical times.

If we do this—and only if we do this—nothing can be more certain in human affairs than that the American people will increasingly enjoy the blessings of prosperity, supported not by unfavorable world conditions but rather by the essential strength and soundness of our own economy. The past illustrates the wisdom of adhering to the principles which have just been outlined. The future will reward us well for so doing.

The potential for further growth and improvement in the American economy, even over the short span of the next ten years, is challenging—in production, in living standards, in correction of inequities, and in stable and more satisfying jobs.

In addition, the opportunity and necessity for economic development in other countries of the free world represent a vastly important new frontier. With all of this we need to sustain our national security lest opportunity be denied us altogether.

Ten years from now a labor force of 76 to 80 million, working more effectively with better tools but somewhat fewer hours per week, could produce annually about 475–500 billion dollars' worth of goods and services, measured in today's prices. This is about 40 per cent above the present level and represents an average increase of slightly over 3 per cent a year.

The consumer portion of total production could then come to about 340–350 billion dollars. This would be about $2,000 for every man, woman, and child in the country, or about 40 per cent more than each person received in 1952. Over the next ten years we should be able to raise the average income of all American families correspondingly.

With a gross national product of about 475–500 billion dollars, well over 40 billion dollars could be spent for new nonfarm plant and equipment; 15 billion or better for new housing; more than 15 billion on schools, highways, hospitals, resources development projects, and other public works. Investment in American agriculture could be substantially larger than the 1952 level of 5.5 billion dollars.

Growth in certain industries, such as plastics, man-made fibres, and electronics, undoubtedly will continue to far outrun average growth. Machinery and electrical lines will have to expand steadily, along with the basic services of transport and electric power. Better housing, more and better automobiles, and a whole range of new or improved fixtures for the home are well within reach over the next decade. A steady improvement in the American diet will take place.

We shall run into some difficulties. Certain raw materials, especially metals, may become scarcer and more costly. The base of natural resources will wear thinner. Consumption expenditures will have to expand persistently, to provide adequate markets for business.

But with intelligent and timely adjustment of private and public policies to serve a fully employed and active economy, we can during the next decade reach the goals set forth above.

The promise ahead is more than reaching certain levels of employment, production, and income. It also involves the further improved distribution of the benefits of economic growth and special care for those who are less fortunately situated.

Despite great progress in raising income levels and distributing these increases in a manner favorable to low and middle income groups, there are still many American families whose incomes are inadequate. In 1951 one quarter of all families had less than $2,000 of spendable money income; forty per cent had less than $3,000.

Some of these families have home-produced fuel and food which raise living standards. Some are aged couples or other families with substantial assets to draw on; some are young single persons whose needs are less. But the picture does not justify complacency. The median liquid asset holding, excluding currency, for the under-$2,000 income group is less than $10; and about one third have debts.

The problem of low-income families is no longer caused by general unemployment, or generally substandard wages, or very low prices for farm products. The problem centers in families with special disabilities; racial minority families, broken families, families with sickness, families where there is lack of sufficent training and education for the principal wage earner, and farm families on substandard farms.

Unskilled and service workers had an average family income of only $2,320 in 1951. We must press forward to reduce these disabilities and to care for them when they are unavoidable.

It is feasible within a decade to raise all the families whose incomes are now below $4,000 annually to that level (measured in present-day prices), plus providing all the new families with this much income, in a full-employment economy. We should set this as a target for a basic American standard of living for all within a decade.

In fact, this would require less than half the total gain in personal incomes that we can achieve, leaving more than half for raising still further the incomes of families already above this basic standard.

In the mid-1930's it was no exaggeration to speak of one third of a nation ill fed, ill clad, and ill housed. Since then the one third has been reduced to one fifth, or maybe less, on the old standards. But as our power to produce increases, our standards and goals rightly increase also. The job ahead of us remains large. About one third of our nonfarm dwelling units and a much higher percentage of our farm housing are substandard. Many families still suffer from malnutrition.

The amounts spent in recent years for schools and hospitals have been far less, as a percentage of total national production, than was spent in 1939. Living conditions in large sections of our cities are distressing, calling for vast slum clearance and redevelopment effort.

Despite much progress in social security since the real beginning of the program in 1935, important gaps remain. Farmers are not covered by old-age insurance. Some 5,000,000 wage and salary workers are still outside the unemployment insurance program. Welfare assistance is not adequate to meet the requirements of many disabled people, uninsured old people, and their dependents. About half of our families find difficulty in meeting the cost of essential medical care.

Standards of adequacy change with the times. What is enough in a 250-billion-dollar economy is not enough in a 350-billion-dollar economy, and will be still less than enough in a 400- or 500-billion-dollar economy.

For example, old-age insurance has not only been insufficiently adjusted for changes in the price level; it has not been brought into line with the fact that the economy of today and tomorrow can afford a higher standard of living among the old than the economy of yesterday. In our long-range programs we should provide for growth as the whole economy grows.

This will have economic as well as social benefits. For if the millions of our people who are beyond working age should be unable to join in the demand for more and better products, the total market would not be adequate to support our expanding productive power. What we do in these fields should not be regarded as measures necessary to save a weak economy from disaster. Instead, we should scale these efforts to what a strong and expanding economy can and should accomplish.

The international responsibilities of the United States are carried out in part through its political and moral influence, and in part through the use of its vast economic strength. The deployment of much of its economic force abroad, in the form of military and economic aid, may appear to be at the expense of lifting living standards at home.

If there be any conflict between these two purposes, it does not permit the choice of one course to the exclusion of the other. Should the United States reduce sharply or prematurely the military and economic aid which is doing so much to strengthen the free world, this country might be forced to abandon the domestic gains which it plans for the future.

For if communism should gain abroad, we would have to become an armed fortress at terrific cost. The prerequisite of a free, strong, and prosperous America is full participation in the effort to create strength and prosperity throughout the free world.

In short, the free world cannot be permanently peaceful until the free world makes further progress toward full and more productive employment—toward release from the burden of the underemployment of its potential resources. Prosperity, like peace, is indivisible, and in our pursuit of a full employment policy at home we must never lose sight of this supremely important truth.

Hence our concern with the economic development of other free countries. This is especially true of the economically less developed countries and areas of the free world, where the provision of capital equipment and managerial and labor skills is a prerequisite to speedup economic growth and improved living standards.

As the momentum of industrial and agricultural growth gathers in these less developed areas, incomes will increase, and they will buy and sell more in other markets. As the level of world trade increases, the benefits to us will involve increased supplies of many raw materials, including critically needed strategic metals.

We must import to live; and we must import more if we want

to export at high and rising levels. We must work with other free nations to remove trade restrictions and to make more effective the sound policy of reciprocal trade. We must not reduce aid so quickly as to undermine the improving foundations for trade.

America is now confronted with the challenge to make its fair contribution toward world peace and security. Happy will be the day when we can rise to the nobler challenge of participating more fully in the advancement of world prosperity. This may be our most significant contribution to human betterment in the second half of the twentieth century.

6. THE NATIONAL HEALTH

One of the foci of controversy in the Fair Deal was the President's plan for federal contribution to the national health. His first comprehensive statement of this plan occurred in a special message of November 19, 1945.

In my message to the Congress of September 6, 1945, there were enumerated in a proposed Economic Bill of Rights certain rights which ought to be assured to every American citizen. One of them was: "The right to adequate medical care and the opportunity to achieve and enjoy good health." Another was the "right to adequate protection from the economic fears of . . . sickness."

Millions of our citizens do not have a full measure of opportunity to achieve and enjoy good health. Millions do not now have protection or security against the economic effects of sickness. The time has arrived for action to help them attain that opportunity and that protection.

The people of the United States received a shock when the medical examinations conducted by the selective service system revealed the widespread physical and mental incapacity among the young people of our nation. We had had prior warnings from eminent medical authorities and from investigating committees. The statistics of the last war had shown the same condition. But the selective service system has brought it forcibly to our attention recently in terms which all of us can understand.

As of April 1, 1945, nearly 5,000,000 male registrants between the ages of 18 and 37 had been examined and classified as unfit for military service. The number of those rejected for military service was about thirty per cent of all those examined. The percentage of rejection was lower in the younger age groups and higher in the higher age groups, reaching as high as 49 per cent for registrants between the ages of 34 and 37.

In addition, after actual induction, about a million and a half men had to be discharged from the Army and Navy for physical or mental disability, exclusive of wounds; and an equal number had to be treated in the armed forces for diseases or defects which existed before induction.

Among the young women who applied for admission to the Women's Army Corps there was similar disability. Over one third of those examined were rejected for physical or mental reasons.

These men and women who were rejected for military service are not necessarily incapable of civilian work. It is plain, however, that they have illnesses and defects that handicap them, reduce their working capacity, or shorten their lives.

It is not so important to search the past in order to fix the blame for these conditions. It is more important to resolve now that no American child shall come to adult life with diseases or defects which can be prevented or corrected at an early age.

In the past the benefits of modern medical science have not been enjoyed by our citizens with any degree of equality. Nor are they today. Nor will they be in the future—unless government is bold enough to do something about it.

People with low or moderate incomes do not get the same medical attention as those with high incomes. The poor have more sickness, but they get less medical care. People who live in rural areas do not get the same amount or quality of medical attentions as those who live in our cities.

Our new economic bill of rights should mean health security for all, regardless of residence, station or race—everywhere in the United States.

We should resolve now that the health of this nation is a national concern; that financial barriers in the way of attaining health shall be removed; that the health of all its citizens deserves the help of all the nation.

There are five basic problems which we must attack vigorously if we would reach the health objectives of our economic bill of rights.

1. The first has to do with the number and distribution of doctors and hospitals. One of the most important requirements for adequate health service is professional personnel—doctors, dentists, public health and hospital administrators, nurses, and other experts.

The United States has been fortunate with respect to physicians. In proportion to population it has more than any large country in the world, and they are well trained for their calling. It is not enough, however, that we have them in sufficient numbers. They should be located where their services are needed. In this respect we are not so fortunate.

The distribution of physicians in the United States has been grossly uneven and unsatisfactory. Some communities have had enough or even too many; others have had too few. Year by year the number in our rural areas has been diminishing. Indeed, in 1940 there were thirty-one counties in the United States, each with more than a thousand inhabitants, in which there was not a single practicing physician. The situation with respect to dentists was even worse.

One important reason for this disparity is that in some communities there are no adequate facilities for the practice of medicine. Another reason, closely allied with the first, is that the earning capacity of the people in some communities makes it difficult if not impossible for doctors who practice there to make a living.

The demobilization of 60,000 doctors and of the tens of thousands of other professional personnel in the armed forces is now proceeding on a large scale. Unfortunately, unless we act rapidly we may expect to see them concentrate in the places with greater financial resources and avoid other places, making the inequalities even greater than before the war.

Demobilized doctors cannot be assigned. They must be attracted. In order to be attracted, they must be able to see ahead of them professional opportunities and economic assurances.

Inequalities in the distribution of medical personnel are matched by inequalities in hospitals and other health facilities. Moreover, there are just too few hospitals, clinics, and health centers to take proper care of the people of the United States.

About 1200 counties, 40 per cent of the total in the country, with some 15,000,000 people, have either no local hospital or none that meets even the minimum standards of national professional associations.

The deficiencies are especially severe in rural and semirural areas and in those cities where changes in population have placed great strains on community facilities.

I want to emphasize, however, that the basic problem in this field cannot be solved merely by building facilities. They have to be staffed; and the communities have to be able to pay for the services. Otherwise the new facilities will be little used.

2. The second basic problem is the need for development of public health services and maternal and child care. The Congress can be justifiably proud of its share in making recent accomplishments possible. Public health and maternal and child health programs already have made important contributions to national health. But large needs remain. Great areas of our country are still without these services. This is especially true among our rural areas; but it is true also in far too many urban communities.

Although local public health departments are now maintained by some 18,000 counties and other local units, many of these have only skeleton organizations, and approximately 40,000,000 citizens of the United States still live in communities lacking full-time local public health service. At the recent rate of progress in developing such service, it would take more than a hundred years to cover the whole nation.

If we agree that the national health must be improved, our cities, towns, and farming communities must be made healthful places in which to live through provision of safe water systems, sewage disposal plants, and sanitary facilities. Our streams and rivers must be safeguarded against pollution. In addition to building a sanitary environment for ourselves and for our children, we must provide those services which prevent disease and promote health.

Services for expectant mothers and for infants, care of crippled or otherwise physically handicapped children, and inoculation for the prevention of communicable diseases are accepted public health functions. So too are many kinds of personal services, such as the diagnosis and treatment of widespread infections like tuberculosis and venereal disease. A large part of the population today lacks many or all of these services.

3. The third basic problem concerns medical research and professional education.

Research, well directed and continuously supported, can do much to develop ways to reduce those diseases of body and mind which now cause most sickness, disability, and premature death—diseases of the heart, kidneys, and arteries, rheumatism, cancer, diseases of childbirth, infancy, and childhood, respiratory diseases, and tuberculosis.

Cancer is among the leading causes of death. It is responsible for over 160,000 recorded deaths a year, and should receive special attention. Though we already have the National Cancer Institute of the Public Health Service, we need still more co-ordinated research on the cause, prevention, and cure of this disease. We need more financial support for research and to establish special clinics and hospitals for diagnosis and treatment of the disease, especially in its early stages. We need to train more physicians for the highly specialized services so essential for effective control of cancer.

There is also special need for research on mental diseases and abnormalities. We have done pitifully little about mental illnesses. Accurate statistics are lacking, but there is no doubt that there are at least two million persons in the United States who are mentally ill, and that as many as ten million will probably need hospitalization for mental illness for some period in the course of their lifetime.

A great many of these persons would be helped by proper care. Mental cases occupy more than one half of the hospital beds, at a cost of about $500,000,000 per year—practically all of it coming out of taxpayers' money. Each year there are 125,000 new mental cases admitted to institutions.

We need more mental disease hospitals, more outpatient clinics. We need more services for early diagnosis, and especially we need much more research to learn how to prevent mental breakdown. Also, we must have many more trained and qualified doctors in this field.

4. The fourth problem has to do with the high cost of individual medical care. The principal reason why people do not receive the care they need is that they cannot afford to pay for it on an individual basis at the time they need it. This is true not only for needy persons. It is also true for a large proportion of normally self-supporting persons.

In the aggregate all health services—from public health agencies, physicians, hospitals, dentists, nurses, and laboratories—absorb only about four per cent of the national income. We can afford to spend more for health.

But four per cent is only an average. It is cold comfort in individual cases. Individual families pay their individual costs, and not average costs. They may be hit by sickness that calls for many times the average cost—in extreme cases for more than their annual income. When this happens they may come face to face with economic disaster. Many families, fearful of expense, delay calling the doctor long beyond the time when medical care would do the most good.

For some persons with very low income or no income at all we now use taxpayers' money in the form of free services, free clinics, and public hospitals. Tax-supported free medical care for needy persons, however, is insufficient in most of our cities and in nearly all of our rural areas. This deficiency cannot be met by private charity or the kindness of individual physicians.

Each of us knows doctors who work through endless days and nights, never expecting to be paid for their services because many of their patients are unable to pay. Often the physician spends not only his time and effort, but even part of the fees he has collected from patients able to pay, in order to buy medical supplies for those who cannot afford them. I am sure that there are thousands of such physicians throughout our country. They cannot, and should not, be expected to carry so heavy a load.

5. The fifth problem has to do with loss of earnings when sickness strikes. Sickness not only brings doctor bills; it also cuts off income.

On an average day there are about 7,000,000 persons so disabled by sickness or injury that they cannot go about their usual tasks. Of these, about 3,250,000 are persons who, if they were not disabled, would be working or seeking employment. More than one half of these disabled workers have already been disabled for six months; many of them will continue to be disabled for years, and some for the remainder of their lives.

Every year four or five hundred million working days are lost from productive employment because of illness and accident among those working or looking for work—about forty times the number of days lost because of strikes on the average during the ten years before the war. About nine tenths of this enormous loss is due to illness and accident that is not directly connected with employment and is therefore not covered by workmen's compensation laws.

To meet these problems I recommend that the Congress adopt a comprehensive and modern health program for the nation, consisting of five major parts, each of which contributes to all the others.

First: Construction of Hospitals and Related Facilities

The federal government should provide financial and other assistance for the construction of needed hospitals, health centers, and other medical, health, and rehabilitation facilities. With the help of federal funds it should be possible to meet deficiencies in hospital and health facilities so that modern services for both prevention and cure can be accessible to all the people. Federal financial aid should be available not only to build new facilities where needed, but also to enlarge or modernize those we now have.

In carrying out this program there should be a clear division of responsibilities between the states and the federal government. The states, localities, and the federal government should share in the financial responsibilities. The federal government should not construct or operate these hospitals. It should, however, lay down minimum national standards for construction and operation and should make sure that federal funds are allocated to those areas and projects where federal aid is needed most. In approving state plans and individual projects and in fixing the national standards the federal agency should have the help of a strictly advisory body that includes both public and professional members.

Adequate emphasis should be given to facilities that are particularly useful for prevention of diseases, mental as well as physical, and to the co-ordination of various kinds of facilities.

The general policy of federal-state partnership which has done so much to provide the magnificent highways of the United States can be adapted to the construction of hospitals in the communities which need them.

Second: Expansion of Public Health, Maternal, and Child Health Services

Our programs for public health and related services should be enlarged and strengthened. The present federal-state co-operative health programs deal with general public health work, tuberculosis and venereal disease control, maternal and child health services, and services for crippled children.

These programs were especially developed in the ten years before the war and have been extended in some areas during the war. They have already made important contributions to national health, but they have not yet reached a large proportion of our rural areas, and in many cities they are only partially developed.

No area in the nation should continue to be without the services of a full-time health officer and other essential personnel. No area should be without essential public health services or sanitation facilities. No area should be without community health services such as maternal and child health care.

Hospitals, clinics, and health centers must be built to meet the needs of the total population and must make adequate provision for the safe birth of every baby and for the health protection of infants and children.

The federal government should co-operate by more generous grants to the states than are provided under present laws for public health services and for maternal and child health care.

The program should continue to be partly financed by the states themselves and should be administered by the states. Federal grants should be in proportion to state and local expenditures and should also vary in accordance with the financial ability of the respective states.

The health of American children, like their education, should be recognized as a definite public responsibility.

In the conquest of many diseases prevention is even more important than cure. A well rounded national health program should, therefore, include systematic and widespread health and physical education and examinations, beginning with the youngest children and extending into community organizations. Medical and dental examinations of school children are now inadequate. A preventive health program, to be successful, must discover defects as early as possible. We should, therefore, see to it that our health programs are pushed most vigorously with the youngest section of the population.

Third: Medical Education and Research

The federal government should undertake a broad program to strengthen professional education in medical and related fields and to encourage and support medical research.

Professional education should be strengthened where necessary through federal grants-in-aid to public and to nonprofit private institutions. Medical research also should be encouraged and supported in the federal agencies and by grants-in-aid to public and nonprofit private agencies.

In my message to the Congress of September 6, 1945, I made various recommendations for a general federal research program. Medical research, dealing with the broad fields of physical and mental illnesses, should be made effective in part through that general program and in part through specific provisions within the scope of a national health program.

Fourth: Prepayment of Medical Costs

Everyone should have ready access to all necessary medical, hospital, and related services.

I recommend solving the basic problem by distributing the costs through expansion of our existing compulsory social insurance system. This is not socialized medicine.

Everyone who carries fire insurance knows how the law of averages is made to work so as to spread the risk and to benefit the insured who actually suffers the loss. If, instead of the costs of sickness being paid only by those who get sick, all the people, sick and well, were required to pay premiums into an insurance fund, the pool of funds thus created would enable all who do fall sick to be adequately served without overburdening anyone. That is the principle upon which all forms of insurance are based.

During the past fifteen years hospital insurance plans have taught many Americans this magic of averages. Voluntary health insurance plans have been expanding during recent years; but their rate of growth does not justify the belief that they will meet more than a fraction of our people's needs. Only about three per cent or four per cent of our population now have insurance providing comprehensive medical care.

A system of required prepayment would not only spread the costs of medical care, it would also prevent much serious disease. Since medical bills would be paid by the insurance fund, doctors would more often be consulted when the first signs of disease occur instead of when the disease has become serious. Modern hospital, specialist, and laboratory services, as needed, would also become available to all and would improve the quality and adequacy of care. Prepayment of medical care would go a long way toward furnishing insurance against disease itself, as well as against medical bills.

Such a system of prepayment should cover medical, hospital, nursing, and laboratory services. It should also cover dental care as fully and for as many of the population as the available professional personnel and the financial resources of the system permit.

The ability of our people to pay for adequate medical care will be increased if, while they are well, they pay regularly into a common health fund, instead of paying sporadically and unevenly when they are sick. This health fund should be built up nationally, in order to establish the broadest and most stable basis for spreading the costs of illness and to assure adequate financial support for doctors and hospitals everywhere. If we were to rely on state-by-state action only, many years would elapse before we had any general coverage. Meanwhile health service would continue to be grossly uneven, and disease would continue to cross state boundary lines.

Medical services are personal. Therefore the nation-wide system must be highly decentralized in administration. The local administrative unit must be the keystone of the system, so as to provide for local services and adaptation to local needs and conditions. Locally as well as nationally, policy and administration should be guided by advisory committees in which the public and the medical professions are represented.

Subject to national standards, methods and rates of paying doctors and hospitals should be adjusted locally. All such rates for doctors should be adequate and should be appropriately adjusted upward for those who are qualified specialists.

People should remain free to choose their own physicians and hospitals. The removal of financial barriers between patient and doctor would enlarge the present freedom of choice. The legal requirement on the population to contribute involves no compulsion over the doctor's freedom to decide what services his patient needs. People will remain free to obtain and pay for medical service outside of the health insurance system if they desire, even though they are members of the system; just as they are free to send their children to private instead of to public schools, although they must pay taxes for public schools.

Freedom of Physicians

Likewise physicians should remain free to accept or reject patients. They must be allowed to decide for themselves whether they wish to participate in the health insurance system full time, part time, or not at all. A physician may have some patients who are in the system and some who are not. Physicians must be permitted to be represented through organizations of their own choosing and to decide whether to carry on in individual practice or to join with other doctors in group practice in hospitals or in clinics.

Our voluntary hospitals and our city, county, and state general hospitals, in the same way, must be free to participate in the system to whatever extent they wish. In any case they must continue to retain their administrative independence.

Voluntary organizations which provide health services that meet reasonable standards of quality should be entitled to furnish services under the insurance system and to be reimbursed for them. Voluntary co-operative organizations concerned with paying doctors, hospitals, or others for health services, but not providing services directly, should be entitled to participate if they can contribute to the efficiency and economy of the system.

None of this is really new. The American people are the most insurance-minded people in the world. They will not be frightened off from health insurance because some people have misnamed it "socialized medicine."

I repeat, what I am recommending is not socialized medicine. Socialized medicine means that all doctors work as employees of government. The American people want no such system. No such system is here proposed.

Under the plan I suggest our people would continue to get medical and hospital services just as they do now—on the basis of their own voluntary decisions and choices. Our doctors and hospitals would continue to deal with diseases with the same professional freedom as now. There would, however, be this all-important difference: whether or not patients get the services they need would not depend on how much they can afford to pay at the time.

I am in favor of the broadest possible coverage for this insurance system. I believe that all persons who work for a living and their dependents should be covered under such an insurance plan. This would include wage and salary earners, those in business for themselves, professional persons, farmers, agricultural labor, domestic employees, government employees and employees of nonprofit institutions, and their families.

Provision for Needy Persons

In addition, needy persons and other groups should be covered through appropriate premiums paid for them by public agencies. Increased federal funds should also be made available by the Congress under the public assistance programs to reimburse the states for part of such premiums, as well as for direct expenditures made by the states in paying for medical services provided by doctors, hospitals, and other agencies to needy persons.

Premiums for present social insurance benefits are calculated on the first $3,000 of earnings in a year. It might be well to have all such premiums, including those for health, calculated on a somewhat higher amount, such as $3,600.

A broad program of prepayment for medical care would need total amounts approximately equal to four per cent of such earnings. The people of the United States have been spending, on the average, nearly this percentage of their incomes for sickness care. How much of the total fund should come from the insurance premiums and how much from general revenues is a matter for the Congress to decide.

The plan which I have suggested would be sufficient to pay most doctors more than the best they have received in peacetime years. The payments of the doctors' bills would be guaranteed, and the doctors would be spared the annoyance and uncertainty of collecting fees from individual patients. The same assurance would apply to hospitals, dentists, and nurses for the services they render.

Federal aid in the construction of hospitals will be futile unless there is current purchasing power so that people can use these hospitals. Doctors cannot be drawn to sections which need them without some assurance that they can make a living. Only a nation-wide spreading of sickness costs can supply such sections with sure and sufficient purchasing power to maintain enough physicians and hospitals. We are a rich nation and can afford many things. But ill health which can be prevented or cured is one thing we cannot afford.

Fifth: Protection Against Loss of Wages from Sickness and Disability

What I have discussed heretofore has been a program for improving and spreading the health services and facilities of the nation and providing an efficient and less burdensome system of paying for them. But no matter what we do, sickness will of course come to many. Sickness brings with it loss of wages.

Therefore, as a fifth element of a comprehensive health program, the workers of the nation and their families should be protected against loss of earnings because of illness. A comprehensive health program must include the payment of benefits to replace at least part of the earnings that are lost during the period of sickness and long-term disability. This protection can be readily and conveniently provided through expansion of our present social insurance system, with appropriate adjustment of premiums.

Insurance for Wage Losses

Insurance against loss of wages from sickness and disability deals with cash benefits, rather than with services. It has to be co-ordinated with the other cash benefits under existing social insurance systems. Such co-ordination should be effected when other social security measures are re-examined. I shall bring this subject again to the attention of the Congress in a separate message on social security.

I strongly urge that the Congress give careful consideration to this program of health legislation now.

Many millions of our veterans, accustomed in the armed forces to the best medical and hospital care, will no longer be eligible for such care as a matter of right except for their service-connected disabilities. They deserve continued adequate and comprehensive health service. And their dependents deserve it, too.

By preventing illness, by assuring access to needed community and personal health services, by promoting medical research, and by protecting our people against the loss caused by sickness, we shall strengthen our national health, our national defense, and our economic productivity. We shall increase the professional and economic opportunities of our physicians, dentists, and nurses. We shall increase the effectiveness of our hospitals and public health agencies. We shall bring new security to our people.

We need to do this especially at this time because of the return to civilian life of many doctors, dentists, and nurses, particularly young men and women.

Appreciation of modern achievements in medicine and public health has created widespread demand that they be fully applied and universally available. By meeting that demand we shall strengthen the nation to meet future economic and social problems; and we shall make a most important contribution toward freedom from want in our land.

§ *Bills to implement this message were immediately introduced by Senator Wagner, Democrat of New York, and Congressman John D. Dingell, Democrat of Michigan. The Journal of the American Medical Association said in an editorial that portions of the Truman plan deserved approval, but that the provisions for compulsory sickness insurance were to be condemned as subjecting physicians to "politically controlled medicine"; and the proposal for federal aid to medical education and research was attacked as putting the government in control of medical education.*

Although Mr. Truman's proposals were repeatedly defeated in Congress, he frequently reasserted them throughout his term of office. Each time the main body of his plan remained the same; relatively minor variations were occasionally added. He never submitted any over-all estimate of the cost. The lack of such an estimate he did not consider especially important, for four per cent of the country's income was going annually for health care, whereas under his plan the three-per-cent payroll tax would finance the country's health needs and, he argued, would pay for more and better care.

The compulsory payroll tax continued to be the main bone of contention and stimulus of rival programs. Widely supported alternatives that came to the fore avoided the controversial payroll tax and called for federal aid to the states instead of national insurance. Under such plans the states would provide direct financial assistance to those unable to pay for medical and hospital expenses or would help them meet the cost of private insurance premiums. This approach was reflected in legislation sponsored by Senator Taft and Senator Lister Hill of Alabama as leaders of a bipartisan coalition.

The final stage in President Truman's campaign was his appointment on December 29, 1951, of the Commission on the Health Needs of the Nation to determine the country's "total health re-

quirements" and report on them within a year. The apparent strategy in setting up this commission was not to present a health program for Congressional action before Mr. Truman's term expired, but to provide a comprehensive statement of one that would be available to the next administration.

The Commission's report urged that complete health services be provided as a "basic human right" through private prepayment plans and federal grants to the states. The compulsory features of the Fair Deal's payroll tax were not a part of the Commission's plan, and there would be no direct federal financing. Federal money would filter down through the states.

President Truman sent the report on to Congress with recommendations that it be translated into legislation—a radical relinquishment of his long-standing insistence on compulsory insurance.

7. UNIVERSAL MILITARY TRAINING

Throughout his term of office Mr. Truman urged, as Franklin Roosevelt had done, the adoption of a program of universal military training. The first major effort of the Truman administration in this direction came on May 16, 1945, when Secretary of War Stimson, General Marshall, and Admiral King recommended in Congressional committee hearings that universal training be established as a foundation of United States military security. But with the advent of V-J day the United States armed forces were being rapidly demobilized under pressure from a public eager to believe that future security could be maintained by United States possession of the atomic bomb and by the efforts of the new United Nations Organization.

Mr. Truman incorporated his ideas on the subject in an urgent message sent to Congress on October 22, 1945.

For years to come the success of our efforts for a just and lasting peace will depend upon the strength of those who are determined to maintain the peace. We intend to use all our moral influence and all our physical strength to work for that kind of peace. We can insure such a peace only so long as we remain strong. We must face the fact that peace must be built upon power, as well as upon good will and good deeds.

Our determination to remain powerful denotes no lack of faith in the United Nations Organization. On the contrary, with all the might we have we intend to back up our obligations and commitments under the United Nations Charter. Indeed, the sincerity of our intention to support the organization will be judged partly by our willingness to maintain the power with which to assist other peace-loving nations to enforce its authority. It is only by strength that we can impress the fact upon possible future aggressors that we will tolerate no threat to peace or liberty.

To maintain that power we must act now. The latent strength of our untrained citizenry is no longer sufficient protection. If attack should come again, there would be no time under conditions of modern war to develop that latent strength into the necessary fighting force.

Never again can we count on the luxury of time with which to arm ourselves. In any future war the heart of the United States would be the enemy's first target. Our geographical security is now gone—gone with the advent of the robot bomb, the rocket, aircraft carriers, and modern air-borne armies.

The surest guarantee that no nation will dare again to attack us is to remain strong in the only kind of strength an aggressor can understand—military power.

To preserve the strength of our nation the alternative before us is clear. We can maintain a large standing army, navy, and air force. Or we can rely on a comparatively small regular army, navy, and air force supported by well trained citizens who in time of emergency could be quickly mobilized.

I recommend the second course—that we depend for our security upon comparatively small professional armed forces, reinforced by a well trained and effectively organized citizen reserve. The backbone of our military force should be the trained citizen who is first and foremost a civilian, and who becomes a soldier or a sailor only in time of danger, and only when the Congress considers it necessary. This plan is obviously the more practical and economical. It conforms more closely to long-standing American tradition.

In such a system, however, the citizen reserve must be a trained reserve. We can meet the need for a trained reserve in only one way—by universal training.

Modern war is fought by experts, from the atomic scientist in his laboratory to the fighting man with his intricate modern weapons.

The day of the Minute Man who sprang to the flintlock hanging on his wall is over. Now it takes many months for men to become skilled in electronics, aeronautics, ballistics, meteorology, and all the other sciences of modern war. If another national emergency should come, there would be no time for this complicated training. Men must be trained in advance.

The sooner we can bring the maximum number of trained men into service, the sooner will be the victory and the less tragic the cost. Universal training is the only means by which we can be prepared right at the start to throw our great energy and our tremendous force into the battle. After two terrible experiences in one generation, we have learned that this is the way—the only way— to save human lives and material resources.

The importance of universal training has already been recognized by the Congress, and the Congress has wisely taken the initiative in this program.

The select Committee of the House of Representatives on Post-War Military Policy has organized hearings and has heard extended testimony from representatives of churches and schools, labor unions, veterans' organizations, the armed services, and many other groups. After careful consideration the Committee has approved the broad policy of universal military training for the critical years ahead. I concur in that conclusion and strongly urge the Congress to adopt it.

In the present hour of triumph we must not forget our anguish during the days of Bataan. We must not forget the anxiety of the days of Guadalcanal. In our desire to leave the tragedy of war behind us we must not make the same mistake that we made after the First World War when we quickly sank back into helplessness.

I recommend that we create a postwar military organization which will contain the following basic elements:

First: A comparatively small regular Army, Navy, and Marine Corps;

Second: A greatly strengthened National Guard and organized reserve for the Army, Navy, and Marine Corps;

Third: A general reserve composed of all the male citizens of the United States who have received training.

The general reserve would be available for rapid mobilization in time of emergency, but it would have no obligation to serve, either in this country or abroad, unless and until called to the service by an act of the Congress.

In order to provide this general reserve I recommend to the Congress the adoption of a plan for universal military training.

Universal military training is not conscription. The opponents of training have labeled it conscription and, by so doing, have confused the minds of some of our citizens. "Conscription" is compulsory service in the Army or Navy in time of peace or war. Trainees under this proposed legislation, however, would not be enrolled in any of the armed services. They would be civilians in training. They would be no closer to membership in the armed forces than if they had no training. Special rules and regulations would have to be adopted for their organization, discipline, and welfare.

Universal training is not intended to take the place of the present selective service system. The selective service system is now being used to furnish replacements in the armed forces for veterans of this war who are being discharged.

Only the Congress could ever draw trainees under a universal training program into the Army and Navy. And if that time ever came, these trainees could be inducted only by selective process, as they were inducted for World War I and World War II. The great difference between having universal training and no training, however, is that in time of emergency those who would be selected for actual military service would already have been basically trained.

That difference may be as much as a year's time. That difference may be the margin between the survival and the destruction of this great nation.

The emphasis in the training of our young men will not be on mere drilling. It will be on the use of all the instruments and weapons of modern warfare. The training will offer every qualified young man a chance to perfect himself for the service of his country in some military specialty.

Under the plan which I propose, provisions should be made within the armed services to help trainees improve their educational status. The year of universal training should provide ample opportunity for self-development. Some part of the training could be used to develop skills which would be useful in future civilian life, just as such skills have been developed during the present war.

The period of training could well be used to raise the physical standards of the nation's manpower, to lower its illiteracy rate, and to develop in our young men ideals of responsible American citizenship.

Medical examinations of the young trainees would do much toward removing some of the minor disabilities which caused the rejection of so many men during this war by the selective service system.

The moral and spiritual welfare of our young people should be a consideration of prime importance, and, of course, facilities for worship in every faith would be available.

But the basic reason for universal training is a very simple one— to guarantee the safety and freedom of the United States against any potential aggressor. The other benefits are all by-products—useful indeed, but still by-products. The fundamental need is, and always will be, the national security of the United States and the safety of our homes and our loved ones.

Since training alone is involved, and not actual military service, no exemptions should be allowed for occupation, dependency, or for any other reason except total physical disqualification.

All men should be included in the training, whether physically qualified for actual combat service or not. There should be a place into which every young American can fit in the service of our country. Some would be trained for combat, others would be trained for whatever war service they are physically and mentally qualified to perform.

I recommend that the training should be for one year. Each young man should enter training either at the age of eighteen or upon his graduation from high school—whichever is later—but in any event before his twentieth birthday. A trainee who completes his high school education in his seventeenth year should be eligible, with parental consent, to enter the course of training.

After the first few months of training, selected trainees who are not physically qualified for military service could be trained in certain skills so that, if war came, they could take their places in shipyards, munitions factories, and similar industrial plants.

Upon completion of the full year's training the trainee would become a member of the general reserve for a period of six years. After that he should be placed in a secondary reserve status.

Present personnel in the Army and Navy reserves would, of course, be retained, and the new trainees would provide the source from which the reserves of the future would draw their personnel.

Commissions would be granted to qualified men who complete the course of training and who then take additional instruction in officer candidate schools, in the Reserve Officers Training Corps or Naval Reserve Officers Training Corps. Outstanding trainees could be selected after an adequate period of training and sent to college with government financial aid, on condition that they return, after graduation and with R.O.T.C. training, as junior officers for a year or more of additional training or service.

Such a system as I have outlined would provide a democratic and efficient military force. It would be a constant bulwark in support of our ideals of government. It would constitute the backbone of defense against any possible future act of aggression.

It has been suggested in some quarters that there should be no universal training until the shape of the peace is better known and until the military needs of this country can be estimated and our commitments under the United Nations Organization can be determined. But it is impossible today to foresee the future. It is difficult at any time to know exactly what our responsibilities will require in the way of force. We do know that, if we are to have available a force when needed, the time to begin preparing is now.

The need exists today—and must be met today.

If at some later time conditions change, then the program can be re-examined and revalued. At the present time we have the necessary organization, the required camp installations, and the essential equipment and the training grounds immediately available for use in a training program. Once we disband and scatter this set-up, it will be much harder and more expensive to re-establish the necessary facilities.

The argument has been made that compulsory training violates traditional American concepts of liberty and democracy, and even that it would endanger our system of government by creating a powerful military caste. The purpose of the program, however, is just the contrary. And it will have just the contrary result. The objective is not to train professional soldiers. It is to train citizens, so that, if and when the Congress should declare it necessary for them to become soldiers, they could do so more quickly and more efficiently. A large trained reserve of peace-loving citizens would never go to war or encourage war if it could be avoided.

It is no valid argument against adopting universal training at this time that there are now millions of trained veterans of this war. No fair-minded person would suggest that we continue to rely indefinitely upon these veterans. They have earned the right to return promptly to civilian life. We must now look to our younger men to constitute the new reserve military strength of our nation.

There are some who urge that the development of rocket weapons and atomic bombs and other new weapons indicates that scientific research, rather than universal training, is the best way to safeguard our security. It is true that, if we are to keep ahead in military preparedness, continuous research in science and new weapons is essential. That is why in my message to the Congress of September 6 I urged that there be created a national research agency one of whose major functions would be to carry on fundamental military research.

Need of Research

It is true that there must be continuous exploration into new fields of science in order to keep ahead in the discovery and manufacture of new weapons. No matter what the cost, we cannot afford to fall behind in any of the new techniques of war or in the development of new weapons of destruction.

Until we are sure that our peace machinery is functioning adequately, we must relentlessly preserve our superiority on land and sea and in the air. Until that time we must also make sure that by planning and by actual production we have on hand at all times sufficient weapons of the latest nature and design with which to repel any sudden attack and with which to launch an effective counterattack.

That is the only way we can be sure—until we are sure that there is another way.

But research, new materials, and new weapons will never, by themselves, be sufficient to withstand a powerful enemy. We must have men trained to use these weapons. As our armed forces become more and more mechanized and as they use more and more complicated weapons, we must have an ever-increasing number of trained men. Technological advances do not eliminate the need for men. They increase the need.

General of the Army George C. Marshall, in his recent report to the Secretary of War, has made this very clear. I quote from his report:

"The number of men that were involved in the delivery of the atomic bomb on Hiroshima was tremendous. First we had to have the base in the Marianas from which the plane took off. This first required preliminary operations across the vast Pacific, thousands of ships, millions of tons of supply, the heroic efforts of hundreds of thousands of men. Further, we needed the B-29s and their fighter escort which gave us control of the air over Japan. This was the result of thousands of hours of training and preparation in the United States and the energies of hundreds of thousands of men.

"The effect of technology on the military structure is identical to its effect on national economy. Just as the automobile replaced the horse and made work for millions of Americans, the atomic explosives will require the services of millions of men if we are compelled to employ them in fighting our battles.

"This war has made it clear that the security of the nation, when challenged by an armed enemy, requires the services of virtually all able-bodied male citizens within the effective age group."

Even the atomic bomb would have been useless to us unless we had developed a strong Army, Navy, and Air Force with which to beat off the attacks of our foe and then fight our way to points within striking distance of the heart of the enemy.

Assume that on December 7, 1941, the United States had had a supply of atomic bombs in New Mexico or Tennessee. What could we have done with them?

Assume that the United States and Japan both had had a supply of bombs on December 7, 1941. Which would have survived?

Suppose that both England and Germany had had the atomic bomb in September of 1940 during the "blitz" over England. Which country would have been destroyed?

The answer is clear that the atomic bomb is of little value without an adequate army, air, and naval force. For that kind of force is necessary to protect our shores, to overcome any attack and to enable us to move forward and direct the bomb against the enemy's own territory. Every new weapon will eventually bring some counter-defense against it. Our ability to use either a new weapon or a counterweapon will ultimately depend upon a strong Army, Navy, and Air Force, with all the millions of men needed to supply them, all quickly mobilized and adequately equipped.

Any system which is intended to guarantee our national defense will, of course, cause some inconvenience—and perhaps even some hardship—to our people. But we must balance that against the danger which we face unless we are realistic and hard-hearted enough to be prepared. Today universal training is the only adequate answer we have to our problem in this troubled world.

There will be better answers, we hope, in the days to come. The United States will always strive for those better answers—for the kind of tried and tested world co-operation which will make for peace and harmony among all nations. It will continue to strive to reach that period quickly. But that time has not yet arrived.

Even from those who are loudest in their opposition to universal training, there has come no other suggestion to furnish the protection and security which we must have—nothing but pious hope and dangerous wishful thinking.

I urge that the Congress pass this legislation promptly, while the danger is still fresh in our minds; while we still remember how close we came to destruction four years ago; while we can vividly recall the horrors of invasion which our allies suffered; and while we can still see all the ravages and ruin of war.

Let us not by a short-sighted neglect of our national security betray those who come after us.

It is our solemn duty in this hour of victory to make sure that in the years to come no possible aggressor or group of aggressors can endanger the national security of the United States of America.

§ *Universal military training was getting nowhere in Congress, and on December 19, 1946, Mr. Truman set up a nine-member commission drawn from the clergy, education, industry, and the law to study and make recommendations for a system of universal training. In May 1947 the commission submitted its report, and in June the President renewed his appeal to Congress, but to no avail. Subsequent appeals met with the same result. This failure meant that until 1950, when the Korean hostilities stepped up selective service recruitment, the United States was conducting the cold war on the* basis of a ten-division army. The Russians were believed to be maintaining on an active footing one hundred and seventy-five combat divisions. But even the crisis of Korea did not bring Congress around to universal military training. In 1951 it contented itself with enunciating the principle and establishing a five-man commission charged with proposing a program to be enacted at a later date.

8. LABOR LEGISLATION

One of the most urgent labor problems that Mr. Truman had to cope with was the strike against the government. There were several such strikes in the railroad industry and in coal mining. All of them were complex; some were dramatic; all deeply involved the President. A signal instance is the railroad strike of May 1946. The dispute involved a request by twenty railroad unions for wage increases averaging $2.50 a day and for forty-five changes in the work rules. Negotiations under the Railway Labor Act failed to prevent Alvanley Johnston, head of the Brotherhood of Locomotive Engineers, and A. F. Whitney, head of the Brotherhood of Railway Trainmen, from ordering a strike to take place on May 18. On May 17 the President seized the railroads. A scant few minutes before the strike deadline he persuaded Johnston and Whitney by telephone to accept a five-day truce on the strength of his professed belief that further progress could be made in negotiations with management. Intensive negotiations at the White House produced a compromise formula—Mr. Truman's—which the eighteen unions accepted, but which Whitney and Johnston rejected. The five-day truce ran out, and the gravest transportation strike in American history began. Thousands of railroad workers left their posts, ignoring the request made by the President when he seized the lines.

After two Cabinet meetings devoted exclusively to the strike Mr. Truman decided to make a strong speech to the nation by radio —an appeal to the striking trainmen and engineers to return to their jobs, a disclosure of facts about the negotiations that he doubted the union leaders had passed along to their membership, and a declaration that he would call out the troops and do anything else within his power to break the strike. The speech was delivered on May 24, 1946.

My fellow countrymen: I come before the American people tonight at a time of great crisis. The crisis of Pearl Harbor was the result of the action by a foreign enemy. The crisis tonight is caused by a group of men within our own country who place their private interests above the welfare of the nation.

As Americans we have the right to look to the President for leadership in this grave emergency. I have accepted the responsibility as I have accepted it in other emergencies.

Every citizen of this country has the right to know what has brought about this crisis. It is my desire to report to you what has already taken place and the action I intend to take.

Negotiations between the unions and the railroad operators started in accordance with the Railway Labor Act. Twenty unions were involved. Eighteen of these unions agreed to arbitrate the wage question, and an award was made.

Alvanley Johnston, president of the Brotherhood of Locomotive Engineers, and A. F. Whitney, president of the Brotherhood of Railway Trainmen, refused to arbitrate the matter for their union and instead took a strike vote.

An emergency board heard the case of these two unions and recommended the same wage increase awarded to the other eighteen unions. Mr. Johnston and Mr. Whitney, however, rejected the emergency board's recommendation in its entirety.

I began conferring with Mr. Whitney and Mr. Johnston as far back as February 21, 1946, in order that every effort should be made to avert a rail strike. When it became evident that the parties themselves were unable to agree, I submitted a compromise proposition to all the parties involved.

Negotiations were made considerably more difficult by the attitude of Mr. Whitney and Mr. Johnston in refusing my request that they meet with the operators and the other eighteen unions in a joint conference in the office of the President of the United States. They agreed to meet with the operators, but not in the presence of the representatives of the other eighteen unions. Accordingly, three separate conferences had to be held in the White House.

The unions had been awarded an increase of 16 cents per hour and certain changes in rules by the arbitration and emergency boards. I recommended that they accept the 16-cent increase awarded by the board, plus 2½ cents in lieu of rule changes. These rule changes had been considered by the emergency board, which recommended that most of them be negotiated by the parties.

After consideration this compromise was accepted by the operators and by eighteen of the unions. These eighteen unions were co-operative. They placed the interests of their country first. The compromise was rejected by the locomotive engineers and the trainmen.

This offer of an increase of 18½ cents per hour was eminently fair. It would have resulted in actually increasing the take-home pay of the union members above the greatest take-home pay which they enjoyed during the war.

In addition, these two unions are among the highest paid unions in the country. It is also important that the suggested increase of 18½ cents was within the wage stabilization formula, and this formula must be maintained.

Instead of accepting this offer as did the eighteen unions and the operators, Mr. Johnston and Mr. Whitney chose to reject it and to call a strike of their unions.

I assume that these two men know the terrible havoc that their decision has caused and the even more extreme suffering that will result in the future.

It is inconceivable that the rank and file of these two unions realize the terrifying situation created by the action of these two men.

The effects of the rail tie-up were felt immediately by industry. Lack of fuel, raw materials, and shipping is bringing about shutdown of hundreds of factories.

Lack of transportation facilities will bring chaos to food distribution. Farmers cannot move food to markets. All of you will see your food supplies dwindle, your health and safety endangered, your streets darkened, your transportation facilities broken down.

The housing program is being given a severe setback by the interruption of shipment of materials. Utilities must begin conservation of fuel immediately. Returning veterans will not be able to get home. Millions of workers will be thrown out of their jobs. The added pressure toward inflation caused by the drop in production cannot be measured.

While the situation in our country is extremely acute, the condition in Europe is tragic. Most of our friends today in liberated Europe are receiving less than one third of the average American consumption of food. We have promised to help the starving nations of Asia and Europe, and we have been helping them. We have been exerting our utmost efforts, and it is necessary for us to increase our shipments. At this minute 100,000 tons of grain are being held up by the strike of these two unions. U.N.R.R.A. has twelve ships scheduled to leave from our ports with grain. These ships cannot sail because the strike of these two unions is keeping the food from reaching the ports. If these ships are held up any longer, it means that the bread supply of 45,000,000 people will be cut off within one week.

These people are living from hand to mouth. They depend upon weekly shipments from us to meet their minimum daily needs. This grain held up in this country by the strike of these few men means the difference between life and death to hundreds of thousands of persons. This is a stark, tragic truth. If the operation of our railroads is not resumed at once thousands of persons both here and abroad will starve.

During these past weeks I have told Mr. Johnston and Mr. Whitney of the tragedy that would result from a strike. They have refused to heed my warning.

I doubt whether the rank and file of their unions have been told these facts. I am telling them now so that each of them can face his conscience and consider the specter of starvation and death that will result from the course which Mr. Whitney and Mr. Johnston are following.

I do not speak tonight of the situation in the coal mines of the nation, where the men are now at work and negotiations for settlement are now taking place between the government and the union.

I am a friend of labor. You men of labor who are familiar with my record in the United States Senate know that I have been a consistent advocate of the rights of labor and of the improvement of labor's position.

I have opposed and will continue to oppose unfair restrictions upon the activities of labor organizations and upon the right of employees to organize and bargain collectively. This has been the basic philosophy of my political career: to advocate those measures that result in the greatest good for the greatest number of our people. I shall always be a friend of labor, but in any conflict that arises between one particular group, no matter who they may be, and the country as a whole, the welfare of the country must come first.

It is inconceivable that in our democracy any two men should be placed in a position where they can completely stifle our economy and ultimately destroy our country.

The government is challenged as seldom before in our history. It must meet the challenge or confess its impotence.

I would regret deeply if the acts of these two leaders of those unions should create such a wave of ill will and the desire for vengeance that there should result ill advised restrictive legislation that would cause labor to lose those gains which it has rightfully made during these years.

As President of the United States I am the representative of 140,000,000 people, and I cannot stand idly by while they are being caused to suffer by reason of the action of these two men.

This is no contest between labor and management. This is a contest between a small group of men and their government. The railroads are now being operated by your government, and the strike of these men is a strike against your government.

The fact is that the action of this small group of men has resulted in millions of other workers losing their wages. The factories of our country are far behind in filling their orders. Our workers have good jobs at high wages, but they cannot earn those wages because of the willful attitude of these few men.

I cannot believe that any right of any worker in our country needs such a strike for its protection. I believe that it constitutes a fundamental attack upon the rights of society and upon the welfare of our country.

It is time for plain speaking.

This strike with which we are confronted touches not only the welfare of a class but vitally concerns the well-being and the very life of all our people.

The railroads must resume operation!

In view of the extraordinary emergency which exists, as President of the United States I call upon the men who are now out on strike to return to their jobs and operate our railroads. To each man now on strike I say that the duty to your country goes beyond any desire for personal gain.

If sufficient workers to operate the trains have not returned by four P.M. tomorrow, as head of your government I have no alternative but to operate the trains by using every means within my power.

I shall call upon the Army to assist the Office of Defense Transportation in operating the trains, and I shall ask our armed forces to furnish protection to every man who heeds the call of his country in this hour of need.

This emergency is so acute and the issue is so vital that I have requested the Congress to be in session tomorrow at four P.M., and I shall appear before a joint session of the Congress to deliver a message on this subject.

§ *The message delivered to the joint session of May 25 was essentially a request for temporary emergency powers to break strikes against the federal government, including authority to draft strikers into the armed forces and to formulate a comprehensive long-range labor policy to reduce the number of strikes.*

I am sure that some of you may think that I should have taken this action earlier and that I should have made this appearance here before today. The reason that I did not do so was that I was determined to make every possible human effort to avoid this strike against the government and to make unnecessary the kind of legislation which I am about to request.

For months, publicly and privately, I have been supervising and directing negotiations between the railroad operators and the twenty different railroad unions. I have been doing the same with respect to the pending labor dispute in the coal mines.

Time and again I have seen the leaders of the unions and the representatives of the operators. Many hours have been spent by me personally and many days have been spent by my representatives in attempting to negotiate settlements of these disputes.

I assure you that it was not easy to be patient. But until the very last moment I made every effort to avert this crisis. In fact, my representatives were in conference with the two striking railroad unions up to two hours before I took my place at the microphone last night.

However, when the strike actually broke against the United States government, which was trying to run the railroads, the time for negotiation definitely had passed and the time for action had arrived. In that action, you, the Congress of the United States, and I, the President of the United States, must work together—and we must work fast.

The action which I have already taken and the action which I shall ask you to take are necessary for the preservation of our government. That action is also necessary to save the great and mighty masses of working men and women from the dangerous effects and the ill advised and misguided acts of some of their own leaders.

This particular crisis has been brought about by the obstinate arrogance of two men—Mr. Alvanley Johnston, president of the Brotherhood of Locomotive Engineers, and Mr. A. F. Whitney, president of the Brotherhood of Railway Trainmen. Eighteen other unions and all of the railroad companies of the nation are ready to run the railroads. And these two men have tried to stop them.

I can well appreciate the attitude of those members of the Congress and those citizens of the United States outside of the Congress who would seek to take vengeance for the unpatriotic acts of these two men. However, I am sure that none of us wishes to take any action which will injure labor.

The contribution of labor to the growth of this country in peace and its victory in war is at least as great as that of any other group in our population. Without well paid, well housed, and well nourished working men and women in this country it would stagnate and decay. I am here not only to urge speedy action to meet the immediate crisis, but also deliberate and weighty consideration of any legislation which might affect the rights of labor.

The benefits which labor has gained in the last thirteen years must be preserved. I voted for all these benefits while I was a member of the Congress. As President of the United States I have repeatedly urged not only their retention but their improvement. I shall continue to do so.

However, what we are dealing with here is not labor as a whole. We are dealing with a handful of men who are striking against their own government and against every one of their fellow citizens, and against themselves. We are dealing with a handful of men who have it within their power to cripple the entire economy of the nation.

I request temporary legislation to take care of this immediate crisis. I request permanent legislation leading to the formulation of a long-range labor policy designed to prevent the recurrence of such crises and generally to reduce the stoppages of work in all industries for the future.

I request that the temporary legislation be effective only for a period of six months after the declaration by the President or by the Congress of the termination of hostilities. It should be applicable only to those few industries in which the President by proclamation declares that an emergency has arisen which affects the entire economy of the United States. It should be effective only in those situations where the President of the United States has taken over the operation of the industry.

In such situations where the President has requested men either to remain at work or to return to work, and where such a request is ignored, the legislation should:

(a) Authorize the institution of injunctive or mandatory proceedings against any union leader, forbidding him from encouraging or inciting members of the union to leave their work or to refuse to return to work, subjecting him to contempt proceeding for failure to obey any order of the court made in such proceedings;

(b) Deprive workers of their seniority rights who, without good cause, persist in striking against the government; provide criminal penalties against employers and union leaders who violate the provisions of the act.

The legislation should provide that, after the government has taken over an industry and has directed men to remain at work or to return to work, the wage scale be fixed either by negotiation or by arbitrators appointed by the President, and when so fixed it shall be retroactive.

This legislation must be used in a way that is fair to capital and labor alike. The President will not permit either side—industry or workers—to use it to further their own selfish interests or to foist upon the government the carrying out of their selfish aims.

Net profits of government operation, if any, should go to the Treasury of the United States.

As a part of this temporary emergency legislation I request the Congress immediately to authorize the President to draft into the armed forces of the United States all workers who are on strike against their government.

[At the conclusion of his address the President, still on the rostrum, was handed a note.]

Word has just been received that the rail strike has been settled on terms proposed by the President.

The measures may appear to you to be drastic. They are. I repeat that I recommend them only as temporary emergency expedients and only in cases where workers are striking against the government.

I take this occasion again to request early action by the Congress to continue the price control and stabilization laws in an effective form. The stoppage of work in many industries has brought about a decline of production which has caused great pressure upon price levels.

We must protect the workers whom we ask to remain on their jobs as well as the millions of workers who have remained on their jobs and the many millions of other American citizens against the extraordinary inflation which may come upon us. Delay by the Congress is daily increasing these pressures, and I urge immediate action.

I have said that I am most anxious—as I am sure that the majority of the members of the Congress are—to do nothing which would injure labor or the cause of labor.

I believe that the time has come to adopt a comprehensive labor policy which will tend to reduce the number of stoppages of work and other acts which injure labor, capital, and the whole population.

The general right of workers to strike against private employers must be preserved. I am sure, however, that adequate study and consideration can produce permanent long-range legislation which will reduce the number of occasions where that ultimate remedy has to be adopted. The whole subject of labor relations should be studied afresh.

I recommend the immediate creation by Congress of a joint committee to make that study. That committee should study the whole problem and, within a period of six months, bring in recommendations for appropriate legislation which would be fair to labor and to industry and to the public at large.

I make these recommendations for temporary and long-range legislation with the same emphasis on each. They should both be part of one program designed to maintain our American system of free enterprise with fairness and justice to all the American citizens who contribute to it.

§ Mr. Truman's announcement that this strike had been settled was received by a wildly cheering Congress. Actually the settlement had been reached by Steelman and the union potentates a few minutes before the President began to talk, and more than one observer of these events has maintained that the President and his associates were indulging themselves in a passage of political histrionics by making the disclosure as they did.

The opposition to the President's proposals entailed one of the strangest combinations of bedfellows in twentieth-century politics. Senator Pepper, whose persuasion was to the left, declared that he would resign his seat before he would give the President's bill his support. From the right Senator Taft characterized the proposal as "the most extreme ever made" and "unconstitutional through calling for involuntary servitude." At a C.I.O. rally in New York City Mr. Truman was called "the number one strikebreaker of the American bankers and railroads."

The House of Representatives rushed his measure through two hours after his appearance by a vote of 306 to 13. Majority Leader Barkley requested immediate action. The administration bill was referred to the Interstate Commerce Committee with instructions to report back "at the earliest practicable hour." But a formidable combination of conservative Republicans, Southern Democrats, and labor sympathizers forced the dropping of the striker draft from the bill and brought about other extreme modifications. At the conference committee stage Mr. Truman renewed his request for the strikebreaking provision, but without success.

In 1946, the big year of the strikes and also of the return of the Republicans to control in Congress for the first time in the Roosevelt-Truman era, many bills were introduced to bring about a drastic redefinition of labor-management relations and of the role of government as established in the Wagner Act. The major bills that emerged, those of Senator Taft and Congressman Fred A. Hartley, Jr., of New Jersey, were actually composites of bills in various stages of enactment in both houses. The resultant Taft-Hartley bill was generally more moderate than its antecedents, and in all its more controversial aspects it reflected the views of Senator Taft. Taft-Hartley, prepared in complete expectation of a presidential veto, was carried through both houses by an imposing bipartisan sweep. The Senate vote was 54 to 17, the House vote 320 to 79.

The President maintained strict silence as the measure advanced through Congress, and even for some time after it had come to his desk he was still biding his counsel. While at Princeton University receiving an honorary degree, two days before he finally acted, he told

of equality. Because of unions the living standards of our working people have increased steadily until they are today the highest in the world.

A bill which would weaken unions would undermine our national policy of collective bargaining. The Taft-Hartley bill would do just that. It would take us back in the direction of the old evils of individual bargaining. It would take bargaining power away from workers and give more power to management. This bill would even take away from our workingmen some bargaining rights which they enjoyed before the Wagner Act was passed twelve years ago. If we weaken our system of collective bargaining, we weaken the position of every workingman in the country.

This bill would again expose workers to the abuses of labor injunctions.

It would make unions liable for damage suits for actions which have long been considered lawful.

This bill would treat all unions alike. Unions which have fine records, with long years of peaceful relations with management, would be hurt by this bill just as much as the few troublemakers.

The country needs legislation which would get rid of abuses. We do not need, and we do not want, legislation which will take fundamental rights away from our working people.

We have been told that the Taft-Hartley bill is a means by which the country can be protected from nation-wide strikes in vital industries. The terms of the bill do not support this claim. Many people are under the impression that this bill would prevent or settle a strike in the coal industry. I sincerely trust that the coal operators and the miners will soon come to an agreement on the terms of a contract and that there will be no interruption of coal mining. But if the miners and the operators do not reach agreement, and if this bill should become law, it is likely that the most that could be accomplished under the complicated procedures of the bill would be the postponement of a strike from July until October.

Under this bill a work stoppage in the coal mines might be prevented for eighty days and then, if agreement had not been reached, the miners would be free to strike, and it would be mandatory for the President to refer the whole matter to the Congress, even if it were not in session. Postponing a strike in the coal industry until the approach of winter, when our need for coal is acute, is certainly not the way to protect the nation against the dangers of a shortage of coal.

The bill would not aid fair and early settlements of disputes in vital industries.

We have been told by the supporters of the Taft-Hartley bill that it would reduce industrial strife. On the contrary, I am convinced that it would increase industrial strife. The bill would soon upset security clauses in thousands of existing agreements between labor and management. These agreements were mutually arrived at and furnish a satisfactory basis for relations between worker and employer. They provide stability in industry. With their present types of agreements outlawed by this bill, the parties would have to find a new basis for agreement. The restrictions in this bill would make the process of reaching new agreements a long and bitter one. The bill would increase industrial strife because a number of its provisions deprive workers of legal protection of fundamental rights. They would then have no means of protecting these rights except by striking.

The bill would open up opportunities for endless lawsuits by employers against unions and by unions against employers. For example, it would make employers vulnerable to an immense number of lawsuits, since grievances, however minor, could be taken into court by dissatisfied workers.

In so far as employers are concerned, I predict that if this bill should become law they would regret the day that it was conceived. It is loaded with provisions that would plague and hamper management. It is filled with hidden legal traps that would take labor relations out of the plant, where they belong, and place them in the courts.

Another defect is that in trying to correct labor abuses the Taft-Hartley bill goes so far that it would threaten fundamental democratic freedoms.

One provision undertakes to prevent political contributions and expenditures by labor organizations and corporations. This provision would forbid a union newspaper from commenting on candidates in national elections. It might well prevent an incorporated radio network from spending any money in connection with the national convention of a political party. It might even prevent the League of Women Voters—which is incorporated—from using its funds to inform its members about the record of a political candidate. I regard this provision of the Taft-Hartley bill as a dangerous challenge to free speech and our free press.

One of the basic errors of this bill is that it ignores the fact that over the years we have been making real progress in labor-management relations. We have been achieving slow but steady improvement in co-operation between employers and workers.

We must always remember that under our free economic system management and labor are associates. They work together for their own benefit and for the benefit of the public. The Taft-Hartley bill fails to recognize these fundamental facts. Many provisions of the bill would have the result of changing employers and workers from members of the same team to opponents on contending teams. I feel deep concern about what this would do to the steady progress we have made through the years.

I fear that this type of legislation would cause the people of our country to divide into opposing groups. If conflict is created, as this bill would create it—if seeds of discord are sown, as this bill would sow them—our unity will suffer and our strength will be impaired.

This bill does not resemble the labor legislation which I have recommended to the Congress. The whole purpose of this bill is contrary to the sound growth of our national labor policy.

There is still time to enact progressive, constructive legislation during the present session. We need such legislation to correct abuses and to further our advances in labor-management relations. We seek in this country today a formula which will treat all men fairly and justly, and which will give our people security in the necessities of life.

As our generous American spirit prompts us to aid the world to rebuild, we must, at the same time, construct a better America in which all can share equitably in the blessings of democracy. The Taft-Hartley bill threatens the attainment of this goal. For the sake of the future of the nation, I hope that this bill will not become law.

§   *The veto message was even more severe in temper. It was studded with such terms as "startling," "dangerous," "far-reaching," "unprecedented," "unworkable," "unique," "complex," "burdensome," "arbitrary," "unnecessary," "impossible," "elaborate," "clumsy," "serious," "drastic," "unwarranted." The bill's sponsors retorted in kind. Senator Taft, in a radio address delivered shortly after Mr. Truman's, said that the President had "completely misrepresented" the character of the bill. Congressman Hartley declared that the veto consisted of "double-talk, sham, distortion, abuse; far-fetched, strained, and tor-*

tured interpretations of clear, simple clauses; hysterical grasping at any argument, however invalid, to thwart the will of Congress."

The Truman forces were desperately rallying in Congress to defend the veto. Senator Wayne Morse filibustered to win time to get the Taft-Hartley issues before the country, but the effort petered out after a mere ten hours. Mr. Truman himself made a last-hour appeal in a letter to Minority Leader Barkley. The letter made little impact. The Senate overrode the veto with six votes to spare, twenty Democrats voting with thirty-eight Republicans to override. Twenty-two Democrats voted to sustain, supported by Republicans Langer, Malone, and Morse.

To President Truman the defeat was merely the beginning of a long and implacable crusade against what was to become one of the most politically useful bêtes noires of his administration. In the 1948 campaign and after, he lost no opportunity to identify the legislation with Republican conservatism, notwithstanding that considerable numbers of Democrats in both houses had voted for its enactment. In a speech at Akron on October 11, 1948, he said:

Now, as I have said time and time again, there is one basic issue in this campaign. That is: The Democratic party and the people against the special interests of the privileged few. . . .

That is our basic philosophy for the people—the greatest good for the greatest number. And upon that philosophy we have erected during the past sixteen years a great progressive body of laws. We call those laws—and I say it proudly—we call them the New Deal.

One of the cornerstones of the New Deal was the Wagner Labor Relations Act, which gave national protection to the right of collective bargaining. Under its provisions the labor movement has grown strong and healthy. The working people of this country were beginning to have something to say about what went on in the United States.

Well, our old mossback reactionary friends didn't like that. . . . They decided that under the pretense of revising the Wagner Act they would load it with provisions which would undermine the strength of labor unions. And that is what they did. They passed, over my veto, one of the most complicated laws that anybody ever saw. That was the Taft-Hartley Law.

The Taft-Hartley Law converts the Wagner Act from a charter

protecting the basic rights of workers into an instrument for union-busting by antilabor employers.

[Speaking of the book by Congressman Hartley, Republican of Michigan, *Our New National Labor Policy: The Taft-Hartley Act and the Next Steps*, Mr. Truman quoted from page 193: "I am well aware of the political difficulties of eliminating the New Deal social legislation. It cannot be repealed at a single stroke. All legislation of this type requires interim treatment."]

Interim treatment. Do you know what that is? That is the Taft-Hartley Law. They call the Taft-Hartley Law interim treatment. After that they take the gloves off and they give you the bare knuckles.

I believe that we should repeal the Taft-Hartley Act.

§ *After his amazing triumph in the 1948 elections and the return of the Democrats to control of Congress the President launched a hopeful drive against Taft-Hartley. Nuclear passages from his State of the Union address of January 5, 1949 indicate his position.*

The working men and women of the nation are unfairly discriminated against by a statute that abridges their rights, curtails their constructive efforts, and hampers our system of free collective bargaining. That statute is the Labor-Management Relations Act of 1947, sometimes called the Taft-Hartley Act.

That Act should be repealed.

The Wagner Act should be re-enacted. However, certain improvements which I recommended to the Congress two years ago are needed. Jurisdictional strikes and unjustifiable secondary boycotts should be prohibited. The use of economic force to decide issues arising out of the interpretation of existing contracts should be prevented. Without endangering our democratic freedoms, means should be provided for settling or preventing strikes in vital industries which affect the public interest.

§ *But the President's plea made no headway against the effective coalition of Republicans and Southern Democrats that succeeded in blocking most of the Fair Deal projects in the 81st Congress.*

Despite his limited legislative success the President had other means, sometimes more rewarding, of coping with what he saw as the limitations of Taft-Hartley and with the labor problems to which it was addressed. For instance, although he opposed the anticommunist affidavit provision of Taft-Hartley he threw the prestige of the presidency into the fierce internal struggles of some unions that were trying to divest themselves of communist leadership. Perhaps the bitterest instance of these purges occurred in the electrical workers' union of the C.I.O. The established United Electrical, Radio, and Machine Workers Union was expelled in November 1949 by the C.I.O. on the ground that it was communist-dominated. Later in November a new International Union of Electrical, Radio, and Machine Workers was established, anticommunist in its orientation, under the chairmanship of James B. Carey. Mr. Truman, in an action rare in the history of the presidency, entered directly into the contention of the two unions for the support of the country's electrical workers. In a letter to Carey the President expressed his confidence that electrical workers would shun "subversive activity" and build a bargaining agency "representative of their hopes and aspirations as loyal American citizens." The President's letter was read by Philip Murray, C.I.O. President, to the delegates of the union convention in Philadelphia to an accompaniment of cheers.

An even more direct attack on the challenge of Taft-Hartley was occasioned by the office of the General Counsel of the National Labor Relations Board. Mr. Truman, in his messages to Congress, neglected no opportunity to propose the abolition of the office in the form given it by Taft-Hartley—of course, to no avail. He did succeed, however, in bringing about the resignation of the General Counsel, Robert Denham, by what is customarily described as "White House pressure." Denham had been continuously at loggerheads with the National Labor Relations Board. He refrained from signing briefs for the Board, although he was its chief law enforcement officer, and he was inclined to a strict interpretation of the law and to the overlooking of policy considerations that carried weight with the Board.

◇

§ The Hobbs Anti-Racketeering Act is one of several pieces of legislation that Mr. Truman approved against the strong protests of organized labor. The Act made it a felony to interfere by robbery or extortion with the movement of goods in interstate commerce. Mr. Truman approved it on July 3, 1946. Concerned lest this legislation

be in any way construed to restrict important rights of labor established in several previous acts of Congress, he accompanied his signature with a statement that said:

The Attorney-General advises me that the present bill does not
in any way interfere with the rights of unions in carrying out their
legitimate objectives. . . .

He makes reference in particular to Title II of the bill. That title
provides that nothing in the bill shall be construed to repeal, modify,
or affect the Railway Labor Act, the Norris-LaGuardia Act, the
Wagner Act, and specified sections of the Clayton Act, i.e. the great
legislative safeguards which the Congress has established for the protection of labor in the exercise of its fundamental rights.

The Attorney-General also advises that the legislative history
shows that the bill is not intended to deprive labor of any of its
recognized rights, including the right to strike and to picket and to
take other legitimate and peaceful concerted action.

Under this understanding I am approving the bill.

§ This statement the President officially transmitted to Congress
along with the signed bill, thereby making a part of the formal record
his construction of ambiguous statutory language that invited a quite
different construction by those hostile to organized labor. His technique was novel; no modern President is known to have adopted it.
Other Presidents, faced with legislation about which they had doubts,
have simply signed it without comment or issued a simultaneous
press release stating the Chief Executive's interpretation.

9. LEGISLATIVE AND PARTY LEADER

Mr. Truman's philosophy and methods of handling Congressional
and party relationships are reflected in a scattering of pronouncements
on various occasions.

From a speech at Washington on March 24, 1946:

Political parties are the instruments through which democracy
works. Our party system remains as one of the massive foundations of
our liberty. Only the free play of political opposition can guarantee
the survival of civil freedom. . . .

Under our party system political responsibility must rest with the

President and with the majority of Congress. To meet this responsibility all our members in the Congress must co-operate wholeheartedly and help carry out our party platform.

From an informal talk to Democratic candidates for Congress, September 25, 1946:

. . . it is absolutely essential, in order that the program of the Democratic party as outlined in the platform adopted in 1944 . . . may be carried out, that we have a Congress that is in sympathy with what that platform calls for.

From an interview by Anthony Leviero, New York Times, December 26, 1952:

"Since Washington's time, Congress has been trying to take over control of the Executive Branch. . . ."

Mr. Truman said that he and President F. D. Roosevelt had had much closer relationships with Congress than any other President. He recalled how he had met every week with four Democratic Congressional leaders.

"If you had a completely rubber stamp Congress or a rubber stamp President it wouldn't be good for the country."

From Mr. Truman's 324th and last presidential press conference, January 15, 1953:

Q. Your views on party obligation: that all elected as Democrats must abide by platform pledges. Suppose (1) you construe a pledge in detail differently from a member of Congress; or (2) he has made a commitment to the contrary prior to the adoption of the platform. Is he recreant as a party man?

A. The President does not expect one-hundred-per-cent support from those elected to Congress on the same platform with him. He recognizes that local situations may require some members to refuse to follow a President on certain matters. As a Senator he reserved the right of independence at times for himself. But he does believe that, after a platform has been duly adopted by a convention, all those who have participated or run on that platform should generally abide by its detailed construction by the national candidate.

Only that national candidate, the President, can translate a platform into actionable terms. There are few chairmen of Congressional committees who follow the platform and the President's construction of it more than 50 per cent of the time, and this is very bad. These chairmen should be the right arm of the administration in orderly government by party. If there is any other way to have a responsible government, he does not know what it is. . . .

Q. It is true that chairmen in Congress get these places through seniority, and it is a bad system. Have you any idea of a better one, or any other that would be operable?

A. The seniority system by which chairmen of committees in Congress are selected is a defective one because the best-qualified men do not always get the jobs. But any substitute that has been proposed is unworkable, and the present system has the merit of keeping order in the legislative process. If the administration were allowed to pick the chairmen, which is one substitute that has been proposed, the Executive would dominate Congress, and this is not only undesirable but contrary to the intent of the Constitution.

Q. Do you think the return of the Republicans to power means a realignment of political parties after four years?

A. No, Mr. Truman said, the Democrats have always been the progressive party and the Republicans the conservative party, and they always would be.

Q. Are you including Southern Democrats?

A. Yes, Mr. Truman said, you would find they would become very progressive when they did not have the chairmanships [laughter].

§ *The first Congress of the Truman administration, the Democratic 79th, rejected virtually all of the Fair Deal program that had then been formulated. The rejections included Mr. Truman's proposals for liberalization of unemployment compensation, a permanent Fair Employment Practices Commission, a rise in the minimum wage, long-range housing legislation, and prepaid medical care. His diagnosis and his displeasure are conveyed in a radio speech of January 4, 1946.*

Now, I intend no blanket criticism of the Congress. Devoted and far-seeing men in both the Senate and the House have labored to make effective a program adequate to our needs. But if they are to succeed, they must be reinforced by you—the people they represent.

And let me make it very clear that when I speak of bills not getting any action it is not the Congress as a whole which is responsible. . . . It is the committees which hold up action on bills . . . often a bare majority of a committee—a handful of men—can prevent a vote by the whole Congress. . . .

When I speak of my recommendations and proposals I also want to make it very clear that I have no pride of authorship in them at all. There are, however, such things as 'must' objectives. It is my responsibility to outline those objectives to the Congress and to you the people. . . .

If the measures which I have recommended . . . do not meet the approval of the Congress . . . it is my fervent wish . . . that the Congress formulate measures of its own to carry out the desired objectives. That is definitely the responsibility of the Congress. What the American people want is action. . . .

I fully appreciate the many problems which Congressmen face. They have done a great wartime job under most trying conditions. The complicated return to peacetime has increased their difficulties.

I seek no conflict with the Congress. I earnestly desire co-operation with the Congress. . . .

We cannot face 1946 in a spirit of drift or irresolution.

The men and women who made this country great and kept it free were plain people with courage and faith.

Let us justify this heritage.

§ *Republican victory in the 1946 Congressional elections marked the end of fourteen years of uninterrupted rule of national politics by the Democratic party. Mr. Truman's first comment on the elections appeared in his State of the Union address of January 6, 1947, in which he outlined the formula by which he thought a Democratic President and a Republican Congress could the most profitably conduct their business.*

I come before you today to report on the state of the Union and, in the words of the Constitution, to recommend such measures as I judge necessary and expedient.

I come, also, to welcome you as you take up your duties and to discuss with you the manner in which you and I should fulfill our obligations to the American people during the next two years.

The power to mold the future of this nation lies in our hands—yours and mine, and they are joined together by the Constitution. . . .

But if we are to realize these ends, the Congress and the President, during the next two years, must work together. It is not unusual in our history that the majority of the Congress represents a party in opposition to the President's party.

I am the twentieth President of the United States who, at some time during his term of office, has found his own party to be in the minority in one or both houses of the Congress. The first one was George Washington, Wilson was number eighteen, and Hoover was number nineteen.

I realize that on some matters the Congress and the President may have honest differences of opinion. Partisan differences, however, did not cause material disagreements as to the conduct of the war. Nor, in the conduct of our international relations during and since the war, have such partisan differences been material.

On some domestic issue we may, and probably shall, disagree. That in itself is not to be feared. It is inherent in our form of government. But there are ways of disagreeing; men who differ can still work together sincerely for the common good. We shall be risking the nation's safety and destroying our opportunities for progress if we do not settle any disagreements in this spirit, without thought of partisan advantage.

§ *How Mr. Truman fared with the 80th Congress—which he did his indefatigable best to pillory as a synonym of evasion and obstruction— is made graphic enough in a simple summary of his proposals that succeeded, those that failed, and those that were more or less drastically modified.*

Successes: interim aid to Europe, Greek-Turkish aid, Marshall Plan, presidential succession, National Security Act, extension of rent control.

Defeats: Department of Welfare, civil rights, housing, Brannan Plan, universal military training, T.V.A. steam plant, health program, federal aid to education, social security extension, increase of old age and survivors' insurance. Against Mr. Truman's wishes Congress passed the Taft-Hartley Act, portal-to-portal pay, and tax reduction.

Modified: selective service (instead of universal military training), extension of reciprocal trade agreements, control of inflation, modified rent control, secondary market for G.I. housing loan.

10. THE ACCOMPLISHMENTS OF THE FAIR DEAL

*Mr. Truman found at the close of his term that, for all his diffi-
culties with the Congress and the defeat of his party in 1952, the
accomplishments of the Fair Deal were substantial. These he summarized in his last State of the Union message on January 7, 1953.*

We are still so close to recent controversies that some of us may
find it hard to understand the accomplishments of these past eight
years. But the accomplishments are real and very great, not as the
President's, not as the Congress', but as the achievements of our
country and all the people in it.

Let me remind you of some of the things we have done since I
first assumed my duties as President of the United States.

I took the oath of office on April 12, 1945. In May of that same
year the Nazis surrendered. Then, in July, that great white flash of
light, man-made at Alamogordo, heralded swift and final victory in
World War II—and opened the doorway to the atomic age.

Consider some of the great questions that were posed for us by
sudden total victory in World War II. Consider also how well we as
a nation have responded.

Would the American economy collapse after the war? That was
one question. Would there be another depression here—a repetition
of 1921 or 1929? The free world feared and dreaded it. The communists hoped for it and built their policies upon that hope. We
answered that question—answered it with a resounding "No."

Our economy has grown tremendously. Free enterprise has flour-
ished as never before. Sixty-two million people are now gainfully
employed, compared with fifty-one million seven years ago. Private
businessmen and farmers have invested more than $200,000,000,000
in new plant and equipment since the end of World War II. Prices
have risen further than they should have done; but incomes, by and
large, have risen even more, so that real living standards are now considerably higher than seven years ago. Aided by sound government
policies, our expanding economy has shown the strength and flexibility
for swift and almost painless reconversion from war to peace, in 1945
and 1946; for quick reaction and recovery—well before Korea—from
the beginnings of recession in 1949. Above all, this live and vital
economy of ours has now shown the remarkable capacity to sustain

a great mobilization program for defense, a vast outpouring of aid to friends and allies all around the world—and still to produce more goods and services for peaceful use at home than we have ever known before.

This has been our answer, up to now, to those who feared or hoped for a depression in this country.

How have we handled our national finances? That was another question arising at war's end. In the administration of the government no problem takes more of the President's time, year in and year out, than fashioning the budget and the related problem of managing the public debt.

Financing World War II left us with a tremendous public debt, which reached $279,000,000,000 at its peak in February 1946.

Beginning in July 1946, when war and reconversion financing had ended, we have held quite closely to the sound standard that in times of high employment and high national income the federal budget should be balanced and the debt reduced. . . .

Now let me turn to another question we faced at the war's end. Would we take up again, and carry forward, the great projects of social welfare—so badly needed, so long overdue—that the New Deal had introduced into our national life? Would our government continue to have a heart for the people, or was the progress of the New Deal to be halted in the aftermath of war as decisively as the progress of Woodrow Wilson's New Freedom had been halted after the First World War?

This question, too, we have answered. We have answered it by doubling old-age insurance benefits and extending coverage to ten million more people. We have answered it by increasing our minimum wage. We have answered by the three million privately constructed homes that the federal government has helped finance since the war and the 155,000 units of low-rent public housing placed under construction since 1949.

We have answered with the 42,000 new hospital beds provided since 1946 through the joint efforts of the federal government and local communities.

We have answered by helping 8,000,000 veterans of World War II to obtain advanced education, 196,000 to start in business, and 64,000 to buy farms.

We have answered by continuing to help farmers obtain electric power, until today nearly ninety per cent of our farms have power line electric service.

In these and other ways we have demonstrated, up to now, that our democracy has not forgotten how to use the powers of the government to promote the people's welfare and security.

Another of the big postwar questions was this: What we would do with the nation's natural resources—its soils and water, forests and grasslands. Would we continue the strong conservation movement of the 1930's, or would we, as we did after the First World War, slip back into the practices of monopoly, exploitation, and waste?

The answer is plain. All across our country the soil conservation movement has spread, aided by government programs, enriching private and public lands, preserving them from destruction, improving them for future use. In our river basins we have invested nearly $5,000,000,000 of public funds in the last eight years—invested them in projects to control floods, irrigate farmlands, produce low-cost power and get it to the housewives and farmers and businessmen who need it. We have been vigilant in protecting the people's property —lands and forests and oil and minerals.

We have had to fight hard against those who would use our resources for private greed; we have met setbacks; we have had to delay work because of defense priorities. But on the whole we can be proud of our record in protecting our natural heritage and in using our resources for the public good.

Here is another question we had to face at the war's close: Would we continue, in peace as well as war, to promote equality of opportunity for all our citizens, seeking ways and means to guarantee for all of them the full enjoyment of their civil rights?

During the war we achieved great economic and social gains for millions of our fellow citizens who had been held back by prejudice. Were we prepared, in peacetime, to keep on moving toward full realization of the democratic promise? Or would we let it be submerged, wiped out, in postwar riots and reactions, as after World War I?

We answered these questions in a series of forward steps at every level of government and in many spheres of private life. In our armed forces, our civil service, our universities, our railway trains, the residential districts of our cities, in stores and factories all across the nation, in the polling booths as well, the barriers are coming down. This is happening, in part, at the mandate of the courts; in part at the insistence of federal, state, and local governments; in part through the enlightened action of private groups and persons in every region and every walk of life.

There has been a great awakening of the American conscience on the issues of civil rights. And all this progress—still far from complete but still continuing—has been our answer, up to now, to those who questioned our intention to live up to the promises of equal freedom for us all.

There was another question posed for us at the war's end, which equally concerned the future course of our democracy: Could the machinery of government and politics in this republic be changed, improved, adapted rapidly enough to carry through, responsibly and well, the vast new complicated undertakings called for in our time?

We have answered this question, too, answered it by tackling the most urgent, most specific problems which the war experience itself had brought into sharp focus. The reorganization of the Congress in 1946; the unification of our armed services, beginning in 1947; the closer integration of foreign and military policy through the National Security Council created that same year; and the executive reorganizations, before and after the Hoover-Acheson Commission report in 1949—these are landmarks in our continuing endeavor to make government an effective instrument of service to the people.

IV
ORGAN OF FOREIGN RELATIONS

President Truman saw national affairs as simply an extension of local affairs, and international affairs as simply an extension of national. A President's understanding of foreign affairs, he believed, can be and must be based on his own experience in dealing with smaller-scale politics. Local issues, he maintained, comprehend the same human attributes and problems as those of the world; the difference is of degree and not of kind. He saw Stalin as essentially another politician, and the Russian situation could be understood "if you understand Jackson county."*

How far the man from Jackson County was a success in his manipulation of our foreign affairs and wherein he failed—these are questions around which disagreements can rage for a long time to come. But most of the disagreements so far heard have completely lost sight of what is undoubtedly the one criterion that Mr. Truman himself would even consider as the measure of his success or failure. That criterion is simply that there has been to date no third world war. It is incontestable that at several junctures the issue of war or

* Quoted in Jonathan Daniels, *The Man of Independence*, Philadelphia, 1950, p. 285.

peace was balanced on a razor's edge. There were periods when practically everyone expected war; there were periods when many of the knowledgeable were predicting when it would come or, as significantly, analyzing the reasons why it had not come quite yet. Through these periods the President strove to do every mortal thing in his power—everything reconcilable with national decency—to preserve the peace. At times when the wrong word or even the wrong intonation could have brought the cold war to incandescence, he said right words with the right intonation, yet with firmness. The threat of a major war must often have been the very greatest of all his worries. No major war has come; and in the face of that overwhelming consideration he would certainly think it senseless and footling to spar for points to prove whether his management of our foreign affairs was a success or a failure.

1. FUNDAMENTALS OF AMERICAN FOREIGN POLICY

The new President made his first comprehensive foreign policy speech on Navy Day, October 27, 1945. In it he adopted, to guide his administration in the coming months, principles to which the administration of Franklin D. Roosevelt had been committed. Indeed, these principles, with one exception, had been classically defined and successfully applied by the United States in the eighteenth and nineteenth centuries. The exception was the internationalism that had replaced the traditionary American isolationism.

The Navy Day speech has the value of a systematic outline of United States policy in its fundamentals, as Mr. Truman conceived these just after the close of the war.

1. We seek no territorial expansion or selfish advantage. We have no plans for aggression against any other state, large or small. We have no objective which need clash with the peaceful aims of any other nations.

2. We believe in the eventual return of sovereign rights and self-government to all peoples who have been deprived of them by force.

3. We shall approve no territorial changes in any friendly part of the world unless they accord with the freely expressed wishes of the people concerned.

4. We believe that all peoples who are prepared for self-government should be permitted to choose their own form of government by their own freely expressed choice, without interference from any foreign source. That is true in Europe, in Asia, in Africa, as well as in the Western Hemisphere.

5. By the combined and co-operative action of our war allies we shall help the defeated enemy states establish peaceful democratic governments of their own free choice. And we shall try to attain a world in which nazism, fascism, and military aggression cannot exist.

6. We shall refuse to recognize any government imposed upon any nation by the force of any foreign power. In some cases it may be impossible to prevent forceful imposition of such a government. But the United States will not recognize any such government.

7. We believe that all nations should have the freedom of the seas and equal rights to the navigation of boundary rivers and waterways and of rivers and waterways which pass through more than one country.

8. We believe that all states which are accepted in the society of nations should have access on equal terms to the trade and the raw materials of the world.

9. We believe that the sovereign states of the Western Hemisphere, without interference from outside the Western Hemisphere, must work together as good neighbors in the solution of their common problems.

10. We believe that full economic collaboration between all nations, great and small, is essential to the improvement of living conditions all over the world, and to the establishment of freedom from fear and freedom from want.

11. We shall continue to strive to promote freedom of expression and freedom of religion throughout the peace-loving areas of the world.

12. We are convinced that the preservation of peace between nations requires a United Nations Organization composed of all the peace-loving nations of the world who are willing jointly to use force if necessary to insure peace.

Now, that is the foreign policy which guides the United States. That is the foreign policy with which it confidently faces the future.

It may not be put into effect tomorrow or the next day. But none the less it is our policy, and we shall seek to achieve it. It may take a long time, and it is worth waiting for, and it is worth striving to attain.

The Ten Commandments themselves have not yet been universally achieved over these thousands of years. Yet we struggle constantly to achieve them, and in many ways we come closer to them each year. Though we may meet setbacks from time to time, we shall not relent in our efforts to bring the Golden Rule into the international affairs of the world.

We are now passing through a difficult phase of international relations. Unfortunately it has always been true after past wars that the unity among allies, forged by their common peril, has tended to wear out as the danger passed.

The world cannot afford any letdown in the united determination of the Allies in this war to accomplish a lasting peace. The world cannot afford to let the co-operative spirit of the Allies in this war disintegrate. The world simply cannot allow this to happen. The people in the United States, in Russia and Britain, in France and China, in collaboration with all the other peace-loving people, must take the course of current history into their own hand and mold it in a new direction—the direction of continued co-operation. It was a common danger which united us before victory. Let it be a common hope which continues to draw us together in the years to come.

The atomic bombs which fell on Hiroshima and Nagasaki must be made a signal, not for the old process of falling apart, but for a new era—an era of ever closer unity and ever closer friendship among peaceful nations.

Building a peace requires as much moral stamina as waging a war. Perhaps it requires even more, because it is so laborious and painstaking and undramatic. It requires undying patience and continuous application. But it can give us, if we stay with it, the greatest reward that there is in the whole field of human effort.

Differences of the kind that exist today among nations that fought together so long and so valiantly for victory are not hopeless or irreconcilable. There are no conflicts of interest among the victorious powers so deeply rooted that they cannot be resolved. But their solution will require a combination of forbearance and firmness. It will require a steadfast adherence to the high principles which we have enunciated.

It will also require a willingness to find a common ground as to the method of applying those principles.

Our American policy is a policy of friendly partnership with all peaceful nations and of full support for the United Nations Organization. It is a policy that has the strong backing of the American people. It is a policy around which we can rally without fear or misgiving.

The more widely and clearly that policy is understood abroad, the better and surer will be the peace. For our own part, we must seek to understand the special problems of other nations. We must seek to understand their own legitimate urge toward security as they see it.

The immediate, the greatest threat to us is the threat of disillusionment, the danger of an insidious skepticism—a loss of faith in the effectiveness of international co-operation. Such a loss of faith would be dangerous at any time. In an atomic age it would be nothing short of disastrous.

There has been talk about the atomic bomb scrapping all navies, armies, and air forces. For the present, I think that such talk is one hundred per cent wrong. Today control of the seas rests in the fleets of the United States and her allies. There is no substitute for them. We have learned the bitter lesson that the weakness of this great republic invites men of ill will to shake the very foundations of civilization all over the world, and we had two concrete lessons in that.

What the distant future of atomic research will bring to the fleet which we honor today, no one can foretell. But the fundamental mission of the Navy has not changed. Control of our sea approaches and of the skies above them is still the key to our freedom and to our ability to help enforce the peace of the world. No enemy will ever strike us directly except across the sea. We cannot reach out to help stop and defeat an aggressor without crossing the sea. Therefore the Navy, armed with whatever weapons science brings forth, is still dedicated to its historic task: control of the ocean approaches to our country and of the skies above them.

The atomic bomb does not alter the basic foreign policy of the United States. It makes the development and application of our policy more urgent than we could have dreamed six months ago. It means that we must be prepared to approach international problems with greater speed, with greater determination, with greater ingenuity, in order to meet a situation for which there is no precedent.

We must find the answer to the problems created by the release of atomic energy—we must find the answers to the many other problems of peace—in partnership with all the peoples of the United Nations. For their stake in world peace is as great as our own.

As I said in my message to the Congress, discussion of the atomic bomb with Great Britain and Canada and later with other nations cannot wait upon the formal organization of the United Nations. These discussions, looking toward a free exchange of fundamental scientific information, will be begun in the near future. But I emphasize again, as I have before, that these discussions will not be concerned with the processes of manufacturing the atomic bomb or any other instruments of war.

In our possession of this weapon, as in our possession of other new weapons, there is no threat to any nation. The world, which has seen the United States in two great recent wars, knows that full well. The possession in our hands of this new power of destruction we regard as a sacred trust. Because of our love of peace, the thoughtful people of the world know that that trust will not be violated, that it will be faithfully executed.

Indeed, the highest hope of the American people is that world co-operation for peace will soon reach such a state of perfection that atomic methods of destruction can be definitely and effectively outlawed forever.

We have sought, and will continue to seek, the attainment of that objective. We shall pursue that course with all the wisdom, patience, and determination that the God of Peace can bestow upon a people who are trying to follow in His path.

2. THE UNITED NATIONS

A key principle of the Truman administration in foreign affairs entailed major support of the United Nations. At many junctures in Mr. Truman's presidency the United Nations became a primary instrument for the conduct of U. S. foreign policy; and as serious weaknesses developed in the functioning of the world organization the United States undertook to lead the way to their correction.

Mr. Truman's attitude toward the United Nations, both during his presidency and since, has been one of unqualified optimism. His New Year's message of 1948 affirms his confidence that the United Nations would preserve the peace. The current vicissitudes of the organization he dismissed as transitory and as comparable to those experienced by the United States in its formative years. And to the Democratic National Convention of 1952 he said: "I am fully convinced that if we keep working at it the United Nations will become . . . the parliament of man and the federation of the world."

While the United Nations Organization was becoming established Mr. Truman's ideas of its proper structure, of its functions, and of the relationship of the United States to it were given expression in his State of the Union message of January 21, 1946.

In his last message on the State of the Union, delivered one year ago, President Roosevelt said:

"This new year of 1945 can be the greatest year of achievement in human history. 1945 can see the final ending of the Nazi-Fascist reign of terror in Europe. 1945 can see the closing in of the forces of retribution about the center of the malignant power of imperialistic Japan. Most important of all—1945 can and must see the substantial beginning of the organization of world peace."

All those hopes, and more, were fulfilled in the year 1945. It was the greatest year of achievement in human history. It saw the end of the Nazi-Fascist terror in Europe, and also the end of the malignant power of Japan. And it saw the substantial beginning of world organization for peace. These momentous events became realities because of the steadfast purpose of the United Nations and of the forces that fought for freedom under their flags. The plain fact is that civilization was saved in 1945 by the United Nations. . . .

Our nation has always been a land of great opportunities for those people of the world who sought to become part of us. Now we have become a land of great responsibilities to all the people of the world. We must squarely recognize and face the fact of those responsibilities. Advances in science, in communication, in transportation have compressed the world into a community. The economic and political health of each member of the world community bears directly on the economic and political health of each other member.

268 The Truman Administration

The evolution of centuries has brought us to a new era in world history in which manifold relationship between nations must be formalized and developed in new and intricate ways.

The United Nations Organization now being established represents a minimum essential beginning. It must be developed rapidly and steadily. Its work must be amplified to fill in the whole pattern that has been outlined. Economic collaboration, for example, already charted, now must be carried on as carefully and as comprehensively as the political and security measures.

It is important that the nations come together as states in the Assembly and in the Security Council and in the other specialized assemblies and councils that have been and will be arranged. But this is not enough. Our ultimate security requires more than a process of consultation and compromise.

It requires that we begin now to develop the United Nations Organization as the representative of the world as one society. The United Nations Organization, if we have the will adequately to staff it and to make it work as it should, will provide a great voice to speak constantly and responsibly in terms of world collaboration and world well-being.

There are many new responsibilities for us as we enter into this new international era. The whole power and will and wisdom of our government and of our people should be focused to contribute to and to influence international action. It is intricate, continuing business. Many concessions and adjustments will be required.

The spectacular progress of science in recent years makes these necessities more vivid and urgent. That progress has speeded internal development and has changed world relationships so fast that we must realize the fact of a new era. It is an era in which affairs have become complex and rich in promise. Delicate and intricate relationships, involving us all in countless ways, must be carefully considered.

§ *The most glowing hopes for a successfully functioning United Nations were quickly dashed by the obstructionism of the Soviet Union. The veto, the walkout, the boycott, and calculated rudeness became standard Soviet tactics, and there was widespread despair even among the original friends of the United Nations, which to many of them now seemed doomed to failure. Mr. Truman, however,*

*took a diametrically opposite position in his speech at San Francisco
on September 22, 1948.*

I have heard from time to time comments by well-meaning but
misinformed Americans that the United Nations is not working.
I think I can understand their concern. All of us have been dis-
appointed in the slowness with which the world is settling down
after World War II. However, I am firmly convinced that our
progress toward peace is much faster than it would have been without the United Nations.

Let me recall for you briefly just what it was we had in mind when
we set up the United Nations. The United Nations was established
for three basic purposes. The first was to prevent future wars by
creating a kind of economic condition throughout the world which
is necessary for peace. The second purpose was to provide the kind
of organization which would help countries settle their differences
peacefully without shooting each other. The third purpose was to
provide an organization by which the peace-loving countries could
act collectively against threats to peace by an aggressive country.

Now that you have in mind the reasons why the United Nations
was set up, let us look at the record of what it has accomplished.
I am sure you will agree that the United Nations has proved its
worth. It has been meeting all three purposes. I think we can hope
for peace in the future.

When the United Nations was less than a year old the Security
Council was faced with the problem of Soviet troops invading the
small and weak country of Iran, located south of the Soviet Union
in the Middle East. Action by the Security Council helped to
persuade the Soviet government to pull its troops out of Iran. Iran
remained an independent country.

The Security Council of the United Nations protected the independence of two other small countries in the Middle East when it
persuaded the British and French governments to withdraw their
troops from Syria and Lebanon.

Greece is still another small nation whose independence has been
maintained with the aid of the United Nations. The United Nations
has taken action against Greece's northern neighbors. Among other
things it has sent a commission to Greece whose job it is to patrol

and to make sure that Greece's neighbors do not invade that country again.

The Security Council of the United Nations secured a truce in the conflict between the Dutch and the Indonesians. A United Nations committee brought about agreement between the Dutch and the Indonesians on a set of principles which are being used as a guide for the creation of a United States of Indonesia. This act alone involved the peace and security of almost sixty million people. The two new countries of India and Pakistan brought their dispute over Kashmir to the United Nations. The United Nations has not yet ended the dispute, but it has succeeded in keeping violence from breaking out into open war.

I have described only a few of the actions which the United Nations has taken since it was founded, but I am sure that those I have mentioned are evidence of the way in which the Security Council and the General Assembly are helping maintain peace in the world.

There are many other activities of the United Nations besides the General Assembly and the Security Council. There is the International Refugee Organization, which is taking care of refugees in Displaced Persons Camps in Europe. There is the International Trade Organization, which is working to increase the flow of trade among all countries. And there are still other organizations, like these two, connected with the United Nations which are successfully working to improve the welfare of all the peoples of the world.

Of course, looking back over the first three years of the United Nations, to ignore the problems which the Soviet tactics have caused would be foolish. I have never, for one moment since I became President, underestimated the multitude of the problems which the Soviet Union could cause if that country were unwilling to join with other nations in working for peace.

At the same time I am so firmly convinced that all the plain people in the world want peace that I have never regarded the Soviet Union's present policies as insuperable obstacles to peace.

Twice in one generation the United States has had the opportunity to lead the countries of the world to peace. After World War I we shirked our responsibilities. World War II taught us a lesson.

All of our efforts for peace—the European Recovery Program, aid to China and Greece and Turkey, support for the Western

European Union, the Inter-American Defense Pacts—all these are in accord with the principles of the United Nations and are in support of its aims.

We shall do everything in our power to strengthen the United Nations, for I believe that the overwhelming majority of the people of this country have confidence in the United Nations that eventually it will be a grand success and will continue to work.

§ *Two years later, in his State of the Union message for January 4, 1950, the President again reviewed the more recent accomplishments of the United Nations and the relevant policies of the United States; and it was clear from what he said that he regarded the United Nations as a primary and focal point of United States foreign policy.*

. . . The events of the past year again showed the value of the United Nations in bringing about the peaceful adjustment of tense international controversies. In Indonesia and in Palestine the efforts of the United Nations have put a stop to bloodshed and paved the way to peaceful settlements.

We are working toward the time when the United Nations will control weapons of mass destruction and will have the forces to preserve international law and order. While the world remains un-settled, however, and as long as our own security and the security of the free world require, we will maintain a strong and well-balanced defense organization. The selective service system is an essential part of our defense plans, and it must be continued.

Under the principles of the United Nations Charter we must continue to share in the common defense of free nations against aggression. At the last session this Congress laid the basis for this joint effort. We now must put into effect the common defense plans that are being worked out.

We shall continue our efforts for world economic recovery, because world prosperity is the only sure foundation for permanent peace.

As an immediate means to this end, we must continue our support of the European Recovery Program. . . .

World prosperity also requires that we do all we can to expand world trade. As a major step in this direction we should promptly join the International Trade Organization. The purpose of this organization, which the United States has been foremost in creating, is to establish a code of fair practice and an international authority for adjusting differences in international commercial relations. It is an effort to prevent the kind of anarchy and irresponsibility in world trade which did so much to bring about the world depression in the 1930's.

An expanding world economy requires the improvement of living standards and the development of resources in areas where human poverty and misery now prevail. Without such improvement the recovery of Europe and the future of our own economy will not be secure. I urge that the Congress adopt the legislation now before it to provide for increasing the flow of technical assistance and capital investment to underdeveloped regions.

It is more essential now than ever, if the ideals of freedom and representative government are to prevail in these areas, and particularly in the Far East, that their people experience in their own lives the benefits of scientific and economic advances. This program will require the movement of large amounts of capital from the industrial nations, and particularly from the United States, to productive uses in the underdeveloped areas of the world. Recent world events make prompt action imperative.

§ *The armed attack on the Korean Republic by North Korean forces in June 1950 confronted the United Nations with its first major test as a security organization established to prevent and suppress acts of aggression. President Truman commented on the significance of this test in his message to Congress of January 8, 1951.*

Korea has tremendous significance for the world. It means that free nations, acting through the United Nations, are fighting together against aggression.

We will understand the importance of this best if we look back into history. If the democracies had stood up against the invasion of Manchuria in 1931, or the attack on Ethiopia in 1935, or the seizure of Austria in 1938; if they had stood together against aggression on these occasions as the United Nations has done in Korea, the whole history of our time would have been different.

The principles for which we are fighting in Korea are right and just. They are the foundations of collective security, of the future of free nations. Korea is not only a country undergoing the torment of aggression; it is also a symbol. It stands for right and justice in the world against oppression and slavery. The free world must always stand for these principles—and we will stand with the free world.

. . . we will continue to work for peaceful settlements in international disputes. We will support the United Nations and remain loyal to the great principles of international co-operation laid down in its Charter.

We are willing, as we have always been, to negotiate honorable settlements with the Soviet Union. But we will not engage in appeasement.

3. PEACE, FREEDOM AND COMMUNIST PENETRATION

Two of the most significant developments in foreign policy launched by the Truman administration were promulgated in the inaugural address of 1949.

The first was the North Atlantic Treaty. The immediate pressures that produced it came from the unhindered consolidation of the Soviet bloc in Europe, the total frustration of United States efforts to negotiate with the Soviet Union, and the Brussels pact of March 17, 1948, by which five Western European nations pledged "all military assistance in their power" to any one of them that might be the object of armed attack in Europe. Coupled with this pact was the resolution introduced by Senator Vandenberg, and passed by the Senate on June 11, 1948, endorsing the association of the United States, under certain conditions, with "regional and other collective arrangements" affecting the national security. In the ensuing summer and fall the Department of State undertook the appropriate negotiations with various Western governments.

The second major innovation declared in the inaugural address was the famous Point Four—the announcement, inspiring to many, of a program of assistance to underdeveloped countries and regions. Although such a program was not actually new—technical assistance to and investment in underdeveloped areas had for some years been the concern of a number of federal, international, and private organizations—the President's proposal gave promise of far exceeding anything accomplished thus far.

Both of these striking departures were conceived by the President *as integral with the larger purpose of promoting peace, freedom, and safeguards against communist penetration, and it was in such a context that his inaugural address presented them.*

Today marks the beginning not only of a new administration, but of a period that will be eventful, perhaps decisive, for us and for the world.

It may be our lot to experience, and in large measure to bring about, a major turning point in the long history of the human race. The first half of this century has been marked by unprecedented and brutal attacks on the rights of man and by the two most frightful wars in history. The supreme need of our time is for men to learn to live together in peace and harmony. . . .

The American people stand firm in the faith which has inspired this nation from the beginning. We believe that all men have a right to equal justice under law and equal opportunity to share in the common good. We believe that all men have the right to freedom of thought and expression. We believe that all men are created equal because they are created in the image of God. From this faith we will not be moved.

The American people desire, and are determined to work for, a world in which all nations and all peoples are free to govern themselves as they see fit and to achieve a decent and satisfying life. Above all else our people desire, and are determined to work for, peace on earth—a just and lasting peace based on genuine agreement freely arrived at by equals.

In the pursuit of these aims the U. S. and other like-minded nations find themselves directly opposed by a regime with contrary aims and a totally different concept of life. That regime adheres to a false philosophy which purports to offer freedom, security, and greater opportunity to mankind. Misled by this philosophy, many peoples have sacrificed their liberties only to learn to their sorrow that deceit and mockery, poverty and tyranny, are their reward.

That false philosophy is communism. Communism is based on the belief that man is so weak and inadequate that he is unable to govern himself and therefore requires the rule of strong masters.

Democracy is based on the conviction that man has the moral and intellectual capacity, as well as the inalienable right, to govern himself with reason and justice.

Communism subjects the individual to arrest without lawful cause, punishment without trial, and forced labor as the chattel of the state. It decrees what information he shall receive, what art he shall produce, what leaders he shall follow, and what thoughts he shall think.

Democracy maintains that government is established for the benefit of the individual and is charged with the responsibility of protecting the rights of the individual and his freedom in the exercise of his abilities.

Communism maintains that social wrongs can be corrected only by violence. Democracy has proved that social justice can be achieved through peaceful change.

Communism holds that the world is so deeply divided into opposing classes that war is inevitable. Democracy holds that free nations can settle differences justly and maintain lasting peace.

These differences between communism and democracy do not concern the United States alone. People everywhere are coming to realize that what is involved is material well-being, human dignity, and the right to believe in and worship God.

I state these differences, not to draw issues of belief as such, but because the actions resulting from the communist philosophy are a threat to the efforts of free nations to bring about world recovery and lasting peace.

Since the end of hostilities the United States has invested its substance and its energy in a great constructive effort to restore peace, stability, and freedom to the world. We have sought no territory and we have imposed our will on none. We have asked for no privileges we would not extend to others. We have constantly and vigorously supported the United Nations and related agencies as a means of applying democratic principles to international relations. We have consistently advocated and relied upon peaceful settlement of disputes among nations. We have made every effort to secure agreement on effective international control of our most powerful weapon, and we have worked steadily for the limitation and control of all armaments. We have encouraged, by precept and example, the expansion of world trade on a sound and fair basis.

Almost a year ago, in company with sixteen free nations of Europe, we launched the greatest co-operative economic program in history. The purpose of that unprecedented effort is to invigorate and strengthen democracy in Europe, so that the free people of that continent can resume their rightful place in the forefront of civilization and can contribute once more to the security and welfare of the world.

Our efforts have brought new hope to all mankind. We have beaten back despair and defeatism. We have saved a number of countries from losing their liberty. Hundreds of millions of people all over the world now agree with us that we need not have war —that we can have peace.

The initiative is ours.

We are moving on with other nations to build an even stronger structure of international order and justice. We shall have as our partners countries which, no longer solely concerned with the problem of national survival, are now working to improve the standards of living of all their people. We are ready to undertake new projects to strengthen the free world.

In the coming years our program for peace and freedom will emphasize four major courses of action.

First, we will continue to give unfaltering support to the U.N. and related agencies, and we will continue to search for ways to strengthen their authority and increase their effectiveness. We believe that the U.N. will be strengthened by the new nations which are being formed in lands now advancing toward self-government under democratic principles.

Second, we will continue our programs for world economic recovery. This means, first of all, that we must keep our full weight behind the European Recovery Program. We are confident of the success of this major venture in world recovery. We believe that our partners in this effort will achieve the status of self-supporting nations once again. In addition we must carry out our plans for reducing the barriers to world trade and increasing its volume. Economic recovery and peace itself depend on increased world trade.

Third, we will strengthen freedom-loving nations against the dangers of aggression.

We are now working out with a number of countries a joint agreement designed to strengthen the security of the North Atlantic area. Such an agreement would take the form of a collective defense arrangement within the terms of the United Nations Charter. We have already established such a defense pact for the Western Hemisphere by the treaty of Rio de Janeiro. The primary purpose of these agreements is to provide unmistakable proof of the joint determination of the free countries to resist armed attack from any quarter. Each country participating in these arrangements must contribute all it can to the common defense.

If we can make it sufficiently clear in advance that any armed attack affecting our national security would be met with overwhelming force, the armed attack might never occur.

I hope soon to send to the Senate a treaty respecting the North Atlantic security plan. In addition we will provide military advice and equipment to free nations which will co-operate with us in the maintenance of peace and security.

Fourth, we must embark on a bold new program for making the benefits of our scientific advances and industrial progress available for the improvement and growth of underdeveloped areas.

More than half the people of the world are living in conditions approaching misery. Their food is inadequate. They are victims of disease. Their economic life is primitive and stagnant. Their poverty is a handicap and a threat both to them and to more prosperous areas. For the first time in history humanity possesses the knowledge and the skill to relieve the suffering of these people.

The U. S. is pre-eminent among nations in the development of industrial and scientific techniques. The material resources which we can afford to use for the assistance of other peoples are limited. But our imponderable resources in technical knowledge are constantly growing and are inexhaustible. I believe that we should make available to peace-loving peoples the benefits of our store of technical knowledge in order to help them realize their aspirations for a better life. And in co-operation with other nations we should foster capital investment in areas needing development.

Our aim should be to help the free peoples of the world, through their own efforts, to produce more food, more clothing, more materials for housing, and more mechanical power to lighten their burdens.

We invite other countries to pool their technological resources in this undertaking. Their contributions will be warmly welcomed. This should be a co-operative enterprise in which all nations work together through the United Nations and its specialized agencies wherever practicable. It must be a world-wide effort for the achievement of peace, plenty, and freedom.

With the co-operation of business, private capital, agriculture, and labor in this country, this program can greatly increase the industrial activity in other nations and can raise substantially their standards of living.

Such new economic developments must be devised and controlled to benefit the peoples of the areas in which they are established. Guarantees to the investor must be balanced by guarantees in the interest of the people whose resources and whose labor go into these developments.

The old imperialism—exploitation for foreign profit—has no place in our plans. What we envisage is a program of development based on the concepts of democratic fair dealing.

All countries, including our own, will greatly benefit from a constructive program for the better use of the world's human and natural resources. Experience shows that our commerce with other countries expands as they progress industrially and economically. Greater production is the key to prosperity and peace. And the key to greater production is a wider and more vigorous application of modern scientific and technical knowledge.

Only by helping the least fortunate of its members to help themselves can the human family achieve the decent, satisfying life that is the right of all people.

Democracy alone can supply the vitalizing force to stir the peoples of the world into triumphant action, not only against their human oppressors, but also against their ancient enemies hunger, misery, and despair.

On the basis of these four major courses of action we hope to help create the conditions that will lead eventually to personal freedom and happiness for all mankind.

If we are to be successful in carrying out these policies, it is clear that we must have continued prosperity in this country and we must keep ourselves strong.

Slowly but surely we are weaving a world fabric of international security and growing prosperity.

We are aided by all who wish to live in freedom from fear—even by those who live today in fear under their own governments.

We are aided by all who want relief from the lies of propaganda—who desire truth and sincerity. We are aided by all who desire self-government and a voice in deciding their own affairs. We are aided by all who long for economic security—for the security and abundance that men in free societies can enjoy. We are aided by all who desire freedom of speech, freedom of religion, and freedom to live their own lives for useful ends. Our allies are the millions who hunger and thirst after righteousness.

In due time, as our stability becomes manifest, as more and more nations come to know the benefits of democracy and to participate in growing abundance, I believe that those countries which now oppose us will abandon their delusions and join with the free nations of the world in a just settlement of international differences.

Events have brought our American democracy to new influence and new responsibilities. They will test our courage, our devotion to duty, and our concept of liberty. But I say to all men, what we have achieved in liberty we will surpass in greater liberty. Steadfast in our faith in the Almighty, we will advance toward a world where man's freedom is secure. To that end we will devote our strength, our resources, and our firmness of resolve. With God's help the future of mankind will be assured in a world of justice, harmony, and peace.

§ *Of the two new components of Mr. Truman's foreign policy— both of which achieved rapid and substantial progress—the first, the North Atlantic Treaty, implementing the Atlantic alliance, was ready for the President's signature on April 4, 1949. In signing it he issued this statement:*

It is altogether appropriate that nations so deeply conscious of their common interests should join in expressing their determination to preserve their present peaceful situation and to protect it in the future.

What we are about to do here is a neighborly act. We are like a group of householders living in the same locality who decide to express their community of interests by entering into a formal association for their mutual self-protection. This treaty is a simple document. The nations who sign it agree to abide by the peaceful principles of the United Nations, to maintain friendly relations and economic co-operation with one another, to consult together whenever the territory or independence of any of them is threatened, and to come to the aid of any one of them who may be attacked.

It is a simple document, but if it had existed in 1914 and in 1939, supported by the nations who are represented here today, I believe it would have prevented the acts of aggression which led to two World Wars.

Each member of the United Nations is under solemn obligation to maintain international peace and security. Each is bound to settle international disputes by peaceful means, to refrain from the threat or use of force against the territory or independence of any country, and to support the United Nations in any action it takes to preserve the peace.

We rededicate ourselves to that obligation, and propose this North Atlantic Treaty as one of the means to carry it out. Through this treaty we undertake to conduct our international affairs in accordance with the provisions of the United Nations Charter.

We undertake to exercise our right of collective or individual self-defense against armed attack, in accordance with Article 51 of the Charter and subject to such measures as the Security Council may take to maintain and restore international peace and security.

Within the United Nations this country and other countries have hoped to establish an international force for the use of the United Nations in preserving peace throughout the world. Our efforts to establish this force, however, have been blocked by one of the major powers.

This lack of unanimous agreement in the Security Council does not mean that we must abandon our attempts to make peace secure. Even without that agreement, which we still hope for, we shall do as much as we can. And every bit that we do will add to the strength of the fabric of peace throughout the world.

In this treaty we seek to establish freedom from aggression and from the use of force in the North Atlantic community. This is the area which has been at the heart of the last two world conflicts. To protect this area against war will be a long step toward permanent peace in the whole world.

There are those who claim that this treaty is an aggressive act on the part of the nations which ring the North Atlantic. That is absolutely untrue. The pact will be a positive, not a negative, influence for peace, and its influence will be felt not only in the area it specifically covers, but throughout the world. Its conclusion does not mean a narrowing of the interests of its members. Under my authority and instructions the Secretary of State has recently made it perfectly clear that the adherence of the United States to this pact does not signify a lessening of American concern for the security and welfare of other areas of the world, such as the Near East. The step we are taking today should serve to reassure peace-loving peoples everywhere and pave the way for the world-wide stability and peaceful development which we all seek.

Twice in recent years nations have felt the sickening blow of unprovoked aggression. Our peoples, to whom our governments are responsible, demand that these things shall not happen again. We are determined that they shall not happen again.

In taking steps to prevent aggression against our own peoples, we have no purpose of aggression against other peoples. The nations represented here are bound together by ties of long standing. We are joined by a common heritage of democracy, individual liberty, and rule of law. These are the ties of a peaceful way of life. In this pact we merely give them formal recognition.

With our common traditions we face common problems. We are, to a large degree, industrial nations, and we face the problem of mastering the forces of modern technology in the public interest. To meet this problem successfully we must have a world in which we can exchange the products of our labor not only among ourselves, but with other nations. We have come together in a great co-operative economic effort to establish this kind of world.

We are determined to work together to provide better lives for our people without sacrificing our common ideals of justice and human worth. But we cannot succeed if our people are haunted by the constant fear of aggression and burdened by the cost of preparing their nations individually against attack. In this pact, we hope to create a shield against aggression and the fear of aggression—a bulwark which will permit us to get on with the real business of government and society, the business of achieving a fuller and happier life for all our citizens.

We shall, no doubt, go about this business in different ways. There are different kinds of governmental and economic systems, just as there are different languages and different cultures. But these differences present no real obstacle to the voluntary association of free nations devoted to the common cause of peace.

We believe that it is possible for nations to achieve unity on the great principles of human freedom and justice and at the same time to permit, in other respects, the greatest diversity of which the human mind is capable. Our faith in this kind of unity is borne out by our experience here in the United States in creating one nation out of the variety of our continental resources and the peoples of many lands.

This method of organizing diverse peoples and cultures is in direct contrast to the methods of the police state, which attempts to achieve unity by imposing the same beliefs and the same rule of force on everyone.

We believe that our method of achieving international unity through the voluntary association of different countries dedicated to a common cause is an effective step toward bringing order to our troubled world.

For us, war is not inevitable. We do not believe that there are blind tides of history which sweep men one way or another. In our own time we have seen brave men overcome obstacles that seemed insurmountable and forces that seemed overwhelming. Men with courage and vision can still determine their own destiny. They can choose slavery or freedom, war or peace.

I have no doubt which they will choose. The treaty we are signing here today is evidence of the path they will follow.

§ *The treaty committed the United States and eleven other signatories (1) to maintain and develop, by means of continuous and effective self-help and mutual aid, their individual and collective capacity to resist attack; (2) to consult together in the event of a threat to the territorial integrity, independence, or security of any of the parties; (3) to consider an armed attack on any one of the parties in the North Atlantic area as an attack against them all; and (4) to assist the party so attacked by taking forthwith, individually and in concert with the other parties, such action as each party should deem necessary, including the use of armed force, to restore the security of the North Atlantic area. The treaty operated as a regional agreement explicitly subordinated to the United Nations Charter.*

In subsequent months the North Atlantic Treaty Organization (NATO) was created as the international entity that would give effect to the treaty. In addition to participating in NATO and assisting in the organization of an integrated NATO force, the United States, under the Mutual Defense Assistance Acts, concluded with individual NATO countries bilateral agreements governing the provision of United States military aid directly to those countries.

Despite numerous difficulties NATO made such progress that its Council meeting in Lisbon in February 1952 dared to plan for a level of some fifty army divisions, half of them on active duty, and also some 4,000 aircraft, by the end of 1952. With the further build-up planned for 1953 and 1954, supplemented by the forces of Greece and Turkey and the expected inclusion of Western Germany in the European Defense Community, the program, as President Truman described it in a message to Congress on March 6, 1952, would "bring within measurable distance the time when even the most foolhardy man in the Kremlin will not dare risk open attack." The President's statement must be read in conjunction with the remarks of General Ridgway, the Supreme Commander, at a later date, October 14, 1952, before the Society of Pilgrims in London: "Although our forces today are far stronger than they were two years ago, . . . we are still far from the minimum we need to deal with an all-out surprise attack . . . We have yet to reach our minimum military requirements. Until we do, military commanders . . . must face the fact that the potential aggressor is capable of moving at any time of his choosing in strength much greater than today we can muster."

It was not until June 1950 that, with the passage of the Act for International Development, the "bold new" Point Four program of January 1949 finally became law. In the first two years of Point Four some 216 technical assistance projects were undertaken in thirty-three countries. The projects followed the principle that the program should be primarily one of teaching and demonstration and that it should attack such basic problems as hunger, illness, and illiteracy. In Burma there was a campaign for the control of infantile diseases that kill three babies out of every ten. A five-hundred-bed hospital and a medical college were under construction, with professors and scientists being exchanged with the University of Pennsylvania. In India a large number of village projects were introduced to improve food production, provide potable water, foster irrigation, introduce fertilizer, teach reading and writing, devise better tools, and improve the forms of land ownership. In Libya ninety citizens attended a technical school opened with Point Four money to learn plumbing, electrical work, and other skilled trades. In Saudi Arabia Point Four geologists located underground water resources. In Brazil United States technicians were working with Brazilians to improve rubber production. In Israel the expansion of fertilizer, potash, petrochemical, and ceramics plants was aided by United States technicians. In Ecuador Point Four aid increased the potato crop sixfold.*

4. COLD WAR

The term "cold war" did not gain currency until 1947, but the fact existed before the phrase. The Truman administration, from its first until its last day, never attained serenity in its relations with the Soviet Union. Well before the Potsdam conference and even before the San Francisco meeting that established the United Nations Organization, Mr. Truman's encounters with Molotov had given him premonitions of serious trouble. When he came into office the United States and the U.S.S.R. were already quarreling over the establishment of a government of Poland representative of the people. At the San Francisco conference more issues arose in the development of the United Nations Organization. Only after bitter and protracted negotiations was agreement reached on a peace treaty for Italy and other lesser allies of Germany. Profound disagreement within the Allied Control Council led finally to the abandonment of four-power rule of Germany.

In the United Nations, United States proposals for the international control of atomic energy, for disarmament, and for the admission of various new members were opposed by the Soviet Union. Most serious of all was the opposition of the Soviet Union to United Nations action to halt aggression in Korea in 1950. Also in opposition to the United States, Russia persistently sought United Nations recognition of Communist China.

The Soviet Union built up with staggering rapidity a ring of satellites in Eastern Europe. In almost no month of the Truman

---

* Data from the survey of Point Four activities in the *New York Times* of January 12, 1953.

administration did the communists fail to have contests of military strength going on somewhere in the world. They fomented guerrilla warfare in Greece, the great logistic test of the Berlin blockade, full-scale strife in Korea and Indochina.

The President's most detailed expression of his own reflections on the cold war is contained in his farewell radio address to the nation on January 15, 1953.

I suppose that history will remember my term in office as the years when the cold war began to overshadow our lives. I have had hardly a day in office that has not been dominated by this all-embracing struggle—this conflict between those who love freedom and those who would lead the world back into slavery and darkness. And always in the background there has been the atomic bomb.

But when history says that my term of office saw the beginning of the cold war, it will also say that in those eight years we have set the course that can win it. We have succeeded in carving out a new set of policies to attain peace—positive policies, policies of world leadership, policies that express faith in other free people. We have averted World War III up to now, and we may already have succeeded in establishing conditions which can keep that war from happening as far ahead as man can see.

These are great and historic achievements that we can all be proud of. Think of the difference between our course now and our course thirty years ago. After the First World War we withdrew from world affairs; we failed to act in concert with other peoples against aggression; we helped to kill the League of Nations; and we built up tariff barriers which strangled world trade.

This time we avoided those mistakes. We helped to found and to sustain the United Nations. We have welded alliances that include the greater part of the free world. And we have gone ahead with other free countries to help build their economies and link us all together in a healthy world trade.

Think back for a moment to the 1930's and you will see the difference. The Japanese moved into Manchuria, and free men did not act. The Fascists moved into Ethiopia, and we did not act. The Nazis marched into the Rhineland, into Austria, into Czecho-slovakia, and free men were paralyzed for lack of strength and unity of will.

Think about those years of weakness and indecision, and World War II which was their evil result. Then think about the speed and courage and decisiveness with which we have moved against the Communist threat since World War II.

The first crisis came in 1945 and 1946, when the Soviet Union refused to honor its agreement to remove its troops from Iran. Members of my Cabinet came to me and asked if we were ready to take the risk that a firm stand involved. I replied that we were. So we took our stand; we made it clear to the Soviet Union that we expected them to honor their agreement; and the Soviet troops were withdrawn.

And then, in early 1947, the Soviet Union threatened Greece and Turkey. The British sent me a message saying they could no longer keep their forces in that area. Something had to be done at once, or the eastern Mediterranean would be taken over by the communists. On March 12 I went before the Congress and stated our determination to help the people of Greece and Turkey maintain their independence. Today Greece is still free and independent; and Turkey is a bulwark of strength at a strategic corner of the world.

Then came the Marshall Plan which saved Europe, the heroic Berlin Airlift, and our military aid programs. We inaugurated the North Atlantic Pact, the Rio Pact binding the Western Hemisphere together, and the defense pacts with countries of the Far Pacific.

Most important of all, we acted in Korea.

I was in Independence, Missouri, in June 1950 when Secretary Acheson telephoned me and gave me the news about the invasion of Korea. I told the Secretary to lay the matter at once before the United Nations, and I came on back to Washington.

Flying back over the flatlands of the Middle West and over the Appalachians that summer afternoon I had a lot of time to think. I turned the problem over in my mind in many ways, but my thoughts kept coming back to the 1930's—to Manchuria—Ethiopia—the Rhineland—Austria—and finally to Munich.

Here was history repeating itself. Here was another probing action, another testing action. If we let the Republic of Korea go under, some other country would be next, and then another. And all the time the courage and confidence of the free world would be ebbing away, just as it did in the 1930's. And the United Nations would go the way of the League of Nations.

When I reached Washington I met immediately with the Secretary of State, the Secretary of Defense and General Bradley, and the other civilian and military officials who had information and advice to help me decide what to do. We talked about the problems long and hard. It was not easy to make the decision that sent American boys again into battle. I was a soldier in the First World War, and I know what a soldier goes through. I knew well the anguish that mothers and fathers and families go through. So I knew what was ahead if we acted in Korea.

But after all this was said, we realized that the issue was whether there would be fighting in a limited area now or on a much larger scale later on—whether there would be some casualties now or many more casualties later. So a decision was reached—the decision I believe was the most important in my time as President. In the days that followed, the most heartening fact was that the American people clearly agreed with the decision.

And in Korea our men are fighting as valiantly as Americans have ever fought—because they know they are fighting in the same cause of freedom in which Americans have stood ever since the beginning of the Republic.

Where free men had failed the test before, this time we met the test. We met it firmly. We met it successfully. The aggression has been repelled. The communists have seen their hopes of easy conquest go down the drain. The determination of free people to defend themselves has been made clear to the Kremlin.

As I have thought about our world-wide struggle with the communists these past eight years, day in and day out, I have never once doubted that you, the people of our country, have the will to do what is necessary to win this terrible fight against communism. I know the people of this country have that will and determination, and I have always depended upon it. Because I have been sure of that, I have been able to make necessary decisions even though they called for sacrifices by all of us. And I have not been wrong in my judgment of the American people. That same assurance of our people's determination will be General Eisenhower's greatest source of strength in carrying on this struggle.

Now, once in a while, I get a letter from some impatient person asking, Why don't we get it over with? Why don't we issue an ultimatum—make all-out war, drop the atomic bomb? For most

Americans, the answer is quite simple: We are not made that way.
We are a moral people. Peace is our goal, with justice and freedom.
We cannot, of our own free will, violate the very principles that
we are striving to defend. The whole purpose of what we are doing
is to prevent World War III. Starting a war is no way to make peace.

But if anyone still thinks that, just this once, bad means can
bring good ends, then let me remind you of this: We are living in
the eighth year of the atomic age. We are not the only nation that
is learning to unleash the power of the atom. A third world war
might dig the grave not only of our communist opponents but also
of our own society, our world as well as theirs. Starting atomic war
is totally unthinkable for rational men.

Then, some of you may ask, when and how will the cold war
ever end? I think I can answer that simply. The communist world
has great resources, and it looks strong. But there is a fatal flaw in
their society. Theirs is a godless system, a system of slavery; there
is no freedom in it, no consent. The Iron Curtain, the secret police,
the constant purges, all these are symptoms of a great basic weakness
—the rulers' fear of their own people. In the long run the strength
of our free society and our ideals will prevail over a system that has
respect for neither God nor men.

Last week, in my State of the Union message to the Congress—
and I hope you will all take the time to read it—I explained how I
think we will finally win through.

As the free world grows stronger, more united, more attractive
to men on both sides of the Iron Curtain—and as the Soviet hopes
for easy expansion are blocked—then there will have to come a time
of change in the Soviet world. Nobody can say for sure when that
is going to be, or exactly how it will come about, whether by revolution, or trouble in the satellite states, or by a change inside the
Kremlin. Whether the Communist rulers shift their policies of their
own free will, or whether the change comes about some other way,
I have not a doubt in the world that the change will occur.

I have a deep and abiding faith in the destiny of free men. With
patience and courage we shall some day move on into a new era—
a wonderful golden age—an age when we can use the peaceful tools
that science has forged for us to do away with poverty and human
misery everywhere on earth.

Think what can be done, once our capital, our skills, our science

—most of all atomic energy—can be released from the tasks of defense and turned wholly to peaceful purposes all around the world. There is no end to what can be done.

I can't help but dream out loud a little here. The Tigris and Euphrates Valley can be made to bloom as it did in the times of Babylon and Nineveh; Israel can be made the country of milk and honey as it was in the time of Joshua. There is a plateau in Ethiopia some six to eight thousand feet high that has sixty-five thousand square miles of land just exactly like the corn belt of northern Illinois. Enough food can be raised there to feed a hundred million people. There are places in South America—places in Colombia and Venezuela and Brazil—just like that plateau in Ethiopia, places where food could be raised for millions of people.

These things can be done, and they are self-liquidating projects. If we can get peace and safety in the world under the United Nations, the developments will come so fast we will not recognize the world in which we now live. This is our dream of the future—our picture of the world we hope to have when the communist threat is overcome.

5. BIPARTISAN FOREIGN POLICY

The principal achievements of the Truman administration in foreign affairs were the result of bipartisan co-operation. Bipartisan-ship drew special force from the fortuitous circumstance that the leading Republican involved, Senator Arthur Vandenberg, a recent convert from isolationism and a man with a strong sense of mission, was committed with idealistic zeal to an internationalist approach. It was only with the aid of the bipartisan coalition of which Senator Vandenberg was the leader that the President could achieve the legislative support necessary to his foreign policy. He was, then, to some extent the captive of Vandenberg.

The scope and coverage of bipartisanship fluctuated. American policy in Japan was not evolved on a bipartisan basis, but in 1951 the Japanese peace treaty was. In the first several years of Mr. Truman's presidency bipartisanship did not apply in Latin America; later it framed the Inter-American Rio treaty. It did not apply to military government in Germany, but it was immediately invoked in the crisis of the Berlin blockade and airlift. Needless to say, bipartisan *policy did not apply to China. The origination of Point Four was not an act of bipartisanship, but a major political stroke of the President. Bipartisanship covered aid to Greece and Turkey, the European Recovery Program, the North Atlantic Pact, and American membership in the United Nations. In general, bipartisanship thrived more vigorously before Mr. Truman's 1948 victory than after.*

The fullest statement of his views about bipartisan foreign policy is in a speech before the National Press Club in Washington on May 10, 1954.

Today I want to talk with you about unity and bipartisanship in foreign policy. I believe very deeply that we must have that unity and bipartisanship to meet the crisis that exists in the world today.

The responsibilities of the United States are vast. Much as we might wish to, we cannot escape them. We cannot escape the fact that our nation is looked to for leadership. And leadership requires taking hard decisions, carrying heavy burdens, making great sacrifices. For our people to join in those decisions and sustain those burdens requires, in turn, a broad measure of agreement and support from both of the great political parties and an overwhelming sense that the national interest is being put above partisan interest in the conduct of our foreign policy.

Everyone seems to agree that we must have national unity in foreign policy, that we must have a nonpartisan or bipartisan approach. But it's one thing to agree upon generalities; it is another to take definite and specific action. It's one thing to give lip service to high-sounding principles; it is another to take practical measures to live up to them.

Bipartisanship goes far deeper than mechanics, important as these are. Under President Roosevelt's administration and my own—under the last five Secretaries of State—all sorts of helpful methods were developed to work with responsible members of the other party in and out of Congress. These not only provided consultation, continuing and thorough, with the opposition, but actual participation in the execution of policy by Republicans—Republicans who were trusted and respected by their own party.

Today I shall not speak further of matters of method, but shall talk briefly of the basis upon which all method must rest. I will talk of the foundation which must exist if a bipartisan foreign policy is to be restored.

The first point I want to make is that this responsibility rests squarely upon the administration in power, and in the very nature of things cannot be discharged by anyone else. It is fundamental, I think, that, however much the minority party wishes to help, its role must be limited to help and co-operation. The responsibility for the conduct of our foreign relations rests and must rest with the administration in power.

More specifically, it rests and must rest where the Constitution places it—with the President of the United States, not with either or both parties in the Congress, nor with the Congress at all. "In this vast external realm," said the Supreme Court, "with its important, complicated, delicate and manifold problems, the President alone has the power to speak or listen as a representative of the nation." [At this point Mr. Truman's text had a reference to a footnote giving the source of the quotation: *United States v. Curtiss-Wright Corporation, 299 U.S. 304, 319.*] "He makes treaties with the advice and consent of the Senate; but he alone negotiates. Into the field of negotiation the Senate cannot intrude; and Congress is powerless to invade it."

Unhappily the court was, of course, referring only to legal power, not lung power.

But the point is that bipartisanship means and must mean that the minority must act within the area which the President makes possible. It can consult, advise, participate, support no more than he and his advisers enable it to. This does not make its obligation any the less, but it may make its opportunity and its ability to co-operate and support considerably less.

The second point I want to make is that in order to have a bipartisan foreign policy there must be a will to co-operate. It is basic to the very meaning of co-operation in foreign policy that those co-operating regard one another as true, loyal, devoted citizens of their common country, trying to do their best for her. This is the only basis on which co-operation can be honorably asked or given.

This does not, of course, mean that the political battle cannot be, or should not be, fought hard on domestic issues or any foreign ones where true and irreconcilable differences develop. I have never complained of an honest political fight, nor have I run away from one. In fact, I rather enjoy the fights. But I never asked a man to co-operate with me whom I called a traitor; and I never called a man a traitor whom I wanted to work with me.

"Traitor" and "treason" are words that you can't use in friendship, even when you smile. There is no smile, grin or otherwise, which goes with them. This is so—regardless of the manners of the dirtiest gutter politics—because the basis of trust and mutual respect dissolves under suspicion born of such reckless talk. False charges about "twenty years of treason" make a very poor steppingstone to bipartisan co-operation.

"True," you may say to me, "but the President of the United States is the one charged with the conduct of our foreign relations, and he is not the one who has said and done these things." But this is not the point. The point is a positive one. If the President wishes a bipartisan foreign policy, it is his responsibility to make one possible. It is his responsibility not to allow it to be made impossible.

No one would suggest that he is able to control all irresponsible and unscrupulous persons who dig out of the dunghill of Hitler's writings the phrase with which he attacked the Weimar Republic— "fourteen years of shame and treason"—and use it as a weapon of political assassination. But there are many things he can do. He hires and fires his own subordinates and need not tolerate political assassins within his own executive branch. He is the leader of his party and can direct that his party chairman follow decent rules of political conduct in the campaign. If there is still a lunatic fringe in his party or in the Congress outside his control, he can at least disavow them.

We can certainly ask: Does the basis for bipartisanship—mutual trust and respect—exist when the administration through its political leadership, which seems to include both the Attorney-General and the chairman of the Republican National Committee, picks up, sponsors, and itself uses both the originators and the content of this infamous campaign of defamation? It most certainly does not. And not because Democrats are sensitive and have their feelings hurt. It is because mutual confidence of Americans in themselves and in their government is undermined and weakened.

It is no cause of satisfaction to Democrats that those who have sown the wind now are reaping the whirlwind. The gravest sufferer is our country. Only a week or two ago a foreign correspondent could write to his paper of our latest attack of political insanity: "I have been watching a circus so fantastic, so degrading, so puerile, and so recklessly dirty that the disgust one feels is matched only by the alarm over the behavior of our closest ally in the conduct of their domestic affairs."

The problem is not who is responsible for starting a course of conduct which destroys the basis for bipartisan foreign policy—perhaps of any foreign policy—but who is responsible for stopping it. There is only one man—the President of the United States.

No greater danger to this country, no greater aid to communism, can be imagined than to permit our people to be split into fiercely partisan groups over issues of foreign policy. For the good of the country and for the good of the cause of freedom, I hope that foreign policy will be taken out of the partisan arena and placed once more on bipartisan foundations. Only then will it be possible to evolve and maintain adequate measures to meet the terrible danger we confront. Only then will the government receive the firm and united support from the whole people which is necessary for an effective foreign policy.

Surely partisan politics should end at the water's edge. But some political attacks, a good way back of the water's edge, are so viciously destructive that they end in destroying our national unity and our nation's position in the world. It isn't enough to deprecate these attacks with pious phrases. It takes vigorous action to stamp them out.

Surely bipartisan foreign policy is as needed now as it ever was. But co-operation between the parties is not made easy when one party officially brands the other as a betrayer of the nation in this very field.

I understand it has been suggested that you gentlemen of the press have been printing more about the news that divides the country than about the news that unites it. I do not want to alarm you unduly by coming to your defense, so I will merely observe that the pickings in the latter field have been pretty thin lately.

The third point I want to make is that if a bipartisan foreign policy must rest upon a spirit of mutual trust, it springs from the firm and consistent leadership in the formulation and execution of foreign policy.

The opposition—indeed the whole American people—must know what the policy is and why it is, before they can support it. They cannot know this if they are subjected to a suggestion of conflicting, vague, and confusing statements, proposals, and acts.

The times are too critical to illustrate what I think is plain enough by drawing upon recent events. But I believe that I am only stating a common experience of my fellow citizens in saying that both on military and foreign policy the pronouncements of recent months have left me very confused indeed.

Deeply as I regret the apparent abandonment or neglect of bipartisan policy, I could, as a citizen, accept this if only an alternative were offered. Bipartisanship is the best approach. But we cannot always have the best. Is it too much to ask that we have at least something in its place—something that could be recognized as a clear-cut administration foreign policy?

The President must give the lead. The loyal opposition can only play a constructive part if that lead is understandable. It cannot furnish the lead. No one knows better than I how complicated and manifold are the problems in that vast external realm. No one is more tolerant of mistakes in statement of policies.

But in all humility, no one knows better than I that this responsibility cannot be delegated, it cannot be avoided. It must be met, and by the President of the United States, or our country and the cause of world peace will be the loser.

So, as one who wishes with all his heart to close ranks to support and strengthen him upon whom now rests the burden which I once bore, I ask for a fully considered and clear lead, however difficult the path may be.

The days and months and perhaps years before us hold dangers and problems of infinite complexity and delicacy. I urge upon my fellow citizens this course. Let us say no word which confuses or obscures the voice of the President as the representative of this nation in our dealings with other nations. Let us ask only that he speak as the representative of all the people, clearly and with weighed words. Let us turn fiercely upon anyone who sets one of us against another, who undermines our faith in one another or in our government.

Let us support with all our power the great principles through which our own Constitution seeks a more perfect union and the blessings of liberty. Let us support with all our power the principle for which so much has been done and suffered in Europe and Asia

—the principle of collective security declared in the United Nations Charter.

6. ASSISTANCE TO FREE NATIONS

The beneficiaries of the earliest major assistance to foreign countries in the Truman administration were Greece and Turkey. They were also the original foci of what became known as the Truman Doctrine and of the policy of containment—a policy that became dominant in the next several years. It was also one of the most successful of all the policies promulgated by the Truman administration. The three crucial tests of it were Greece, the Berlin blockade, and Korea; and of these, two have to be called victorious tests, and the third not a defeat. Greece was pacified and the Communist threat quashed; the Berlin blockade was roundly beaten by the airlift; and Korea, a stalemate by military criteria, was a success in the sense that Southern Korea is today not communized.

Affairs in Greece had been in varying states of crisis since the country's liberation in 1944. The British, whose forces had come in when the Germans moved out, had labored unsuccessfully for three years to restore stability and to end the Communist-fomented civil war. On February 24, 1947, the British Ambassador in Washington informed the Department of State that after March 31 Britain would have to discontinue her economic assistance to Greece and also to Turkey. Subsequently the British government announced that its troops in Greece would have to be altogether withdrawn. The Truman administration, though aware of the economic plight that dictated these moves, was surprised that Britain had run out her string so fast and was providing so short a deadline for her withdrawal.

Mr. Truman did not take the matter to Congress until nearly three weeks after the British notification. The procrastination is a political curiosity made the more curious by the fact that the President's message, when it came, requested action on the Greek-Turkish crisis before the end of March. One reason for his delay was the mauling that Congress had given the recent British loan. He feared that at best Greek-Turkish aid would face great uncertainty in the Congress. An even more important factor was his deliberate intention to make his message coincide with the arrival of Secretary of State Marshall in Moscow for conferences in which he was to impress it upon the Russians that the days of the soft policy were over and that Russian good faith would no longer be assumed by the United States. What Mr. Truman meant by the Marshall mission and the message of Greek-Turkish aid was a double-barreled declaration that the United States would stand up to the Russians and resist their systematic grabbing of areas vital to our security.

The President's message of March 12 said:

The gravity of the situation which confronts the world today necessitates my appearance before a joint session of the Congress. The foreign policy and the national security of this country are involved.

One aspect of the present situation, which I wish to present to you at this time for your consideration and decision, concerns Greece and Turkey. The United States has received from the Greek government an urgent appeal for financial and economic assistance. Preliminary reports from the American Economic Mission now in Greece and reports from the American Ambassador in Greece corroborate the statement of the Greek government that assistance is imperative if Greece is to survive as a free nation. I do not believe that the American people and the Congress wish to turn a deaf ear to the appeal of the Greek government.

Greece is not a rich country. Lack of sufficient natural resources has always forced the Greek people to work hard to make both ends meet. Since 1940 this industrious and peace-loving country has suffered invasion, four years of cruel enemy occupation, and bitter internal strife.

When forces of liberation entered Greece they found that the retreating Germans had destroyed virtually all the railways, roads, port facilities, communications, and merchant marine. More than a thousand villages had been burned. Eighty-five per cent of the children were tubercular. Livestock, poultry, and draft animals had almost disappeared. Inflation had wiped out practically all savings. As a result of these tragic conditions a military minority, exploiting human want and misery, was able to create political chaos which, until now, has made economic recovery impossible.

Greece is today without funds to finance the importation of those goods which are essential to bare subsistence. Under these circumstances the people of Greece cannot make progress in solving their problems of reconstruction. Greece is in desperate need of financial and economic assistance to enable it to resume purchases of food, clothing, fuel, and seeds. These are indispensable for the subsistence of its people and are obtainable only from abroad. Greece must have help to import the goods necessary to restore internal order and security, so essential for economic and political recovery.

The Greek government has also asked for the assistance of experienced American administrators, economists, and technicians to insure that the financial and other aid given to Greece shall be used effectively in creating a stable and self-sustaining economy and in improving its public administration.

The very existence of the Greek state is today threatened by the terrorist activities of several thousand armed men, led by communists, who defy the government's authority at a number of points, particularly along the northern boundaries. A commission appointed by the United Nations Security Council is at present investigating disturbed conditions in northern Greece and alleged border violations along the frontier between Greece on the one hand and Albania, Bulgaria, and Yugoslavia on the other. Meanwhile, the Greek government is unable to cope with the situation. The Greek army is small and poorly equipped. It needs supplies and equipment if it is to restore the authority of the government throughout Greek territory.

Greece must have assistance if it is to become a self-supporting and self-respecting democracy. The United States must supply that assistance. We have already extended to Greece certain types of relief and economic aid, but these are inadequate. There is no other country to which democratic Greece can turn. No other nation is willing and able to provide the necessary support for a democratic Greek government.

The British government, which has been helping Greece, can give no further financial or economic aid after March 31. Great Britain finds itself under the necessity of reducing or liquidating its commitments in several parts of the world, including Greece.

We have considered how the United Nations might assist in this crisis. But the situation is an urgent one requiring immediate action, and the United Nations and its related organizations are not in a position to extend help of the kind that is required.

It is important to note that the Greek government has asked for our aid in utilizing effectively the financial and other assistance we may give to Greece and in improving its public administration. It is of the utmost importance that we supervise the use of any funds made available to Greece, in such a manner that each dollar spent will count toward making Greece self-supporting and will help to build an economy in which a healthy democracy can flourish.

No government is perfect. One of the chief virtues of a democracy, however, is that its defects are always visible and under democratic processes can be pointed out and corrected. The government of Greece is not perfect. Nevertheless it represents 85 per cent of the members of the Greek Parliament who were chosen in an election last year. Foreign observers, including 692 Americans, considered this election to be a fair expression of the views of the Greek people.

The Greek government has been operating in an atmosphere of chaos and extremism. It has made mistakes. The extension of aid by this country does not mean that the United States condones everything that the Greek government has done or will do. We have condemned in the past, and we condemn now, extremist measures of the Right or the Left. We have in the past advised tolerance, and we advise tolerance now.

Greece's neighbor Turkey also deserves our attention. The future of Turkey as an independent and economically sound state is clearly no less important to the freedom-loving peoples of the world than the future of Greece. The circumstances in which Turkey finds itself today are considerably different from those of Greece. Turkey has been spared the disasters that have beset Greece. And during the war the United States and Great Britain furnished Turkey with material aid.

Nevertheless, Turkey now needs our support. Since the war Turkey has sought financial assistance from Great Britain and the United States for the purpose of effecting that modernization necessary for the maintenance of its national integrity. That integrity is essential to the preservation of order in the Middle East. The British Government has informed us that, owing to its own difficulties, it can no longer extend financial or economic aid to Turkey. As in the case of Greece, if Turkey is to have the assistance it needs the United States must supply it. We are the only country able to provide that help.

I am fully aware of the broad implications involved if the United States extends assistance to Greece and Turkey, and I shall discuss these implications with you at this time.

One of the primary objectives of the foreign policy of the United States is the creation of conditions in which we and other nations will be able to work out a way of life free from coercion. This was a fundamental issue in the war with Germany and Japan. Our victory was won over countries which sought to impose their will and their way of life upon other nations.

To ensure the peaceful development of nations, free from coercion, the United States has taken a leading part in establishing the United Nations. The United Nations is designed to make possible lasting freedom and independence for all its members. We shall not realize our objectives, however, unless we are willing to help free people to maintain their free institutions and their national integrity against aggressive movements that seek to impose upon them totalitarian regimes. This is no more than a frank recognition that totalitarian regimes imposed on free peoples, by direct or indirect aggression, undermine the foundations of international peace and hence the security of the United States.

The peoples of a number of countries of the world have recently had totalitarian regimes forced upon them against their will. The government of the United States has made frequent protests against coercion and intimidation in violation of the Yalta agreement, in Poland, Rumania, and Bulgaria. I must also state that in a number of other countries there have been similar developments.

At the present moment in world history nearly every nation must choose between alternative ways of life. The choice is too often not a free one.

One way of life is based upon the will of the majority, and is distinguished by free institutions, representative government, free elections, guarantees of individual liberty, freedom of speech and religion, and freedom from political oppression.

The second way of life is based upon the will of a minority forcibly impressed upon the majority. It relies upon terror and oppression, a controlled press and radio, fixed elections, and the suppression of personal freedoms.

I believe that it must be the policy of the United States to support free peoples who are resisting attempted subjugation by armed minorities or by outside pressures. I believe that we must assist free peoples to work out their own destinies in their own way. I believe that our help should be primarily through economic and financial aid, which is essential to economic stability and orderly political processes.

The world is not static, and the status quo is not sacred. But we cannot allow changes in the status quo in violation of the Charter of the United Nations by such methods as coercion, or by such subterfuges as political infiltration. In helping free and independent nations to maintain their freedom the United States will be giving effect to the principles of the Charter of the United Nations.

It is necessary only to glance at a map to realize that the survival and integrity of the Greek nation are of grave importance in a much wider situation. If Greece should fall under the control of an armed minority, the effect upon its neighbor Turkey would be immediate and serious. Confusion and disorder might well spread throughout the entire Middle East.

Moreover, the disappearance of Greece as an independent state would have a profound effect upon those countries in Europe whose peoples are struggling against great difficulties to maintain their freedoms and their independence while they repair the damages of war. It would be an unspeakable tragedy if these countries, which have struggled so long against overwhelming odds, should lose that victory for which they sacrificed so much. Collapse of free institutions and loss of independence would be disastrous not only for them but for the world. Discouragement and possibly failure would quickly be the lot of neighboring peoples striving to maintain their freedom and independence.

Should we fail to aid Greece and Turkey in this fateful hour, the effect will be far-reaching to the West as well as to the East. We must take immediate and resolute action.

I therefore ask the Congress to provide authority for assistance to Greece and Turkey in the amount of $400,000,000 for the period ending June 30, 1948. In requesting these funds I have taken into consideration the maximum amount of relief assistance which would be furnished to Greece out of the $350,000,000 which I recently requested that the Congress authorize for the prevention of starvation and suffering in countries devastated by the war.

In addition to funds I ask the Congress to authorize the detail of American civilian and military personnel to Greece and Turkey, at the request of those countries, to assist in the tasks of reconstruction and for the purpose of supervising the use of such financial and material assistance as may be furnished. I recommend that authority also be provided for the instruction and training of selected Greek and Turkish personnel.

Finally, I ask that the Congress provide authority which will permit the speediest and most effective use, in terms of needed commodities, supplies, and equipment, of such funds as may be authorized.

If further funds, or further authority, should be needed for purposes indicated in this message, I shall not hesitate to bring the situation before the Congress. On this subject the executive and legislative branches of the government must work together.

This is a serious course upon which we embark. I would not recommend it except that the alternative is much more serious.

The United States contributed $341,000,000,000 toward winning World War II. This is an investment in world freedom and world peace. The assistance that I am recommending for Greece and Turkey amounts to little more than one tenth of one per cent of this investment. It is only common sense that we should safeguard this investment and make sure that it was not in vain.

The seeds of totalitarian regimes are nurtured by misery and want. They spread and grow in the evil soil of poverty and strife. They reach their full growth when the hope of a people for a better life has died. We must keep that hope alive. The free peoples of the world look to us for support in maintaining their freedoms. If we falter in our leadership, we may endanger the peace of the world —and we shall surely endanger the welfare of our own nation.

Great responsibilities have been placed upon us by the swift movement of events. I am confident that the Congress will face these responsibilities squarely.

§ In Congress the Truman message was on the whole enthusiastically received, though with reservations in some quarters. Senators Taft and Byrd and others opposed sending military advisers to Greece and Turkey on the ground that it would be tantamount to dominating those countries. Byrd, as an inveterate economizer, was concerned over the expense of the Truman program. Vandenberg was dismayed at the haste demanded; the deadline of March 31 gave Congress only nineteen days to act on a project the implications of which were both enormous and enigmatic.

There was criticism in and out of Congress to the effect that the President was by-passing the United Nations, or that he had at least erred in not sufficiently explaining his reasons for leaving the United

Nations out of the picture. Senator Vandenberg introduced an amendment, which was adopted, to provide that the program of aid should lapse whenever the General Assembly or the Security Council should decide that action taken by the United Nations had rendered the continuance of United States aid unnecessary or undesirable, and that, if the question came before the Security Council, the United States would waive its right of veto.

Other provisions of the legislation passed by Congress called for aid in the form of loans or grants and for the dispatch to Greece and Turkey of civilian and military advisers to help the recipient governments make effective use of the aid. The President was required to withdraw any or all aid if requested to do so by either the Greek or the Turkish government. The recipient governments were required to give free access to United States officials and to the press, that they might observe how the aid was being used. Full publicity was to be given to the programs of aid within each country.

The Truman doctrine, though faced with numerous and formidable difficulties, achieved its fundamental aim of keeping Greece and Turkey out of the Soviet orbit. By the close of January 1948 over 90,000 tons of American military equipment had been sent to Greece. At the request of the Greek government American military advisers were sent into the field to advise directly in operations. Toward the end of 1949 hostilities came to an end in Greece, and attention shifted to the country's very serious economic problems—disastrous inflation, severe unemployment, and the almost desperate circumstances of wage earners and white-collar workers.

As to Turkey, President Truman's quarterly reports on the program in 1949 expressed satisfaction with the progress toward the objective of a smaller but more effective Turkish armed force—one better matched to the resources of Turkey.

7.   EUROPEAN RECOVERY PROGRAM

The European Recovery Program (ERP) was heralded by Under Secretary of State Dean Acheson in a little-noticed speech in Cleveland, Mississippi, on May 8 and in the address of Secretary of State Marshall at Harvard on June 5, 1947.

European recovery was hardly a fresh subject in 1947. Since the end of the war the United States had poured assistance into Europe under various programs, chiefly the former United Nations Relief and Rehabilitation Administration. Britain, France, Norway, the Netherlands, and Belgium had achieved remarkable economic recoveries since the war, but some countries had made little progress. Italian production was about fifty per cent of 1937, with Austria and Germany below that level. A retarded Germany threatened to nullify the progress made by other nations.

Europe's worst problems were food and dollars. Severe winters and shortages of farm equipment and of fertilizers resulted in crops not exceeding seventy per cent of the prewar average. The winter of 1946–47 was so severe that rations in many countries had to be cut, and there were food riots in the Ruhr. The dollar shortage resulted from the postwar trade disequilibrium between Europe and the United States, which put Europe in a position such that it could get needed American goods only by gifts or loans from America.

ERP had also its political background. In the spring of 1947 strong Communist forces were pressing hard in France and Italy. Prolonged cabinet crises in those countries resulted in governments, not including communists, that faced the possible counteraction of strikes and the paralysis of vital industries by communist-dominated trade unions. Ramadier in France and de Gasperi in Italy were depending on improved economic conditions and on American aid to pull them through.

A number of Truman measures preceded the President's address to Congress on European aid. On October 1 he urged the call of key Congressional committees "at the earliest possible date to prepare measures for stop-gap relief in Europe." He set up the President's Citizens Food Committee, with Charles Luckman as Chairman. He called on the nation to forego meat on Tuesday and poultry and eggs on Thursday, to aid Europe. He had to deny that the Marshall Plan was imperialism, as the U.S.S.R. was charging. He accused the reborn Comintern of conspiring to forestall the economic recovery of Europe. On October 24 he made a radio speech to the nation setting forth the objectives of the European Recovery Program and stressing the importance of curbing inflation. On the same day he presided over a White House conference of one hundred business and labor leaders to explain the program of aid and to anticipate *criticisms based on the supposed effect on the American economy.*

These preparatory steps led up to the address to Congress delivered on December 19, 1947.

It is of vital importance to the United States that European recovery be continued to ultimate success. The American tradition of extending a helping hand to people in distress, our concern for the building of a healthy world economy which can make possible ever-increasing standards of living for our people, and our overwhelming concern for the maintenance of a civilization of free men and free institutions, all combine to give us this great interest in European recovery.

The people of the United States have shown, by generous contributions since the end of hostilities, their great sympathy and concern for the many millions in Europe who underwent the trials of war and enemy occupation. Our sympathy is undiminished, but we know that we cannot give relief indefinitely, and so we seek practical measures which will eliminate Europe's need for further relief.

Considered in terms of our own economy, European recovery is essential. The last two decades have taught us the bitter lesson that no economy, not even one so strong as our own, can remain healthy and prosperous in a world of poverty and want.

In the past the flow of raw materials and manufactured products between Western Europe, Latin America, Canada, and the United States has integrated these areas in a great trading system. In the same manner Far Eastern exports to the United States have helped pay for the goods shipped from Europe to the Far East. Europe is thus an essential part of a world trading network. The failure to revive fully this vast trading system, which has begun to function again since the end of the war, would result in economic deterioration throughout the world. The United States, in common with other nations, would suffer.

Our deepest concern with European recovery, however, is that it is essential to the maintenance of the civilization in which the American way of life is rooted. It is the only assurance of the continued independence and integrity of a group of nations who constitute a bulwark for the principles of freedom, justice, and the dignity of the individual.

The economic plight in which Europe now finds itself has intensified a political struggle between those who wish to remain free men living under the rule of law and those who would use economic distress as a pretext for the establishment of a totalitarian state.

The next few years can determine whether the free countries of Europe will be able to preserve their heritage of freedom. If Europe fails to recover, the peoples of these countries might be driven to the philosophy of despair—the philosophy which contends that their basic wants can be met only by the surrender of their basic rights to totalitarian control. Such a turn of events would constitute a shattering blow to peace and stability in the world. It might well compel us to modify our own economic system and to forego, for the sake of our own security, the enjoyment of many of our freedoms and privileges.

It is for these reasons that the United States has so vital an interest in strengthening the belief of the people of Europe that freedom from fear and want will be achieved under free and democratic governments.

Origins of the European Recovery Program

The end of the fighting in Europe left that continent physically devastated and its economy temporarily paralyzed. The immediate problem was to prevent widespread starvation and disease and to make a start toward economic recovery. In the first year and a half after V-E day the people of Western Europe, by their own diligent efforts and with the aid of the United States and other nations, made remarkable progress toward these objectives.

At the beginning of 1947, however, they were still short of the goal of economic recovery. Their difficulties were greatly increased during the present year, chiefly by a bitter winter followed by floods and droughts which cut Western Europe's grain crop to the lowest figure in generations and hampered production of many other products. Nevertheless it was clear by last spring that Europe had achieved sufficient political and economic stability to make possible an over-all plan for recovery.

European recovery is essentially a problem for the nations of Europe. It was therefore apparent that it could not be solved, even with outside aid, unless the European nations themselves would find a joint solution and accept joint responsibility for its execution. Such a co-operative plan would serve to release the full productive resources of Europe and provide a proper basis for measuring the need and effectiveness of further aid from outside Europe, and in particular from the United States.

These considerations led to the suggestion by the Secretary of State on June 5, 1947, that further help from the United States should be given only after the countries of Europe had agreed upon their basic requirements and the steps which they would take in order to give proper effect to additional aid from us.

In response to this suggestion representatives of sixteen European nations assembled in Paris in July, at the invitation of the British and French governments, to draw up a co-operative program of European recovery. They formed a Committee of European Economic Co-operation. The countries represented were Austria, Belgium, Denmark, France, Greece, Iceland, Ireland, Italy, Luxembourg, the Netherlands, Norway, Portugal, Sweden, Switzerland, Turkey, and the United Kingdom. Although Western Germany was not formally represented on the Committee, its requirements as well as its ability to contribute to European economic recovery were considered by the Committee.

The Recovery Program Proposed by the European Countries

The report of the European Committee was transmitted to the government of the United States late in September. The report describes the present economic situation of Europe and the extent to which the participating countries can solve their problem by individual and joint efforts. After taking into account these recovery efforts, the report estimates the extent to which the sixteen countries will be unable to pay for the imports they must have.

The report points out that the peoples of Western Europe depend for their support upon international trade. It has been possible for some 270,000,000 people occupying this relatively small area to enjoy a good standard of living only by manufacturing imported raw materials and exporting the finished products to the rest of the world. They must also import foodstuffs in large volume, for there is not enough farmland in Western Europe to support its population even with intensive cultivation and with favorable weather. They cannot produce adequate amounts of cotton, oil, and other raw materials.

Unless these deficiencies are met by imports, the productive centers of Europe can function only at low efficiency if at all.

In the past these necessary imports were paid for by exports from Europe, by the performance of services such as shipping and banking, and by income from capital investments abroad. All these elements of international trade were so badly disrupted by the war that the people of Western Europe have been unable to produce in their own countries, or to purchase elsewhere, the goods essential to their livelihood. Shortages of raw materials, productive capacity, and exportable commodities have set up vicious circles of increasing scarcities and lowered standards of living.

The economic recovery of Western European countries depends upon breaking through these vicious circles by increasing production to a point where exports and services can pay for the imports they must have to live. The basic problem in making Europe self-supporting is to increase European production.

The sixteen nations presented in their report a recovery program designed to enable them and Western Germany to become economically self-supporting within a period of four years and thereafter to maintain a reasonable minimum standard of living for their people without special help from others. The program rests upon four basic points:

(1) A strong production effort by each of the participating countries.

(2) Creation of internal financial stability by each country.

(3) Maximum and continuing co-operation among the participating countries.

(4) A solution of the problem of the participating countries' trading deficit with the American continents, particularly by increasing European exports.

The nations represented on the European Committee agreed at Paris to do everything in their power to achieve these four aims. They agreed to take definite measures leading to financial, economic, and monetary stability, the reduction of trade barriers, the removal of obstacles to the free movement of persons within Europe, and a joint effort to use their common resources to the best advantage.

These agreements are a source of great encouragement. When the representatives of sixteen sovereign nations with diverse peoples, histories, and institutions jointly determine to achieve closer economic ties among themselves and to break away from the self-defeating actions of narrow nationalism, the obstacles in the way of recovery appear less formidable.

The report takes into account the productive capacities of the participating nations and their ability to obtain supplies from other parts of the world. It also takes into account the possibilities of obtaining funds through the International Bank for Reconstruction and Development, through private investment, and in some instances by the sale of existing foreign assets. The participating countries recognized that some commodities, particularly food, will remain scarce for years to come, and the diet they have set as their goal for 1951 is less adequate in most cases than their prewar diet. The report assumes that many countries will continue restrictions on the distribution of shortage items such as food, clothing, and fuel.

When all these factors had been considered the European Committee concluded that there will still be a requirement for large quantities of food, fuel, raw materials, and capital equipment for which the financial resources of the participating countries will be inadequate. With successful execution of the European recovery program, this requirement will diminish in each of the four years ahead, and the Committee anticipated that by 1952 Europe could again meet its needs without special aid.

Appraisal of the European Problem

The problem of economic recovery in Western Europe is basically of the character described in the report of the sixteen nations. A successful European recovery program will depend upon two essentials. The first is that each nation separately and all the nations together should take vigorous action to help themselves. The second essential is that sufficient outside aid should be made available to provide the margin of victory for the recovery program.

The necessary imports which the sixteen countries cannot finance without assistance constitute only a small proportion, in terms of value, of their total national production—some five per cent over the four years of the program. These imports, however, are of crucial importance in generating recovery. They represent the difference between ever-deepening stagnation and progressive improvement.

Most of the necessary outside aid, if it is to come at all, must come from the United States. It is a simple fact that we are the only nation with sufficient economic strength to bridge the temporary gap between minimum European needs and war-diminished European resources.

We expect that other countries which have it within their power will also give what assistance they can to Europe. Canada, for example, has been lending assistance to Europe fully as great in proportion to its capacity as that which we have given. We also expect that international institutions, particularly the International Bank, will provide such assistance as they can within their charters. But the fact remains: only the United States can provide the bulk of the aid needed by Europe over the next four years.

It is necessarily a complex and difficult task to determine the extent and nature of this aid.

In some respects, the situation has changed significantly since the report of the sixteen countries was completed. Some of these changes have been unfavorable, including price increases in the United States and other countries where Europe makes purchases, a serious drought in Europe, and aggressive activities by communists and communist-inspired groups aimed directly at the prevention of European recovery.

There have also been favorable changes. In the last few months coal production in the Ruhr district of Western Germany has increased from 230,000 tons a day to 290,000 tons a day. Similarly, coal production in the United Kingdom has risen markedly in recent weeks. Iron and steel production has correspondingly increased. Such increases in production, which lie at the heart of industrial recovery, are of far-reaching importance. Further changes in the situation, now unpredictable, are to be expected as European recovery progresses.

All our plans and actions must be founded on the fact that the situation we are dealing with is flexible and not fixed, and we must be prepared to make adjustments whenever necessary. Weather conditions will largely determine whether agricultural goals can be met. Political events in Europe and in the rest of the world cannot be accurately foreseen. We must not be blind to the fact that the communists have announced determined opposition to any effort to help Europe get back on its feet. There will unquestionably be further incitements to strike, not for the purpose of redressing the legitimate grievances of particular groups, but for the purpose of bringing chaos in the hope that it will pave the way for totalitarian control.

On the other hand, if confidence and optimism are re-established soon the spark they provide can kindle united efforts to a degree which would substantially accelerate the progress of European recovery.

Despite these many imponderables, the dimensions of the necessary assistance by the United States can now be determined within reasonable limits. We can evaluate the probable success of a bold concept of assistance to the European economy. We can determine the principles upon which American aid should be based. We can estimate the probable magnitude of the assistance required and judge whether we can safely and wisely provide that assistance.

Extensive consideration has been given to these problems. Congressional committees and individual members of the Congress have studied them at home and abroad during the recent Congressional recess. The report of the European nations has been carefully analyzed by officials of our government. Committees of the executive branch and a group of distinguished private citizens have given their best thought to the relationship between Europe's needs and our resources.

Program for United States Aid

In the light of all these factors an integrated program for United States aid to European recovery has been prepared for submission to the Congress. In developing this program, certain basic considerations have been kept in mind:

First, the program is designed to make genuine recovery possible within a definite period of time, and not merely to continue relief indefinitely.

Second, the program is designed to insure that the funds and goods which we furnish will be used most effectively for European recovery.

Third, the program is designed to minimize the financial cost to the United States, but at the same time to avoid imposing on the European countries crushing financial burdens which they could not carry in the long run.

Fourth, the program is designed with due regard for conserving the physical resources of the United States and minimizing the impact on our economy of furnishing aid to Europe.

Fifth, the program is designed to be consistent with other international relationships and responsibilities of the United States.

Sixth, the administration of the program is designed to carry out wisely and efficiently this great enterprise of our foreign policy.

I shall discuss each of these basic considerations in turn.

Recovery—Not Relief

The program is designed to assist the participating European countries in obtaining imports essential to genuine economic recovery which they cannot finance from their own resources. It is based on the expectation that with this assistance European recovery can be substantially completed in about four years.

The aid which will be required from the United States for the first fifteen months—from April 1, 1948, to June 30, 1949—is now estimated at $6.8 billion.

These funds represent careful estimates of the cost of the goods and services which will be required during this period to start Europe on the road to genuine economic recovery. The European requirements as they were stated in the Paris report have been closely reviewed and scaled downward where they appeared to include non-essentials or where limited supplies will prevent their full satisfaction.

The requirements of the remaining three years of the program are more difficult to estimate now, but they are expected to decrease year by year as progress is made toward recovery. Obviously price changes, weather and crop conditions, and other unpredictable factors will influence the over-all cost of our aid. Nevertheless the inherent nature of this enterprise and the long-range planning necessary to put it into effect on both sides of the Atlantic require that this government indicate its plans for the duration and the general magnitude of the program, without committing itself to specific amounts in future years. The best estimates we can now make indicate that appropriations of about $10.2 billion will be required for the last three years.

I recommend that legislation providing for United States aid in support of the European recovery program authorize the appropriation of $17 billion from April 1, 1948, to June 30, 1952. Appropriation for the period from April 1, 1948, to June 30, 1949, should be made in time for the program to be put into effect by April 1, 1948. Appropriations for the later years should be considered subsequently by the Congress on an annual basis.

The funds we make available will enable the countries of Europe to purchase goods which will achieve two purposes—to lift the standard of living in Europe closer to a decent level, and at the same time to enlarge European capacity for production. Our funds will enable them to import grain for current consumption, and fertilizer and agricultural machinery to increase their food production. They will import fuel for current use and mining machinery to increase their coal output. In addition they will obtain raw materials, such as cotton, for current production, and some manufacturing and transportation equipment to increase their productive capacity.

The industrial goods we supply will be primarily to relieve critical shortages at a few strategic points which are now curtailing the great productive powers of Europe's industrial system.

The fundamental objective of further United States aid to European countries is to help them achieve economic self-support and to contribute their full share to a peaceful and prosperous world. Our aid must be adequate to this end. If we provide only half-hearted and halfway help, our efforts will be dissipated and the chances for political and economic stability in Europe are likely to be lost.

Insuring Proper Use of United States Aid

A second basic consideration with regard to this program is the means by which we can insure that our aid will be used to achieve its real purposes—that our goods and our dollars will contribute most effectively to European recovery. Appropriate agreements among the participating countries and with the United States are essential to this end.

At the Paris conference the European nations pledged themselves to take specific individual and co-operative actions to accomplish genuine recovery. While some modification or amplification of these pledges may prove desirable, mutual undertakings of this nature are essential. They will give unity of purpose and effective co-ordination to the endeavors of the peoples of the sixteen nations.

In addition each of the countries receiving aid will be expected to enter into an agreement with the United States affirming the pledges which it has given to the other participating countries, and making additional commitments.

Under these agreements each country would pledge itself to take the following actions, except where they are inapplicable to the country concerned:

(1) To promote increased industrial and agricultural production in order to enable the participating country to become independent of abnormal outside economic assistance.

(2) To take financial and monetary measures necessary to stabilize its currency, establish or maintain a proper rate of exchange, and generally to restore or maintain confidence in its monetary system.

(3) To co-operate with other participating countries to reduce barriers to trade among themselves and with other countries, and to stimulate an increasing interchange of goods and services.

(4) To make efficient use, within the framework of a joint program for European recovery, of the resources of the participating country, and to take the necessary steps to assure efficient use in the interest of European economic recovery of all goods and services made available through United States aid.

(5) To stimulate the production of specified raw materials, as may be mutually agreed upon, and to facilitate the procurement of such raw materials by the United States for stock-piling purposes from the excess above the reasonable domestic usage and commercial export requirements of the source country.

(6) To deposit in a special account the local currency equivalent of aid furnished in the form of grants, to be used only in a manner mutually agreed between the two governments.

(7) To publish domestically and to furnish to the United States appropriate information concerning the use made of our aid and the progress made under the agreements with other participating countries and with the United States.

The United States will, of course, retain the right to determine whether aid to any country is to be continued if our previous assistance has not been used effectively.

Financial Arrangements

A third basic consideration in formulating the program of United States aid relates to the financial arrangements under which our aid is to be provided.

One of the problems in achieving the greatest benefit from United

States aid is the extent to which funds should be made available in the form of grants as contrasted with loans. It is clear that we should require repayment to the extent that it is feasible and consistent with the objectives of the program, in order that no unnecessary burden be imposed upon the people of the United States. It is equally clear that we should not require repayment where it would impose paralyzing financial obligations on the people of Europe and thus defeat the basic purpose of making Europe self-supporting.

Recovery for Europe will not be achieved until its people are able to pay for their necessary imports with foreign exchange obtained through the export of goods and services. If they were to have additional burdens to bear in the form of interest and amortization payments in future years, they would have to plan for an even higher level of exports to meet these obligations. This would necessarily increase the requirements of the recovery program and delay the achievement of economic stability.

It is also important that an increasing portion of the financial needs of Europe be met by dollar loans from the International Bank and by the revival of private financing. This prospect would be seriously jeopardized if the United States, as part of the recovery program, were to impose all that the traffic will bear in the form of debt obligations.

I recommend that our aid should be extended partly in the form of grants and partly in the form of loans, depending primarily upon the capacity of each country to make repayments and the effect of additional international debt upon the accomplishment of genuine recovery. No grants should be made to countries able to pay cash for all imports or to repay loans.

At a later date it may prove desirable to make available to some of the European countries special loans to assist them in attaining monetary stability. I am not now requesting authorization for such loans, since it is not possible at this time to determine when or to what extent such loans should be made.

As economic conditions in Europe improve and political conditions become more stable, private financing can be expected to play an increasingly important role. The recommended program of United States aid includes provisions to encourage private financing and investments.

Impact on the United States Economy

A fourth basic consideration is the effect of further aid for Europe upon the physical resources of the United States and upon our economy.

The essential import requirements of the 270,000,000 people of Western Europe cover a wide range of products. Many of these requirements can be met by the United States and other countries without substantial difficulty. However, a number of the commodities which are most essential to European recovery are the same commodities for which there is an unsatisfied demand in the United States. Sharing these commodities with the people of Europe will require some self-denial by the people of the United States. I believe that our people recognize the vital importance of our aid program and are prepared to share their goods to insure its success.

While the burden on our people should not be ignored or minimized, neither should it be exaggerated. The program of aid to Europe which I am recommending is well within our capacity to undertake. Its total cost, though large, will be only about five per cent of the cost of our effort in the recent war. It will cost less than three per cent of our national income during the life of the program. As an investment toward the peace and security of the world and toward the realization of hope and confidence in a better way of life for the future, this cost is small indeed.

A committee under the chairmanship of the Secretary of the Interior was appointed last summer to study the effect of a foreign aid program upon the natural resources of our country. Its study has shown that our resources can safely meet the demands of a program such as I am now recommending. Such demands could not, however, be supplied indefinitely. Our program of aid to Europe recognizes this fact. Our exports to Europe will decrease during the succeeding years of the program as trade is revived along realistic patterns which will make available from other sources an increasing share of Europe's requirements.

Actually, our position with respect to some raw materials of which we have inadequate domestic resources will be improved, since, under our program of aid to Europe, an increased amount of these materials will be made available to us.

During recent months the Council of Economic Advisers made an intensive study of the impact of foreign aid on our domestic economy. The Council concluded that a program of the size now contemplated is well within our productive capacity and need not produce a dangerous strain on our economy.

At the same time a group of distinguished private citizens under the chairmanship of the Secretary of Commerce considered the extent and nature of foreign aid which the United States can and should provide. The conclusion of this group was that a program of the scope I am recommending is a proper, wise, and necessary use of United States resources.

The reports submitted to me by the Council of Economic Advisers and the committees under the chairmanship of the Secretary of the Interior and the Secretary of Commerce all emphasized that specific measures should be taken to prevent our foreign aid program from imposing unnecessary burdens on our economy.

If the United States were to supply from its own production all the essential commodities needed to meet European requirements, unnecessary scarcities and unnecessary inflationary pressures would be created within our economy. It is far wiser to assist in financing the procurement of certain of these commodities from other countries, particularly the other food-producing countries in the Western Hemisphere. The funds we make available to aid European recovery therefore should not be restricted to purchases within the United States.

Under the proposed program of aid to Europe the total exports to the whole world from this country during the next year are expected to be no greater than our total exports during the past twelve months.

This level of exports will nevertheless have an important impact on our markets. The measures I have already proposed to the Congress to fight general domestic inflation will be useful, as well, in cushioning the impact of the European aid program.

The effect of aid to Europe upon our economy, as well as its financial cost, will be significantly affected by the arrangements we make for meeting shipping requirements.

The interest of the United States will be served best by permitting the sale or temporary transfer of some of our war-built merchant ships to the European countries. Because of world steel shortages the sale or temporary transfer of ships should be linked with a reduction or deferment of the projected shipbuilding schedules of the participating countries. These arrangements should be consistent with their long-range merchant marine requirements. They should also be consistent with our long-range objectives of maintaining an adequate merchant marine and shipbuilding industry for the United States.

Making these vessels available to the European countries will materially reduce the cost of United States aid both by lowering shipping costs and by reducing the use of scarce materials for new ship construction overseas.

Relationship to Other International Questions

A fifth basic consideration is the relationship of our aid to the European recovery program to other international questions.

I have already mentioned that the requirements and resources of Western Germany were included in the considerations of the sixteen countries at Paris. Our program of United States aid also includes Western Germany.

The productive capacity of the highly industrialized areas of Western Germany can contribute substantially to the general co-operative effort required for European recovery. It is essential that this productive capacity be effectively utilized, and it is especially important that the coal production of the Ruhr continue to increase rapidly.

Every precaution must of course be taken against a resurgence of military power in Germany. The United States has made clear on many occasions its determination that Germany shall never again threaten to dominate Europe or endanger the peace of the world. The inclusion of Western Germany in the European recovery program will not weaken this determination.

As an occupying power in Western Germany, the United States has a responsibility to provide minimum essentials necessary to prevent disease and unrest. Separate appropriations will be requested for this purpose for the period through June 30, 1949. Above this minimum level, amounts needed to assist in the rehabilitation of Western Germany are included in the over-all estimates for aid to European recovery.

Another significant area of the world which has been considered in developing the recovery program is Eastern Europe. A number of the governments of Eastern Europe which were invited to participate in the work of the Paris Conference on Economic Co-operation chose not to do so. Their failure to join in the concerted effort for recovery makes this effort more difficult and will undoubtedly prolong their own economic difficulties. This should not, however, prevent the restoration of trade between Eastern and Western Europe to the mutual advantage of both areas. Both the report of the sixteen nations and the program now submitted to the Congress are based on the belief that over the next few years the normal pattern of trade between Eastern and Western Europe will be gradually restored. As this restoration of trade is achieved the abnormal demands on the Western Hemisphere, particularly for food and fuel, should diminish.

The relationship between this program and the United Nations deserves special emphasis because of the central importance in our foreign policy of support of the United Nations. Our support of European recovery is in full accord with our support of the United Nations. The success of the United Nations depends upon the independent strength of its members and their determination and ability to adhere to the ideals and principles embodied in the Charter. The purposes of the European recovery program are in complete harmony with the purposes of the Charter—to insure a peaceful world through the joint efforts of free nations. Attempts by any nation to prevent or sabotage European recovery for selfish ends are clearly contrary to these purposes.

It is not feasible to carry out the recovery program exclusively through the United Nations. Five of the participating countries are not yet members of the United Nations. Furthermore, some European members are not participating in the program. We expect, however, that the greatest practicable use will be made of the facilities of the United Nations and its related agencies in the execution of the program. This view is shared by all the participating countries.

Our intention to undertake a program of aid for European recovery does not signify any lessening of our interest in other areas of the world. Instead, it is the means by which we can make the quickest and most effective contribution to the general improvement of economic conditions throughout the world. The workshops of Europe, with their great reservoir of skilled workers, must produce the goods to support peoples of many other nations.

I wish to make especially clear that our concentration on the task in Western Europe at this time will not lessen our long-established interest in economic co-operation with our neighbors in the Western Hemisphere. We are first of all a member of an American community of nations in which co-operative action, similar to that which the European nations are now undertaking, is required to increase production, to promote financial stability, and remove barriers to trade. Fortunately we in the Americas are further advanced along this road, but we must not overlook any opportunity to make additional progress. The European recovery program will require procurement of supplies in many nations of this hemisphere. This will act as a stimulant to production and business activity and promote the re-establishment of world trade, upon which the prosperity of all of us depends.

While our present efforts must be devoted primarily to Western Europe, as the most important area in the world at this time for the future of peace, we also have a special concern for the war-torn areas of Asia. In Japan and Korea the United States has supplied extensive aid to support life and commence reconstruction. Since the war's end we have provided China with varied and important assistance which has aided that nation substantially.

The United States should continue to do all it appropriately can to assist in the restoration of economic stability as a basis for recovery in the Far East. Extensive study has been given during the last few months to the means by which we might best aid in meeting the special needs for relief and rehabilitation in China. I expect to make recommendations on that subject to the Congress during its next session.

Administrative Arrangements

I have set forth several basic considerations which should govern our aid to the recovery of Europe. One further consideration which vitally affects all the others is the necessity for effective administrative arrangements adapted to the particular requirements of the program. If the work to be done is not well organized and managed, the benefits of our aid could be largely dissipated.

The administration of our aid will involve the performance of several major functions. The needs of the participating countries must be reviewed in close co-operation with them. Continued relationships must be maintained with the United Nations and with an organization of the participating nations. The requirements for each commodity or service under the program must be carefully evaluated in relation to United States supplies and domestic needs and to the resources of other nations which can help. Decisions must be reached as to the best means of supplying aid and the conditions of aid for each country. Assistance must be given to facilitate the procurement, transportation, and efficient use of goods. A constant review must be maintained over the use of our aid and the execution of agreements. The results of the program must be evaluated and reported to all concerned—the President, the Congress, and the people.

While these activities are complex, they are not comparable in magnitude or in character to our wartime supply activities. Under this program most of the operations can be carried out through private channels and existing government agencies.

Nevertheless, the scope and importance of the program warrant the creation of a new organization to provide central direction and leadership. I therefore recommend the establishment of a new and separate agency, the Economic Co-operation Administration, for this purpose. It should be headed by an Administrator appointed by the President and directly responsible to him. The Administrator should be subject to confirmation by the Senate.

The Economic Co-operation Administration will sponsor the European aid requirements as they are reviewed and adjusted, with other governmental agencies, to form a practical program in the light of available supplies and capacities. The Economic Co-operation Administration will be responsible for initiating the approved program project by project and nation by nation and for regulations as to supervision, co-operative assistance, and other policy matters which will guide the program at every point. In keeping with the importance and nature of its task, the new agency should have flexibility in the determination of operating methods, the use of funds, and the hiring of key personnel.

The relationship of the Economic Co-operation Administration to the existing governmental establishment is of crucial importance. In the determination of programs for the several countries, the assessment of individual projects, and many other matters involving our activities abroad, the Economic Co-operation Administration must work closely with the Department of State. Similarly on many actions affecting our domestic economy the Administration must work with, rather than supplant, existing agencies. For example, the Department of Agriculture should be relied upon for any required government action in the procurement and allocation of food, and the Department of Commerce for the allocation of certain other commodities in short supply and for continued administration of export controls. The facilities of these agencies will in some cases need to be strengthened, but no major changes in governmental organization to perform important domestic functions will be required.

Under these circumstances, I expect that the Economic Co-operation Administration will need only a small staff. No vast new agency or corporation is needed to perform functions for which government facilities now exist.

It is essential to realize that this program is much more than a commercial operation. It represents a major segment of our foreign policy. Day in and day out its operations will affect and be affected by foreign policy judgments. We shall be dealing with a number of countries in which there are complex and widely varying economic and political situations. This program will affect our relationships with them in matters far beyond the outline of the program itself. Its administration must therefore be fully responsive to our foreign policy. The Administrator must be subject to the direction of the Secretary of State on decisions and actions affecting our foreign policy.

The United States activities in Europe under the program will constitute essentially an extension of our present relationships with the participating countries. In order to maintain unity of United States representation abroad our ambassador in each country must retain responsibility for all matters requiring contacts with the government to which he is accredited, including operations under this program. Some additional personnel, technically qualified to perform specialized functions arising out of the program, should be placed in the embassies to represent and carry out the responsibilties of the Economic Co-operation Administration abroad.

In addition I recommend that provision be made for a special United States Representative for the European Recovery Program. He would represent the United States at any continuing organization of the participating countries, and he would exercise general co-ordination of our operations in Europe under the program. He should be appointed by the President, subject to confirmation by the Senate, and have ambassadorial rank. Because of the joint interest of the

Secretary of State and the Administrator in his activities, the special Representative must serve both as the President may direct. The activities of this Representative in promoting mutual self-help among the European nations will be of the utmost importance in achieving the success of the European Recovery Program.

The administrative arrangements I have described are in keeping with the character of the job to be done and will provide the most efficient and economical means for its performance.

Conclusion

In proposing that the Congress enact a program of aid to Europe I am proposing that this nation contribute to world peace and to its own security by assisting in the recovery of sixteen countries which, like the United States, are devoted to the preservation of free institutions and enduring peace among nations. It is my belief that United States support of the European Recovery Program will enable the free nations of Europe to devote their great energies to the reconstruction of their economies. On this depend the restoration of a decent standard of living for their peoples, the development of a sound world economy, and continued support for the ideals of individual liberty and justice.

In providing aid to Europe we must share more than goods and funds. We must give our moral support to those nations in their struggle to rekindle the fires of hope and strengthen the will of their peoples to overcome their adversities. We must develop a feeling of teamwork in our common cause of combating the suspicions, prejudices, and fabrications which undermine co-operative effort, both at home and abroad.

This joint undertaking of the United States and a group of European nations, in devotion to the principles of the Charter of the United Nations, is proof that free men can effectively join together to defend their free institutions against totalitarian pressures and to promote better standards of life for all their peoples.

I have been heartened by the widespread support which the citizens of the United States have given to the concept underlying the proposed aid to European recovery. Workers, farmers, businessmen, and other major groups have all given evidence of their confidence in its noble purpose and have shown their willingness to give it full support.

I recommend this program of United States support for European recovery to the Congress in full confidence of its wisdom and necessity as a major step in our nation's quest for a just and lasting peace.

§ Along with his message the President submitted a draft bill to transform the European Recovery Program into legislation. Senator Vandenberg, with his great bargaining power, was able to effect certain changes in those items of the President's proposal with which he did not agree. Among these was the provision of the administration draft bill for a $17,000,000,000 four-year authorization. Vandenberg objected that future Congresses could not be committed to any specific sum. The administration agreed to eliminate the provision, and appropriations were made on an annual basis.

The progress of the European Recovery Program is reflected in the datum that the total production of goods and services in the participating European countries rose by nearly one fourth between 1947 and 1949. The general index of industrial production, based on 1938, rose to 115 in 1949; it had been 77 in 1946 and 87 in 1947. Good harvests helped speed agricultural recovery. Production of bread grains in the crop year 1948–49 was 57 per cent above the previous year. Foreign trade of the participating countries rose from 74 per cent of the 1938 level in the first quarter of 1948 to 100 per cent of 1938 (measured at constant prices) a year later. Unfortunately, much of this increase was in trade among the ERP countries themselves and too little with other countries of the world, especially the United States.*

In its political objectives ERP was an unqualified success. In France, Italy, and other Western countries the threat of local communism to come into power was effectively halted.

8. ISRAEL

United States policy bearing on Israel was largely evolved in the President's own chambers. Mr. Truman outlined its main features in an address on October 28, 1948:

It's my responsibility to see that our policy in Israel fits in with our foreign policy throughout the world. . . . it is my desire to help

---

* From Council on Foreign Relations, The United States in World Affairs, 1949, New York, 1950, p. 119.

build in Palestine a strong, prosperous, free, and independent state. It must be large enough, free enough, and strong enough to make its people self-supporting and secure. As President of the United States, back in 1945 I was the first to call for the immediate opening of Palestine to immigration to the extent of at least 100,000 persons. The United States, under my administration, led the way in November 1947 and was responsible for the resolution of the United Nations setting up Israel, not only as a homeland but as a free and independent political state. The United States was the first to give full and complete recognition to the new state of Israel in April 1948, and recognition to its provisional government. I have never changed my position on Palestine or Israel. As I have previously announced, I have stood, still stand, on the present Democratic platform of 1948. [Mr. Truman added that the platform of 1948 goes a little farther than the platform of 1944.] What we need now is to help the people of Israel, and they've proved themselves in the best traditions of hardy pioneers. They have created out of a barren desert a modern and efficient state with the highest standards of Western civilization. They've demonstrated that Israel deserves to take its place in the family of nations. That's our objective. We shall work toward it, but will not work toward it in a partisan and political way. I am confident that that objective will be reached. And I know of no American citizen, of whatever race or religion, who would want us to deal with the question of Palestine on any other basis than the welfare of all Americans of every race and faith.

9. THE JAPANESE PEACE TREATY

The Japanese peace treaty is a unique document: it not only imposed terms on a vanquished enemy, but also brought that former enemy into a structure of collective security as a major ally. With the Korean struggle at full flood, Japan was in 1951 both the principal base of American operations in Korea and an integral part of the American defense perimeter extending along the shores of Asia from the Aleutians to the Philippines and beyond.

The principal architect of the Japanese peace treaty was John Foster Dulles, who conducted negotiations with Japan and the other interested powers, including the Soviet Union, with both dexterity and privacy. United States views about the treaty were laid down in broad outline in a memorandum of late 1950 that was circulated to the thirteen member nations of the Far Eastern Commission. Underlying the memorandum and the eventual peace treaty was the assumption that Japan had turned over a new leaf, assisted in the process by the far-reaching policies evolved during the stewardship of General MacArthur.

The upshot of Mr. Dulles' labors included, in addition to the Japanese treaty, an interlocking rudimentary security system that linked Japan with the United States, and the United States with Australia, New Zealand, and the Philippines, the chief military powers in the remoter Pacific. These arrangements are referred to by President Truman in his remarks of September 4, 1951 to the delegates who gathered in San Francisco to consider the proposed treaty.

Six years ago the nations represented at this conference were engaged in a bitter and costly war. Nevertheless these nations and others came together here, in this very hall, to set up the United Nations as the first essential step toward a firm and lasting peace.

The treaty we are gathered here to sign has not been drawn in a spirit of revenge. The treaty reflects the spirit in which we carried on the war. The principles for which we fought were clearly set forth by President Franklin D. Roosevelt right after Pearl Harbor. On December 9, 1941, in a broadcast to the American people, he said:

"When we resort to force, as now we must, we are determined that this force shall be directed toward ultimate good as well as against immediate evil. . . . We are now in the midst of a war, not for conquest, not for vengeance, but for a world in which this nation, and all that this nation represents, will be safe for our children."

That's our purpose here today as we gather to sign the peace treaty. We are trying to build a world in which the children of all nations can live together in peace. We hope we are attaining the ultimate good to which President Roosevelt referred.

Unfortunately, today, the world is faced with new threats of aggression. Many of the countries represented here are now engaged in a hard fight to uphold the United Nations against international lawbreaking. There are thugs among nations just as among individuals. But we have not forgotten that our goal is peace. We will not let the present conflict deter us from taking every step we can toward peace. We will not let that happen now, any more than we let the existence of war in 1945 hold up our efforts for the creation of the United Nations. . . .

Since the fighting ended in 1945 Japan has been an occupied country. The occupation was designed by the wartime allies to prevent future Japanese aggression and to establish Japan as a peaceful and democratic country, prepared to return to the family of nations. The United States, as the principal occupying power, was given a special responsibility to carry out these objectives. It is our judgment that they have been achieved.

I wish on this occasion to express the pride that my countrymen and I feel in the way in which the Allied occupation has been carried out. Its success has been due to the devoted efforts of many thousands of people serving under the outstanding leadership of General of the Army Douglas MacArthur and his able successor General Matthew Ridgway.

I would also like to pay tribute to the impressive effort put forward by the people of Japan in this period. They have fully complied with the surrender terms. They have co-operated fully in carrying out the purposes of the occupation.

The result has been a remarkable and unprecedented period of progress in Japanese history. Japan today is a very different country from what it was six years ago. The old militarism has been swept away. This has been done not just by occupation edict, but by the overwhelming will of the Japanese people themselves. The secret police and the police state methods used by the former government have been abolished. The new Japanese Constitution provides a bill of rights for all citizens and establishes a government truly representative of the people. The Japanese people now have universal suffrage and they are taking a vigorous part in their government. In recent local elections more than ninety per cent of those eligible have voted. I wish that same percentage would obtain in the United States. Japanese women now vote and take part in the government, and enjoy full democratic rights for the first time. Free and independent labor unions have been established and farm co-operatives have been greatly expanded. The monopolies that used to have such a strangle hold on Japanese economy have been substantially broken up. Remarkable progress has been made in land reform. Over 5,000,000 acres of land have been purchased from the old landlords and sold to working farmers. Today about ninety per cent of all the cultivated land belongs to those who work on it—land that means freedom and liberty. That compares with less than fifty per cent in 1945. This is a great achievement, full of meaning for all Asia.

Through these and other reforms the Japanese people have been developing a stable economy and a democratic society. They still have a long way to go, but they are well on the road to building a new Japan, dedicated to the arts of peace and the well-being of the people. Because of these accomplishments it is possible at this time to restore full sovereignty to the Japanese people.

This does not mean that the slate has been wiped clean. The United States has not forgotten Pearl Harbor or Bataan, and many of the other nations represented here have similar memories that will not easily be erased. The new Japan will not find the world entirely friendly and trusting. It will have to keep on working to win the friendship and trust of other peoples over the years to come. But the foundations for a peaceful future have been laid. It is now time to move ahead with the restoration of normal relations between Japan and the rest of the world.

There were, of course, differences of opinion among the nations concerned as to many of the matters covered by this treaty. The text of the treaty now before us is the product of long and patient negotiations among the nations, which were undertaken to reconcile these differences.

I think it is fair to say that it is a good treaty. It takes account of of the principal desires and ultimate interests of all the participants. It is fair to both victor and vanquished.

But more than that, it is a treaty that will work. It does not contain the seeds of another war; it is a treaty of reconciliation which looks to the future, and not to the past.

The treaty re-establishes Japan as a sovereign independent nation. It provides for the restoration of Japanese trade with other nations, and it imposes no restrictions upon Japan's access to raw materials. The treaty recognizes the principle that Japan should make reparations to the countries which suffered from its aggression. But it does not saddle the Japanese people with a hopeless burden of reparations which would crush their economy in the years to come. In all these respects the treaty takes account of the peaceful advances the Japanese people have made in recent years and seeks to establish the conditions for further progress.

However, there is one thing we must all recognize. There can be no progress unless the Japanese people and their neighbors in the Pacific are made secure against the threat of aggression. And at the present time the Pacific area is gravely affected by outright aggression and by the threat of further armed attack. One of our primary concerns in making peace with Japan, therefore, is to make Japan secure against aggression and to provide that Japan, in its turn, will so conduct itself as not to endanger the security of other nations. To accomplish this it is important to bring Japan under the principles of the United Nations and within the protection of the mutual obligations of the United Nations members.

The treaty expresses Japan's intention to apply for membership in the United Nations. The other countries who sign the treaty can be counted on to work for the admission of Japan to membership. But, even so, there may be delays before Japan can be admitted. Under the treaty, therefore, the Japanese people bind themselves to accept immediately the basic obligations of a United Nations member —namely, to refrain from aggression, to settle disputes peacefully, and to support the efforts of the United Nations to maintain peace. At the same time the other nations who sign the treaty specifically recognize that Japan is entitled to the protection of the United Nations Charter.

In a sense these provisions are the heart of the treaty. Under them Japan becomes a part of the community of nations, pledged to outlaw aggression and to support a world order based on justice.

This tying together of the Japanese Peace Treaty and the United Nations Charter is a long step toward building security in the Pacific. But more than this is needed.

In the present world situation it has been necessary to buttress the peaceful principles of the United Nations Charter with regional arrangements for the common defense against aggression. If real security is to be attained in the Pacific, the free nations in that area must find means to work together for common defense.

The United States recognizes that fact. Our people have suffered from past aggression in the Pacific and are determined that this country shall do its part for peace in that locality. In recent days we have joined with other Pacific nations in important mutual security agreements. Last Thursday the Philippines and the United States signed a treaty of mutual defense. Under this treaty each country recognizes that an armed attack on the other in the Pacific area would be dangerous to its own peace and safety and declares that it would act to meet the common danger. Last Saturday a similar security treaty was signed by Australia, New Zealand, and the United States. These treaties are initial steps toward the consolidation of peace in the Pacific.

It is vital that Japan be included as soon as possible in the appropriate security arrangements for keeping the peace in the Pacific. This is necessary for her own protection and the protection of other countries. The peace treaty, therefore, recognizes that Japan, as a sovereign nation, must possess the right of self-defense and the right to join in defense arrangements with other countries under the United Nations Charter.

The development of regional arrangements for defense in the Pacific will mean that such Japanese defense forces as may be created would be associated with the defense forces of other nations in that area. Japan's security would not depend exclusively on Japanese forces but on interrelated security arrangements with other countries. The Japanese contribution, by itself, would not constitute an offensive threat. But Japanese forces, together with the forces of other nations, would provide mutual security against threats to the independence of the nations of the Pacific, including Japan.

At present, of course, Japan is totally unarmed. In view of the open aggression taking place near Japan, the Japanese government has requested the United States to enter into a bilateral treaty for Japan's immediate security. Under such a treaty the United States would maintain armed forces in Japan for the time being as a contribution to international peace and to Japan's defense against attack. Security arrangements are essential in a world in danger. In the Pacific, as in other parts of the world, social and economic progress is impossible unless there is a shield which protects men from the paralysis of fear. But our great goal, our major purpose, is not just to build bigger and stronger shields. What we want to do is to advance, as rapidly as we can, to the great constructive tasks of human progress.

We in the United States respect and support the many new free and independent nations in the Pacific area and Asia. We want to see them grow and prosper as equal partners in the community of independent nations both East and West. We want to co-operate with them and to help them in their agricultural and industrial development. We wish to see these nations attain in dignity and freedom a better life for their people, for that is the road to world peace.

These countries have a rich historical and cultural heritage. Today their people are experiencing great economic and social changes. They are stirred by a new zeal for progress and independence. Already we have seen some of the progress that can be made—progress in stamping out malaria, in building schools and training teachers, in growing more food and creating new industries. Immense opportunities lie ahead if these countries can pursue their national destinies in a partnership of peace, free from the fear of aggression. Under this peace treaty we believe that Japan can and will join in this partnership of peace.

We look forward to the contribution which the new Japan, with its rich culture and its dedication to peace, can bring to the community of nations. We expect this contribution to grow over the years, for the signing of a peace treaty is but one part of the process of making peace. When aggression and war have severed relations between nations, many ties which bind one nation to the others is cut. Making peace is like repairing the many strands of an intercontinental cable; each strand must be spliced separately and patiently, until the full flow of communication has been restored.

There is no other way to bring about lasting peace than this slow and patient progress, step by step, of mending and strengthening the cables of communication and of understanding between nations.

In this San Francisco conference we have the opportunity to take one vital step toward lasting peace. Our specific task here is to conclude the treaty of peace with Japan. This will be a great step toward general peace in the Pacific. There are other steps which need to be taken. The most important of these is the restoration of peace and security in Korea. With Japan returned to its place in the family of nations and with the people of Korea secure, free, and united, it should be possible to find ways to settle other problems in the Pacific which now threaten the peace. The United States has made clear on many occasions its desire to explore with other governments, at the proper time and in the proper forum, how this might be accomplished. There are many well established ways in which next steps can be explored, if there is a genuine desire for peace in all quarters.

But these are not matters which can be dealt with in this present conference. We've come here to take a single step, but a step of utmost importance.

The treaty now before us offers more than talk of peace; it offers action for peace. This conference will show, therefore, who seeks to make peace and who seeks to prevent it; who wishes to put an end to war and who wishes to continue it.

We believe this treaty will have the support of all those nations that honestly desire to reduce the tensions which now grip the world.

I pray that we shall be united in taking this step to advance us toward greater harmony and understanding.

As we approach the peace table let us be free of malice and hate, to the end that from here on there shall be neither victors nor vanquished among us, but only equals in the partnership of peace.

§ *Opposition to the peace treaty came principally from India, Yugoslavia, Red China, and the U.S.S.R. with its satellites. With India, which declined to attend the San Francisco conference, opposition was a further manifestation of her established aloofness toward the cold war and her championship of the ideas of Asian nationalism. Somewhat surprisingly, the Soviet Union sent to San Francisco a delegation which Mr. Dulles, before the conference, said he hoped would not become a wrecking crew. To avoid that eventuality the United States, with the concurrence of Great Britain, the cosponsor of the conference, drew up special rules of debate that carefully limited the possibilities of parliamentary sabotage.*

In Japan, with few exceptions, the opinions expressed were favorable to the treaty. In Congress the treaty was so well received that President Truman was able to name a bipartisan delegation that included several of the most vehement Republican critics of the administration's Far East policy. On September 8, 1951 the treaty was signed at San Francisco. The Senate approved it on March 20, 1952 by a vote of 58 to 9, and the President ratified it on April 15, 1952.

V
COMMANDER IN CHIEF

§ Significant shifts of emphasis occurred during the Truman administration in the use of the President's military powers as these are provided for in the Constitution and by statute. The principal occasions of these shifts were the hostilities in Korea, the development of the atomic bomb, the dismissal of General MacArthur, and the reorganization of the armed services under the National Security Act of 1947 and under its amendment in 1949.

These matters are successively presented in the passages that follow.

1. ATOMIC ENERGY

On November 15, 1945 the President joined with the Prime Minister of the United Kingdom and the Prime Minister of Canada—the other two countries known to possess the knowledge essential for the use of atomic energy—in the making of a three-power proposal for the control of atomic energy. One essential requirement of the proposal was that a commission be set up under the United Nations to formulate recommendations. On January 24, 1945 the General

Assembly, in a rare display of unanimity, voted 52 to 0 to establish an atomic energy commission accountable to the Security Council.

In the meantime Mr. Truman had appointed a five-man committee, headed by Under-Secretary of State Dean Acheson, assisted by David Lilienthal, to study the question of international controls, and on March 28, 1946 the group issued its Report on the International Control of Atomic Energy. This became the basis of proposals issued by Bernard Baruch, United States Representative to the United Nations Atomic Energy Commission, on June 14, 1946. These provided, among other things, that there should be a strong and comprehensive system of control and inspection—a schedule of stages leading to full establishment of an international control to be exercised by an international agency with broad and flexible authority to control nuclear fuels and the means of producing them. This agency's decisions would govern the operation of national agencies for atomic energy; it would have positive developmental responsibilities and the exclusive right to carry on atomic research for destructive purposes. These proposals were incorporated in the report and recommendations of the United Nations Atomic Energy Commission on December 31, 1946. The recommendations were supported by ten members of the Commission, but were opposed by the Soviet Union and Poland.

The Soviet position, as advanced on June 19, 1946 by Andrei Gromyko, Representative to the United Nations Atomic Energy Commission, demanded outlawing the production and use of atomic weapons and the destruction of existing stock piles. The United States, mindful of the danger from the Soviet Union, was unwilling to accede to these proposals.

In ensuing months the Western powers advanced further proposals, but these were consistently blocked by the Russians. President Truman's own summary and evaluation of these happenings are to be found in a campaign speech at Milwaukee on October 14, 1948.

Ever since the discovery of atomic energy, Mr. Truman said—

. . . it has been my constant aim to prevent its use for war and to hasten its use for peace.

Three months after the bomb was used I met in Washington with Prime Minister Attlee of Great Britain and Prime Minister MacKenzie King of Canada. These two great countries were our partners in developing the atomic bomb.

After this conference our three governments proposed that a United Nations commission be established to work out a plan for the international control of atomic energy—a plan which would further the welfare rather than the destruction of mankind. We were joined by France, China, and the Soviet Union in sponsoring the establishment of such a commission.

The commission first met in June 1946. The United States offered to stop making atomic bombs when an effective system of international control had been set up. We offered to dispose of our existing bombs and to turn over to an international agency full information on the production of atomic energy.

I believe that these proposals by the United States government will be regarded by history as one of the world's greatest examples of political responsibility and moral leadership. In these proposals lies the best assurance for world peace and for the security of this nation.

There has been no change in the American position. We still want atomic energy to be placed under international control, and on a practical, realistic basis that means the control will work. Only on this basis can atomic energy be removed as an ominous threat to mankind and turned to the purpose which has been in my heart from the beginning: peace, prosperity, and progress for all nations and all people everywhere.

Until the right kind of international control is assured, we have no choice but to proceed with the development of atomic weapons. We Americans are not a warlike people. We hunger for peace. The world knows that the United States will never use the atomic bomb to wage aggressive war.

But in the hands of a nation bent on aggression, the atomic bomb could spell the end of civilization on this planet. That must not happen. The fearful power of atomic weapons must be placed beyond the reach of any irresponsible government or any power-mad dictator.

You know of the difficulties we have encountered in trying to achieve international control. The great majority of the countries on the United Nations Atomic Energy Commission agreed upon a plan for an international agency with powers of ownership, operation, management, and inspection which would make effective control possible. But the Soviet Union rejected such a plan as an intrusion upon its national sovereignty. The majority of the nations felt that the control agency ought not to be subject to a veto by any nation. The Soviet Union insisted upon its right to veto.

The issues which have thus far blocked agreement are serious. But I do not regard the situation as hopeless. Even now, in Paris, discussions are under way in the United Nations on this subject. It is our hope that the Soviet Union and all members of the United Nations will see the wisdom, logic, and necessity for adopting the plan of control so overwhelmingly supported by the United Nations Commission.

The conscience of humanity will not permit the awful force of atomic energy to be used for the self-destruction of the human race.

Of course, there is a price to be paid for the mutual security of nations against the horrors of an atomic war. All nations must reckon with that price. The plain fact is that the international control of atomic energy does demand some sacrifice of national sovereignty. The atom is no respecter of the sovereignty of nations.

From the moment the atomic bomb became a reality the United States has stood ready to do its share, to make its sacrifice, so that a lasting peace can be achieved.

But we will not make a one-sided sacrifice. The United States will not be satisfied with anything less than a plan of international control which is clearly meant to work, and which will work. A make-believe control would be worse than none.

While we are making these efforts toward international control of atomic energy, we have also been working to strengthen our atomic security and to hasten the use of atomic energy for peaceful purposes.

§ *President Truman did not abate his efforts to secure effective international control of atomic energy. In 1949, for example, when he laid the cornerstone of the United Nations headquarters, his principal point was that the proposal approved by the United Nations Atomic Energy Commission should be adopted "unless a better one is offered."*

2. HOSTILITIES IN KOREA

On June 25, 1950 at four A.M. *Korean time, troops of the so-called Democratic People's Republic crossed the 38th parallel in an unprovoked surprise attack on the Republic of Korea. President Truman* decided to lay the crisis before a special meeting of the United Nations Security Council convened on June 25. The Security Council, with the Soviet delegate absent, adopted a resolution (1) calling for the immediate cessation of hostilities, with the North Koreans withdrawing at once to the 38th parallel; (2) requesting the United Nations Commission on Korea to submit recommendations and verify the execution of the resolution; and (3) calling on all United Nations members "to render every assistance to the United Nations in the execution of this resolution and to refrain from giving assistance to the North Korean authorities."

But the fighting continued, and on June 27 the Council adopted a second resolution recommending that the "Members of the United Nation furnish such assistance to the Republic of Korea as may be necessary to repel the armed attack and to restore international peace and security in the area."

Mr. Truman responded by ordering United States air and sea forces to give the Republic of Korea government troops "cover and support." Then, in a move made independently of the United Nations and in behalf of the security of the United States, the President announced that he had ordered the Seventh Fleet to prevent any attack on Formosa, United States forces in the Philippines to be increased, and military aid to the Philippine government and to the forces of France and the Associated States in Indochina to be accelerated. On June 27 it was also revealed that he had instructed Ambassador Alan Kirk in Moscow to request that the Soviet government use its good offices to end hostilities. This request was interpreted as a face-saving device for the Russians and as a feeler to determine their real intentions.

In a press conference on June 29 Mr. Truman offered his own legal analysis of the Korean problem in its relation to presidential power when he commented that the United States was not at war and that our combat operations in Korea were a police action undertaken for the United Nations as a result of a bandit attack on South Korea.

Meanwhile the North Koreans, well equipped with Soviet-made tanks, aircraft, and heavy artillery and aided by seaborne landings on the Korean east coast, were rolling rapidly onward. More drastic United States measures were clearly necessary, or the North Koreans would control the peninsula in short order. On June 30, on Mr. Truman's authorization, United States ground forces were flown in to South Korea, and the Air Force for the first time was undertaking, in the President's words, "missions on specific military targets in Northern Korea wherever militarily necessary," i.e. beyond the 38th parallel.

On July 7 the Security Council, acting on a resolution introduced by Britain and France, set up a unified command in Korea. The resolution requested the United States "to designate the commander of such forces," authorized the unified command to display the United Nations flag in operations against the North Korean forces "concurrently with the flags of the various nations participating," and requested the United States to "provide the Security Council with reports as appropriate on the course of action taken under the unified command." General Douglas MacArthur was appointed by the President to the United Nations post.

Thus far Mr. Truman had sent no message to Congress about Korea and had made no address to the people. On July 19 he broke his silence with an address to Congress during the day, and in the evening he made to the people the address that follows. It constituted both his report on developments in Korea and a statement of his mobilization plans.

My fellow citizens: At noon today I sent a message to the Congress about the situation in Korea. I want to talk to you tonight about that situation, and about what it means to the security of the United States and to our hopes for peace in the world.

Korea is a small country, thousands of miles away, but what is happening there is important to every American.

On Sunday, June 25, Communist forces attacked the Republic of Korea. This attack has made it clear beyond all doubt that the international communist movement is willing to use armed invasion to conquer independent nations. An act of aggression such as this creates a very real danger to the security of all free nations.

The attack upon Korea was an outright breach of the peace and a violation of the Charter of the United Nations. By their actions in Korea communist leaders have demonstrated their contempt for the basic moral principles on which the United Nations is founded.

This is a direct challenge to the efforts of free nations to build the kind of world in which men can live in freedom and peace. This challenge has been presented squarely. We must meet it squarely.

It is important for all of us to understand the essential facts as to how the situation in Korea came about.

Before and during World War II Korea was subject to Japanese rule. When the fighting stopped it was agreed that troops of the Soviet Union would accept the surrender of the Japanese soldiers in the northern part of Korea and that American forces would accept the surrender of the Japanese in the southern part. For this purpose the 38th parallel was used as the dividing line.

Later the United Nations sought to establish Korea as a free and independent nation. A commission was sent out to supervise a free election in the whole of Korea. However, this election was held only in the southern part of the country, because the Soviet Union refused to permit an election for this purpose to be held in the northern part. Indeed, Soviet authorities even refused to permit the United Nations Commission to visit Northern Korea.

Nevertheless the United Nations decided to go ahead where it could. In August 1948 the Republic of Korea was established as a free and independent nation in that part of Korea south of the 38th parallel.

In December 1948 the Soviet Union stated that it had withdrawn its troops from Northern Korea and that a local government had been established there. However, the communist authorities never have permitted the United Nations observers to visit Northern Korea to see what was going on behind that part of the Iron Curtain. It was from that area, where the communist authorities have been unwilling to let the outside world see what was going on, that the attack was launched against the Republic of Korea on June 25. That attack came without provocation and without warning. It was an act of raw aggression, without a shadow of justification.

I repeat that it was an act of raw aggression. It had no justification whatever.

The communist invasion was launched in great force, with planes, tanks, and artillery. The size of the attack and the speed with which it was followed up make it perfectly plain that it had been plotted long in advance.

As soon as word of the attack was received, Secretary of State Acheson called me at Independence, Missouri, and informed me that, with my approval, he would ask for an immediate meeting of the United Nations Security Council. The Security Council met just twenty-four hours after the communist invasion began.

One of the main reasons the Security Council was set up was to act in such cases as this—to stop outbreaks of aggression in a hurry before they develop into general conflicts. In this case the Council passed a resolution which called for the invaders of Korea to stop fighting and withdraw. The Council called on all members of the United Nations to help carry out this resolution. The communist invaders ignored the action of the Security Council and kept right on with their attack.

The Security Council then met again. It recommended that the members of the United Nations help the Republic of Korea repel the attack and help restore peace and security in that area. Fifty-two of the fifty-nine countries which are members of the United Nations have given their support to the action taken by the Security Council to restore peace in Korea.

These actions by the United Nations and its members are of great importance. The free nations have now made it clear that lawless aggression will be met with force. The free nations have learned the fateful lesson of the 1930's. That lesson is that aggression must be met firmly. Appeasement leads only to further aggression and ultimate war.

The principal effort to help the Koreans preserve their independence and to help the United Nations restore peace has been made by the United States. We have sent land, sea, and air forces to assist in these operations. We have done this because we know that what is at stake here is nothing less than our own national security and the peace of the world.

So far two other nations, Australia and Great Britain, have sent planes to Korea; and six other nations, Australia, Canada, France, Great Britain, the Netherlands, and New Zealand, have made naval forces available. Under the flag of the United Nations a unified command has been established for all forces of the members of the United Nations fighting in Korea. General Douglas MacArthur is the commander of this combined force.

The prompt action of the United Nations to put down lawless aggression and the prompt response to this action by free peoples all over the world will stand as a landmark in mankind's long search for a rule of law among nations.

Only a few countries have failed to indorse the efforts of the United Nations to stop the fighting in Korea. The most important of these is the Soviet Union. The Soviet Union has boycotted the meetings of the United Nations Security Council. It has refused to support the actions of the United Nations with respect to Korea. The United States requested the Soviet government, two days after the fighting started, to use its influence with the North Koreans to have them withdraw. The Soviet government refused. The Soviet government has said many times that it wants peace in the world, but its attitude toward this act of aggression against the Republic of Korea is in direct contradiction of its statements.

For our part, we shall continue to support the United Nations action to restore peace in the world. We know that it will take a hard, tough fight to halt the invasion, to drive the communists back. The invaders have been provided with enough equipment and supplies for a long campaign. They overwhelmed the lightly armed defense forces of the Korean Republic in the first few days and drove southward. Now, however, the Korean defenders have been reorganized and are making a brave fight for their liberty, and an increasing number of American troops have joined them. Our forces have fought a skillful rear guard delaying action, pending the arrival of reinforcements. Some of these reinforcements are now arriving; others are on the way from the United States.

I should like to read you a part of a report I have received from General Collins, Chief of Staff of the United States Army. General Collins and General Vandenberg, Chief of Staff of the Air Force, have just returned from an inspection trip to Korea and Japan. This is what General Collins had to say:

"United States armed forces in Korea are giving a splendid account of themselves.

"Our Far Eastern forces were organized and equipped primarily to perform peaceful occupation duties in Japan. However, under General MacArthur's magnificent leadership, they have quickly adapted themselves to meet the deliberately planned attack of the North Korean Communist forces, which are well equipped, well led, and battle-trained, and which have at times outnumbered our troops by as much as twenty to one.

"Our Army troops, ably supported by tactical aircraft of the United States Air Force and Navy and our Australian friends, flying under the most adverse conditions of weather, have already distinguished themselves in the most difficult of military operations—a delaying action. The fact that they are preventing the communists from overrunning Korea—which this calculated attack had been designed to accomplish—is a splendid tribute to the ability of our armed forces to convert quickly from the peaceful duties of occupation to the grim duties of war.

"The task that confronts us is not an easy one, but I am confident of the outcome."

I should also read to you a part of a report that I received from General MacArthur within the last few hours. General MacArthur says:

"It is, of course, impossible to predict with any degree of accuracy the future incidents of a military campaign. Over a broad front involving continuous local struggles, there are bound to be ups and downs, losses as well as successes. . . . But the issue of battle is now fully joined and will proceed along lines of action in which we will not be without choice.

"Our hold upon the southern part of Korea represents a secure base. Our casualties, despite overwhelming odds, have been relatively light. Our strength will continually increase while that of the enemy will relatively decrease. His supply line is insecure. He has had his great chance and failed to exploit it. We are now in Korea in force, and with God's help we are there to stay until the constitutional authority of the Republic of Korea is fully restored."

These and other reports I have received show that our armed forces are acting with close teamwork and efficiency to meet the problem facing us in Korea. These reports are reassuring, but they also show that the job ahead of us in Korea is long and difficult.

Furthermore, the fact that communist forces have invaded Korea is a warning that there may be similar acts of aggression in other parts of the world. Free nations must be on their guard more than ever before against this kind of sneak attack. It is obvious that we must increase our military strength and preparedness immediately. There are three things we need to do.

First, we need to send more men, equipment, and supplies to General MacArthur.

Second, in view of the world situation, we need to build up our own Army, Navy, and Air Force over and above what is needed in Korea.

Third, we need to speed up our work with other countries in strengthening our common defenses.

To help meet these needs I have already authorized increases in the size of our armed forces. These increases will come in part from volunteers, in part from selective service, and in part from the National Guard and the Reserves.

I have also ordered that military supplies and equipment be obtained at a faster rate.

The necessary increases in the size of our armed forces and the additional equipment they must have will cost about ten billion dollars, and I am asking the Congress to appropriate the amount required. These funds will be used to train men and equip them with tanks, planes, guns, and ships, in order to build the strength we need to help assure peace in the world.

When we work out with other free countries an increased program for our common defense I shall recommend to the Congress that additional funds be provided for this purpose. This is of great importance. The free nations face a world-wide threat. It must be met with a world-wide defense. The United States and other free nations can multiply their strength by joining with one another in a common effort to provide this defense. This is our best hope for peace.

The things we need to do to build up our military defense will require considerable adjustment in our domestic economy. We have a tremendously rich and productive economy, and it is expanding every year. Our job now is to divert to defense purposes more of that tremendous productive capacity—more steel, more aluminum, more of a good many things. Some of the additional production for military purposes can come from making fuller use of plants which are not operating at capacity. But many of our industries are already going full tilt, and until we can add new capacity some of the resources we need for the national defense will have to be taken from civilian uses.

This requires us to take certain steps to make sure that we obtain the things we need for national defense, and at the same time guard against inflationary price rises. The steps that are needed now must be taken promptly. In the message which I sent to the Congress today I described the economic measures which are required at this time.

First, we need laws which will insure prompt and adequate supplies for military and essential civilian use. I have therefore recommended that the Congress give the Government power to guide the flow of materials into essential uses, to restrict their use for nonessential purposes, and to prevent the accumulation of unnecessary inventories.

Second, we must adopt measures to prevent inflation and to keep our government in a sound financial condition. One of the major causes of inflation is the excessive use of credit. I have recommended that the Congress authorize the government to set limits on installment buying and to curb speculation in agricultural commodities. In the housing field, where government credit is an important factor, I have already directed that credit restraints be applied, and I have recommended that the Congress authorize further controls.

As an additional safeguard against inflation and to help finance our defense needs it will be necessary to make substantial increases in taxes. This is a contribution to our national security that every one of us should stand ready to make. As soon as a balanced and fair tax program can be worked out I shall lay it before the Congress. This tax program will have as a major aim the elimination of profiteering.

Third, we should increase the production of goods needed for national defense. We must plan to enlarge our defense production, not just for the immediate future, but for the next several years. This will be primarily a task for our business men and workers. However, to help obtain the necessary increases, the government should be authorized to provide certain types of financial assistance to private industry to increase defense production.

Our military needs are large, and to meet them will require hard work and steady effort. I know that we can produce what we need if each of us does his part—each man, each woman, each soldier, each civilian. This is a time for all of us to pitch in and work together.

I have been sorry to hear that some people have fallen victims to rumors in the last week or two and have been buying up various things they have heard would be scarce. That is foolish. I say that's foolish, and it's selfish, very selfish, because hoarding results in entirely unnecessary local shortages.

Hoarding food is especially foolish. There is plenty of food in this country. I have read that there have been runs on sugar in some cities. That's perfectly ridiculous. We now have more sugar available than ever before. There are ample supplies of our other basic foods also. Now, I sincerely hope that every American house-wife will keep this in mind when she does her daily shopping.

If I had thought that we were actually threatened by shortages of essential consumer goods, I should have recommended that price control and rationing be immediately instituted. But there's no such threat. We have to fear only those shortages which we ourselves artificially create.

Every business man who is trying to profiteer in time of national danger, every person who is selfishly trying to get more than his neighbor, is doing just exactly the thing that any enemy of this country would want him to do.

If prices should rise unduly because of excessive buying or specu-lation, I know our people will want the government to take action, and I will not hesitate to recommend rationing and price control.

We have the resources to meet our needs. Far more important, the American people are unified in their belief in democratic freedom. We are united in detesting communist slavery. We know that the cost of freedom is high. But we are determined to preserve our freedom, no matter what the cost.

I know that our people are willing to do their part to support our soldiers and sailors and airmen who are fighting in Korea. I know that our fighting men can count on each and every one of you.

Our country stands before the world as an example of how free men, under God, can build a community of neighbors, working together for the good of all.

That is the goal we seek not only for ourselves, but for all people. We believe that freedom and peace are essential if men are to live as our Creator intended us to live. It is this faith that has guided us in the past, and it is this faith that will fortify us in the stern days ahead.

3.   CHANGE OF COMMAND IN KOREA

By November 1950 United Nations forces had the North Koreans in full retreat, only to find the Chinese communists feeding so-called volunteer troops and matériel into Korea on a scale that caused General MacArthur to declare that "a new war" had come about in Korea that "not only jeopardizes, but threatens the ultimate destruction of the forces under my command." The MacArthur plan of retaliation against the Chinese communists was set forth in a memorandum to the Joint Chiefs of Staff on December 30, 1950:

a. Blockade the coast of China.
b. Destroy through naval gunfire and air bombardment China's industrial capacity to wage war;
c. Secure appropriate reinforcements from the Nationalist garrison on Formosa; and
d. Release existing restrictions upon the Formosa garrison for diversionary action (possibly leading to counterinvasion) against vulnerable areas of the Chinese mainland.

President Truman rejected these proposals as being unacceptable to the United Nations and as involving undue risk of general war.

In succeeding months General MacArthur reasserted his views on various occasions, and the administration's resistance included journeys of several high-level emissaries, and eventually of the President himself, across the Pacific to confer with MacArthur in an effort to reconcile his views as Supreme Commander with those of the United States government and the other noncommunist members of the United Nations. But the General persisted in his advocacy, even to the point of framing a letter to Minority Leader Joseph W. Martin, Jr. Read on the floor of the House on April 5, this letter, embodying General MacArthur's convictions about foreign policy, evoked numerous expressions of anxiety in foreign capitals.

On April 10 Mr. Truman concluded that decisive action was unavoidable if the established policy and the constitutional structure of the United States were to be upheld. On this date the

White House released the President's announcement of General MacArthur's removal and disclosed secret documents that had been sent as instructions to MacArthur, which, the administration asserted, he had violated. In rejoinder an aide of General MacArthur declared that the General had "complied meticulously with all directives he received."

On the evening of the same day that the order of removal was announced Mr. Truman made a radio address to the people to explain the background and purpose of his decision.

My fellow Americans:

I want to talk to you tonight about what we are doing in Korea and about our policy in the Far East.

In the simplest terms what we are doing in Korea is this: We are trying to prevent a third world war.

I think most people in this country recognized that fact last June. And they warmly supported the decision of the government to help the Republic of Korea against the communist aggressors. Now many persons, even some who applauded our decision to defend Korea, have forgotten the basic reason for our action.

It is right for us to be in Korea now. It was right last June. It is right today.

I want to remind you why this is true.

The communists in the Kremlin are engaged in a monstrous conspiracy to stamp out freedom all over the world. If they were to succeed, the United States would be numbered among their principal victims. It must be clear to everyone that the United States cannot and will not sit idly by and await foreign conquest. The only question is: When is the best time to meet the threat and how?

The best time to meet the threat is in the beginning. It is easier to put out a fire in the beginning when it is small than after it has become a roaring blaze.

And the best way to meet the threat of aggression is for the peace-loving nations to act together. If they don't act together, they are likely to be picked off one by one.

If they had followed the right policies in the 1930's—if the free countries had acted together to crush the aggression of the dictators, and if they had acted in the beginning, when the aggression was small—there probably would have been no World War II.

If history has taught us anything, it is that aggression anywhere in the world is a threat to the peace everywhere in the world. When that aggression is supported by the cruel and selfish rulers of a powerful nation who are bent on conquest, it becomes a clear and present danger to the security and independence of every free nation.

This is a lesson that most people in this country have learned thoroughly. This is the basic reason why we have joined in creating the United Nations. And since the end of World War II we have been putting that lesson into practice—we're working with other free nations to check the aggressive designs of the Soviet Union before they can result in a third world war.

That is what we did in Greece, when that nation was threatened by the aggression of international Communists. The attack against Greece could have led to general war. But this country came to the aid of Greece. The United Nations supported Greek resistance. With our help the determination and efforts of the Greek people defeated the attack on the spot.

Another big Communist threat to peace was the Berlin blockade. That, too, could have led to war. But again it was settled because free men would not back down in an emergency.

The aggression against Korea is the boldest and most dangerous move the Communists have yet made. The attack on Korea was part of a greater plan for conquering all of Asia.

I would like to read to you from a secret intelligence report which came to us after the attack. I have that report here. It is a report of a speech a communist army officer in North Korea gave to a group of spies and saboteurs last May, one month before South Korea was invaded. The report shows in great detail how this invasion was a part of a carefully prepared plot. Here is a part of what the communist officer, who had been trained in Moscow, told his men:

"Our forces," he said, "are scheduled to attack South Korean forces about the middle of June. . . . The coming attack on South Korea marks the first step toward the liberation of Asia."

Notice that he used the word "liberation." This is communist double-talk meaning "conquest."

I have another secret intelligence report here. This one tells what another communist officer in the Far East told his men several months before the invasion of Korea. And here's what he said: "In order to successfully undertake the long awaited world revolution, we must first unify Asia. . . . Java, Indochina, Malaya, India, Tibet, Thailand, Philippines, and Japan are our ultimate targets. . . . The United States is the only obstacle on our road to the liberation of all countries in Southeast Asia. In other words, we must unify the people of Asia and crush the United States." Again, liberation in Commie language means conquest.

That's what the communist leaders are telling their people, and that is what they've been trying to do. They want to control all Asia from the Kremlin.

This plan of conquest is in flat contradiction to what we believe. We believe that Korea belongs to the Koreans. We believe that India belongs to the Indians. We believe all the nations of Asia should be free to work out their affairs in their own way. This is the basis of peace in the Far East, and it is the basis of peace everywhere else.

The whole communist imperialism is back of the attack on peace in the Far East. It was the Soviet Union that trained and equipped the North Koreans for aggression. The Chinese communists massed forty-four well trained and well equipped divisions on the Korean frontier. These were the troops they threw into battle when the North Korean communists were beaten.

The question we have had to face is whether the communist plan of conquest can be stopped without a general war. Our government and other countries associated with us in the United Nations believe that the best chance of stopping it without a general war is to meet the attack in Korea and defeat it there. That is what we have been doing. It is a difficult and bitter task. But so far it has been successful. So far, we have prevented World War III. So far, by fighting a limited war in Korea we have prevented aggression from succeeding, and bringing on a general war. And the ability of the whole free world to resist communist aggression has been greatly improved.

We have taught the enemy a lesson. He has found out that aggression is not cheap or easy. Moreover, men all over the world who want to remain free have been given new courage and new hope. They know now that the champions of freedom can stand up and fight and that they will stand up and fight. Our resolute stand in Korea is helping the forces of freedom now fighting in Indochina and other countries in that part of the world. It has already slowed down the timetable of conquest.

In Korea itself there are signs that the enemy is building up his ground forces for a new mass offensive. We also know that there have been large increases in the enemy's available air forces. If a new attack comes, I feel confident it will be turned back. The United Nations fighting forces are tough and able and well equipped. They are fighting for a just cause. They are proving to all the world that the principle of collective security will work. We are proud of all these forces for the magnificent job they have done against heavy odds. We pray that their efforts may succeed, for upon their success may hinge the peace of the world.

The communist side must now choose its course of action. The communist rulers may press the attack against us. They may take further action which will spread the conflict. They have that choice, and with it the awful responsibility for what may follow. The communists also have the choice of a peaceful settlement which could lead to a general relaxation of the tensions in the Far East. The decision is theirs, because the forces of the United Nations will strive to limit the conflict if possible.

We do not want to see the conflict in Korea extended. We are trying to prevent a world war, not to start one. And the best way to do that is to make it plain that we and the other free countries will continue to resist the attack.

But you may ask, Why can't we take other steps to punish the aggressor? Why don't we bomb Manchuria and China itself? Why don't we assist the Chinese Nationalist troops to land on the mainland of China?

If we were to do these things we would be running a very grave risk of starting a general war. If that were to happen, we would have brought about the exact situation we are trying to prevent. If we were to do these things we would become entangled in a vast conflict on the continent of Asia, and our task would become immeasurably more difficult all over the world. What would suit the ambitions of the Kremlin better than for our military forces to be committed to a full-scale war with Red China?

It may well be that, in spite of our best efforts, the communists may spread the war. But it would be wrong, tragically wrong, for us to take the initiative in extending the war.

The dangers are great. Make no mistake about it. Behind the North Koreans and Chinese communists in the front lines stand additional millions of Chinese soldiers. And behind the Chinese stand the tanks, the planes, the submarines, the soldiers, and the scheming rulers of the Soviet Union.

Our aim is to avoid the spread of the conflict. The course we have been following is the one best calculated to avoid an all-out war. It is the course consistent with our obligation to do all we can to maintain international peace and security. Our experience in Greece and Berlin shows that it is the most effective course of action we can follow.

First of all, it is clear that our efforts in Korea can blunt the will of the Chinese communists to continue the struggle. The United Nations forces have put up a tremendous fight in Korea and have inflicted very heavy casualties on the enemy. Our forces are stronger now than they have been before. These are plain facts which may discourage the Chinese communists from continuing their attack.

Second, the free world as a whole is growing in military strength every day. In the United States, in Western Europe, and throughout the world free men are alert to the Soviet threat and are building their defenses. This may discourage the communist rulers from continuing the war in Korea and from undertaking new acts of aggression elsewhere. If the communist authorities realize they cannot defeat us in Korea, if they realize it would be foolhardy to widen the hostilities beyond Korea, then they may recognize the folly of continuing their aggression. A peaceful settlement may then be possible. The door is always open. Then we may achieve a settlement in Korea which will not compromise the principles and purposes of the United Nations.

I have thought long and hard about this question of extending the war in Asia. I have discussed it many times with the ablest military advisers in the country. I believe with all my heart that the course we are following is the best course.

I believe that we must try to limit the war to Korea for these vital reasons: to make sure that the precious lives of our fighting men are not wasted; to see that the security of our country and the free world is not needlessly jeopardized; and to prevent a third world war.

A number of events have made it evident that General MacArthur did not agree with that policy. I have therefore considered it essential to relieve General MacArthur so that there would be no doubt or confusion as to the real purpose and aim of our policy.

It was with the deepest personal regret that I found myself compelled to take this action. General MacArthur is one of our greatest military commanders. But the cause of world peace is more important than any individual.

The change in commands in the Far East means no change whatever in the policy of the United States. We will carry on the fight in Korea with vigor and determination in an effort to bring the war to a speedy and successful conclusion. The new commander, Lieutenant General Matthew Ridgway, has already demonstrated that he has the good qualities of military leadership needed for the task.

We are ready at any time to negotiate for a restoration of peace in the area. But we will not engage in appeasement. We are only interested in real peace. Real peace can be achieved through a settlement based on the following factors:

1. The fighting must stop.
2. Concrete steps must be taken to insure that the fighting will not break out again.
3. There must be an end of the aggression.

A settlement founded upon these elements would open the way for the unification of Korea and the withdrawal of all foreign forces.

In the meantime I want to be clear about our military objective. We are fighting to resist an outrageous aggression in Korea. We are trying to keep the Korean conflict from spreading to other areas. But at the same time we must conduct our military activities so as to insure the security of our forces. This is essential if they are to continue the fight until the enemy abandons its ruthless attempt to destroy the Republic of Korea. That is our military objective— to repel attack and to restore peace.

In the hard fighting in Korea we are proving that collective action among nations is not only a high principle but a workable means of resisting aggression. Defeat of aggression in Korea may be the turning point in the world's search for a practical way of achieving peace and security.

The struggle of the United Nations in Korea is a struggle for peace. The free nations have united their strength in an effort to prevent a third world war. That war can come if the communist rulers want it to come. But this nation and its allies will not be responsible for its coming.

We do not want to widen the conflict. We will use every effort to prevent that disaster. And in so doing we know that we are following the great principles of peace, freedom, and justice.

§ As the President had anticipated, the immediate response to his action was decidedly adverse. Letters to the White House and to Congress followed a pattern of protest, and so did the comments of the press. But Mr. Truman was said to feel that, if he was right, the people would in time give him their support; and he was certain that he was right now.

On April 19 General MacArthur addressed the Congress and advanced his well-known ideas with what his admirers regarded as superb oratorical skill and his detractors as question-begging bombast. In May the Senate Armed Services and Foreign Relations Committees started a joint investigation of the dismissal. The testimony of the top military unqualifiedly supported the President's action.

4. UNIFICATION OF THE ARMED SERVICES

President Truman's interest in the unification of the armed services dates back to his years in the Senate. In the reports of his wartime investigating committee he was a frequent critic of "the scrambled professional military setup," which was to him "an open invitation to catastrophe." In a magazine article during his vice-presidential campaign he described himself as "an ardent champion of a single authority over everything that pertains to American safety."

As was to be expected, the several services had conflicting views on unification. The Navy was opposed to the creation of a single department out of apprehension that its own status would become secondary and defense be weakened. The Air Force was opposed to the existing two-department arrangement because it subordinated *the air arm to the War Department and to the Army General Staff, which in the past had been dominated by ground officers. The Air Force wanted equal status with Army and Navy and thought that unification was the best way to achieve it. The Army ground forces were opposed to any three-department idea. They feared that they would receive the leavings of the other two services in the budget; they therefore favored a unified department.*

Mr. Truman's own conclusions were incorporated in a special message to Congress on December 19, 1945.

One of the lessons which have most clearly come from the costly and dangerous experience of this war is that there must be unified direction of land, sea, and air forces at home as well as in all other parts of the world where our armed forces are serving.

We did not have that kind of direction when we were attacked four years ago—and we certainly paid a high price for not having it.

In 1941 we had two completely independent organizations with no well established habits of collaboration and co-operation between them. If disputes arose, if there was failure to agree on a question of planning or a question of action, only the President of the United States could make a decision effective on both. Besides, in 1941 the air power of the United States was not organized on a par with the ground and sea forces.

Our expedient for meeting these defects was the creation of the Joint Chiefs of Staff. On this committee sat the President's Chief of Staff and the chiefs of the land forces, the naval forces, and the air forces. Under the Joint Chiefs were organized a number of committees bringing together personnel of the three services for joint strategic planning and for co-ordination of operations. This kind of co-ordination was better than no co-ordination at all, but it was in no sense a unified command.

In the theaters of operation, meanwhile, we went farther in the direction of unity by establishing unified commands. We came to the conclusion—soon confirmed by experience—that any extended military effort required over-all co-ordinated control in order to get the most out of the three armed forces. Had we not early in the war adopted this principle of a unified command for operations, our efforts, no matter how heroic, might have failed.

But we never had comparable unified direction or command in Washington. And even in the field our unity of operations was greatly impaired by the differences in training, in doctrine, in communication systems, and in supply and distribution systems that stemmed from the division of leadership in Washington.

It is true, we were able to win in spite of these handicaps. But it is now time to take stock, to discard obsolete organizational forms, and to provide for the future the soundest, the most effective, and the most economical kind of structure for our armed forces of which this most powerful nation is capable.

I urge this as the best means of keeping the peace. . . .

Whether we like it or not, we must all recognize that the victory which we have won has placed upon the American people the continuing burden of responsibility for world leadership. The future peace of the world will depend in large part upon whether or not the United States shows that it is really determined to continue in its role as a leader among nations. . . . Together with the other United Nations we must be willing to make the sacrifices necessary to protect the world from future aggressive warfare. In short, we must be prepared to maintain in constant and immediate readiness sufficient military strength to convince any future potential aggressor that this nation, in its determination for a lasting peace, means business.

The Joint Chiefs of Staff are not a unified command. It is a committee which must depend for its success upon the voluntary co-operation of its member agencies. During the war period of extreme national danger there was, of course, a high degree of co-operation. In peacetime the situation will be different. It must not be taken for granted that the Joint Chiefs of Staff as now constituted will be as effective in the apportionment of peacetime resources as they have been in the determination of war plans and in their execution. As national defense appropriations grow tighter and conflicting interests make themselves felt in major issues of policy and strategy, unanimous agreements will become more difficult to reach.

It was obviously impossible in the midst of conflict to reorganize the armed forces of the United States along the lines here suggested. Now that our enemies have surrendered, I urge the Congress to proceed to bring about a reorganization of the management of the armed forces.

To me the most important reasons for combining the two existing departments are these:

1. We should have integrated strategic plans and a unified military program and budget.

We cannot have the sea, land, and air members of our defense team working at what may turn out to be cross purposes, planning their programs on different assumptions as to the nature of the military establishment we need, and engaging in an open competition for funds.

From experience as a member of the Congress, I know the great difficulty of appraising properly the over-all security needs of the nation from piecemeal presentations by separate departments appearing before separate Congressional committees at different times. It is only by combining the armed forces into a single department that the Congress can have the advantage of considering a single co-ordinated and comprehensive security program.

2. We should realize the economies that can be achieved through unified control of supply and service functions.

Instances of duplication among Army and Navy activities and facilities have been brought to the attention of the Congress on many occasions. . . . There is no question that the extent of waste through lack of co-ordination between the two departments is very much greater than the waste resulting from faulty co-ordination within each. If we can attain as much co-ordination among all the services as now exists within each department, we shall realize extensive savings.

Businessmen have to deal with separate buyers, who may use separate specifications for items which could as well have the same specifications. Separate inspectors are stationed in their plants. During this war instances occurred where the purchase of all available quantities of certain items by one service resulted in acute shortages in the other service. Parallel transportation and storage system required extra overhead.

As the war progressed, it is true that increased co-operation reduced the extent of waste and conflict. But voluntary co-operation in such matters can never be expected to be fully effective. A single authority at the top would inevitably achieve a greater degree of economy than would be obtained under divided direction.

3. We should adopt the organizational structure best suited to fostering co-ordination between the military and the remainder of the government. Our military policy, for example, should be completely consistent with our foreign policy. It should be designed to support and reflect our commitments to the United Nations Organization. It should be adjusted according to the success or lack of success of our diplomacy. It should reflect our fullest knowledge of the capabilities and intentions of other powers. Likewise, our foreign policy should take into account our military capabilities and the strategic power of our armed forces.

4. We should provide the strongest means for civilian control of the military.

Civilian control of the military establishment—one of the most fundamental of our democratic concepts—would be strengthened if the President and the Congress had but one Cabinet member with clear and primary responsibility for the exercise of that control. When the military establishment is divided between two civilian secretaries, each is limited necessarily to a restricted view of the military establishment. Consequently, on many fundamental issues where the civilian point of view should be controlling the secretaries of the two departments are cast in the role of partisans of their respective services, and real civilian control can be exercised by no one except the President or the Congress.

During and since the war the need for joint action by the services and for objective recommendations on military matters has led inevitably to increasing the authority of the only joint organization and the most nearly objective organization that exists—the Joint Chiefs of Staff. But the Joint Chiefs of Staff are a strictly military body. Responsibility for civilian control should be clearly fixed in a single full-time civilian below the President. This requires a Secretary for the entire military establishment, aided by a strong staff of civilian assistants.

There is no basis for the fear that such an organization would lodge too much power in a single individual—that the concentration of so much military power would lead to militarism. There is no basis for such fear as long as the traditional policy of the United

States is followed that a civilian, subject to the President, the Congress, and the will of the people, be placed at the head of this department.

5. We should organize to provide parity for air power. Air power has been developed to a point where its responsibilities are equal to those of land and sea power, and its contribution to our strategic planning is as great. . . .

The Cabinet is not merely a collection of executives administering different governmental functions. It is a body whose combined judgment the President uses to formulate the fundamental policies of the administration. In such a group, which is designed to develop teamwork wisdom on all subjects that affect the political life of the country, it would be inappropriate and unbalanced to have three members representing three different instruments of national defense.

The President, as Commander in Chief, should not personally have to co-ordinate the Army and Navy and Air Force. With all the other problems before him the President cannot be expected to balance either the organization, the training, or the practice of the several branches of national defense. He should be able to rely for that co-ordination upon civilian hands at the Cabinet level.

6. We should establish the most advantageous framework for a unified system of training for combined operations of land, sea, and air.

Whatever the form which any future war may take, we know that the men of our separate services will have to work together in many kinds of combinations for many purposes. The Pacific campaign of the recent war is an outstanding example of common and joint effort among land, sea, and air forces. Despite its successes that campaign proved that there is not adequate understanding among the officers and men of any service of the capabilities, the uses, the procedures, and the limitations of the other services. This understanding is not something that can be created overnight whenever a combined operation is planned and a task force organized. The way men act in combat is determined by the sum total of all their previous training, indoctrination, and experience.

What we seek is a structure which can best produce an integrated training program, carry on merged training activities where that is appropriate, and permit officers to be assigned in such a way that

an individual officer will learn first-hand of other services besides
the one in which he has specialized. The organizational framework
most conducive to this kind of unified training and doctrine is a
unified department.

7. We should allocate systematically our limited resources for
scientific research.

No aspect of military preparedness is more important than
scientific research. Given the limited amount of scientific talent that
will be available for military purposes, we must systematically apply
that talent to research in the most promising lines and on the
weapons with the greatest potentiality, regardless of the service in
which these weapons will be used. We cannot afford to waste any
of our scientific resources in duplication of effort.

This does not mean that all Army and Navy laboratories would
be immediately or even ultimately consolidated. The objectives
should be to preserve initiative and enterprise while eliminating
duplication and misdirected effort.

8. We should have unity of command in outlying bases.

All military authority at each of our outlying bases should be
placed under a single commander who will have clear responsibility
for security, who can be held clearly accountable, and whose orders
come from a single authority in Washington. Reconnaissance planes,
radar sets, and intelligence and counterintelligence measures at a
United States outpost are not intended to serve separate services
for different purposes. Unification of the services offers a far greater
guarantee of continued unity in the field than does our present
organization.

9. We should have consistent and equitable personnel policies.

There have been differences in personnel policies between the
Army and the Navy during the war. They began with competitive
recruitment for certain types of persons and continued in almost
every phase of personnel administration. In rates of promotion, in
ways of selecting officers, in the utilization of reserve officers, in
awards and decorations, in allowances, and in point systems for
discharge the two services have followed different policies. This
inconsistency is highly undesirable. It will be reduced to a minimum
under a unified organization.

I recommend that the reorganization of the armed services be
along the following broad lines:

(1) There should be a single department of national defense. This department should be charged with the full responsibility for armed national security. It should consist of the armed and civilian forces that are now included within the War and Navy departments.

(2) The head of this department should be a civilian, a member of the President's Cabinet, to be designated as the Secretary of National Defense. Under him there should be a civilian under-secretary and several civilian assistant secretaries.

(3) There should be three co-ordinated branches of the Department of National Defense: one for the land forces, one for the naval forces, and one for the air forces, each under an assistant secretary. The Navy should, of course, retain its own carrier-, ship-, and water-based aviation, which has proved so necessary for efficient fleet operation. And, of course, the Marine Corps should be continued as an integral part of the Navy.

(4) The under-secretary and the remaining assistant secretaries should be available for assignment to whatever duties the President and the Secretary may determine from time to time.

(5) The President and the Secretary should be provided with ample authority to establish central co-ordinating and service organizations, both military and civilian, where these are found to be necessary.

I do not believe that we can specify at this time the exact nature of these organizations. They must be developed over a period of time by the President and the Secretary as a normal part of their executive responsibilities. . . . The President and the Secretary should not be limited in their authority to establish department-wide co-ordinating and service organizations.

(6) There should be a chief of staff of the Department of National Defense. There should also be a commander for each of the three component branches—Army, Navy, and Air.

(7) The Chief of Staff and the commanders of the three co-ordinate branches of the department should together constitute an advisory body to the Secretary of National Defense and to the President. There should be nothing to prevent the President, the Secretary, and other civilian authorities from communicating with the commanders of any of the components of the department on such vital matters as basic military strategy and policy and the division of the budget.

Furthermore, the key staff positions in the department should be filled with officers drawn from all the services, so that the thinking of the department would not be dominated by any one or two of the services.

As an additional precaution, it would be wise if the post of Chief of Staff were rotated among the several services, whenever practicable and advisable, at least during the period of evolution of the new unified department. The tenure of the individual officer designated to serve as Chief of Staff should be relatively short—two or three years—and should not, except in time of a war emergency declared by the Congress, be extended beyond that period.

Unification of the services must be looked upon as a long-term job. We all recognize that there will be many complications and difficulties. Legislation of the character outlined will provide us with the objective and with the initial means whereby forward-looking leadership in the department, both military and civilian, can bring real unification into being.

Unification is much more than a matter of organization. It will require new viewpoints, new doctrine, and new habits of thinking throughout the departmental structure. But in the comparative leisure of peacetime, and utilizing the skill and experience of our staff and field commanders who brought us victory, we should start at once to achieve the most efficient instrument of national safety.

Once a unified department has been established, other steps necessary to the formulation of a comprehensive national security program can be taken with greater ease. Much more than a beginning has already been made in achieving consistent political and military policy through the establishment of the State-War-Navy co-ordinating committee.

The American people have all been enlightened and gratified by the free discussion which has taken place within the services and before the committees of the Senate and the House of Representatives. The Congress, the people, and the President have benefited from a clarification of the issues that could have been provided in no other way.

I can assure the Congress that, once unification has been determined upon as the policy of this nation, there is no officer or civilian in any service who will not contribute his utmost to make the unification a success.

§ After the President's message a special subcommittee of the Senate Military Affairs committee, with Elbert D. Thomas of Utah as chairman, set out to draft a bill. Months of intensified argument followed among the armed services, their supporters in Congress, and the press. In January 1947 the White House announced that Army and Navy had resolved their differences on unification. It was agreed that there should be a single Secretary of Defense with co-ordinating powers, with the War and Navy Departments keeping their own secretaries and military chiefs, the departments to function as individual units. There was still to be a National Security Council, a small War Council, a National Security Resources Board, a Central Intelligence Agency, and a command structure headed by the Joint Chiefs of Staff. It was also agreed that the specific roles and missions among the three proposed services should be dealt with not by statute but by executive order. A draft order was prepared that gave the Navy primary responsibility for its own land-based reconnaissance and patrol aircraft, and the Marines were accorded primary responsibility for the techniques of amphibious warfare. It was in this form that legislation was enacted in midsummer 1947.

The rocky road traversed in the application of unification cannot be retraced here. At one stage, in February 1948, the obstinate bitterness of service rivalries impelled the President to designate General Eisenhower, then President of Columbia University, to serve temporarily as presiding officer of the Joint Chiefs of Staff. A year later the Hoover Commission made extensive recommendations calling for a Department of Defense as "a regular executive department" with the Secretary having the necessary statutory authority, which he then lacked, "to run his department and control the separate military establishments." Mr. Truman recommended that the Congress take action accordingly.

In the following August the necessary legislation was enacted, and the President approved it. The military establishment was converted into the Department of Defense, and a Chairman of the Joint Chiefs of Staff was created. Also adopted was a performance budget that allowed the Department of Defense and the three armed forces more flexible control of appropriations.

There is still an aftermath of lingering resentment in some quarters.

CONCLUSION
TRANSITION: FROM TRUMAN TO EISENHOWER

Mindful of the awkward hiatus in the passage from the Roosevelt administration to his own, Mr. Truman labored conscientiously and imaginatively to make the transition to the incoming Eisenhower administration smooth and effective. The outgoing President in his last State of the Union message on January 7, 1953 made his report to the Congress in a vein of solicitous forethought and good will.

This is the eighth such report that, as President, I have been privileged to present to you and to the country. On previous occasions it has been my custom to set forth proposals for legislative action in the coming year. But that is not my purpose today. The presentation of a legislative program falls properly to my successor, not to me, and I would not infringe upon his responsibility to chart the forward course. . . .

In just two weeks General Eisenhower will be inaugurated as President of the United States and I will resume—most gladly— my place as a private citizen of this republic. The Presidency last changed hands eight years ago this coming April. That was a tragic time, a time of grieving for President Roosevelt—the great and gallant human being who had been taken from us; a time of unrelieved anxiety to his successor, thrust so suddenly into the complexities and burdens of the presidential office.

Not so this time. This time we see the normal transition under our democratic system. One President, at the conclusion of his term, steps back to private life; his successor, chosen by the people, begins his tenure of the office. And the presidency of the United States continues to function without a moment's break.

Since the election I have done my best to assure that the transfer from one administration to another shall be smooth and orderly. From General Eisenhower and his associates I have had friendly and understanding collaboration in this endeavor. I have not sought to thrust upon him—nor has he sought to take—the responsibility which must be mine until twelve o'clock noon on January twentieth. But together I hope and believe we have found means whereby the incoming President can obtain the full and detailed information he will need to assume the responsibility the moment he takes the oath of office.

§ *And to the people the President said in his last radio address from the White House on January 15, 1953:*

Inauguration Day will be a great demonstration of our democratic process. . . . The whole world will have a chance to see how simply and how peacefully our American system transfers the vast power of the presidency from my hands to his. It is a good object lesson in democracy. . . .

During the last two months I have done my best to make this transfer an orderly one. I have talked with my successor on the affairs of the country, both foreign and domestic, and my Cabinet officers have talked with their successors. . . . Such an orderly transfer from one party to another has never taken place before in our history. I think a real precedent has been set.

§ *The precedent was one of many parts, more numerous than Mr. Truman reported and covering a longer period than the two months of preparation he described. Actually, he had begun working toward the transition during the campaign by having the Central Intelligence Agency send General Eisenhower weekly reports on the understanding that they would not limit the Republican candidate's "freedom to discuss or analyze the foreign programs as my [Eisenhower's] judgment indicates."*

On the day after the election Mr. Truman invited his successor to the White House for consultation on the problems confronting the country, and General Eisenhower accepted the invitation. Mr. Truman also urged the President-elect to send to Washington a representative who would be concerned with the budget in the next administration and to designate his Secretary of State and Secretary of Defense at the earliest possible moment so that they might have time to familiarize themselves with the work of their departments. The appointments were made, and the conferences ensued.

The President also presented to the President-elect three large volumes prepared by the National Security Council, containing (1) a summary, country by country, of current United States policies; (2) an estimate of critical trouble spots; (3) "eyes only" plans for dealing with an all-out Communist attack in Korea, Yugoslavia, or Iran.

In addition to his budget message Mr. Truman delivered two other messages to the new Congress that convened in January 1953, shortly before the inauguration. In both—the State of the Union message and the Economic Report—he chose to limit himself to generalities and to leave a clear stage to his successor. The budget contained no recommendations of new legislation.

Mr. Truman arranged for his trusted assistant, Steelman, to stay on indefinitely at the White House until the new administration had found its bearings. And the retiring President left office with his desk completely clear, inside and out. The last act that he was seen to perform was to walk down the hallway to return a pad that a staff member had forgotten and left on the President's desk.

INDEX

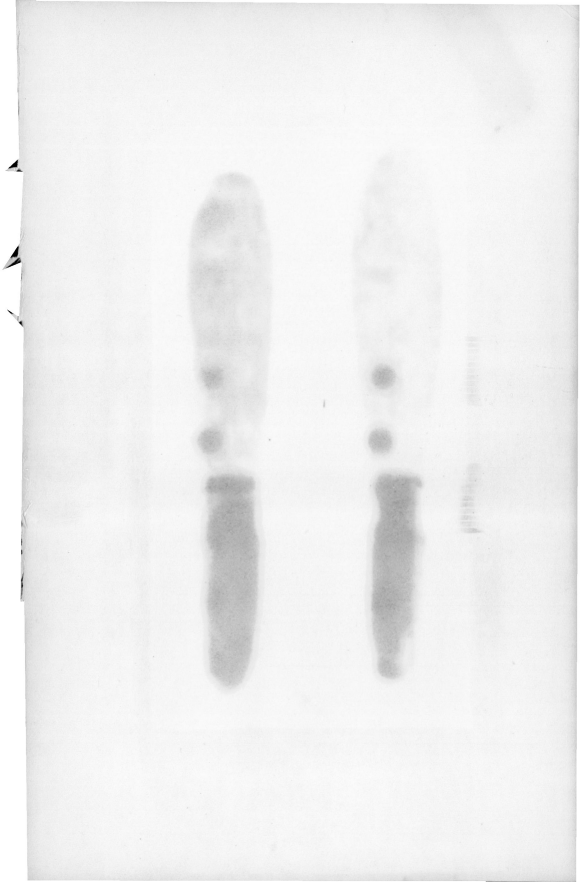

10/11/56